LUSITANIA

An Irish Tragedy

Fishing boats, trawlers, rowboats and a naval vessel picking up Lusitania survivors (The Graphic). In reality the rescue was late, inadequate and chaotic.

LUSITANIA

An Irish Tragedy

SENAN MOLONY

MERCIER PRESS
Douglas Village, Cork
www.mercierpress.ie

Trade enquiries to COLUMBA MERCIER DISTRIBUTION,
55a Spruce Avenue, Stillorgan Industrial Park, Blackrock, Dublin

Also by Senan Molony: *The Irish Aboard Titanic, Celtic Mists, A Ship Accused.*
See www.titanicbooksite.com. Author email sennbrig@indigo.ie

ISBN: 1 85635 452 0

10 9 8 7 6 5 4 3 2 1

To Amelia

Mercier Press receives financial assistance from
the Arts Council/An Chomhairle Ealaíon

Printed in Ireland by Colour Books Ltd.

Contents

Doomed off the Old Head: The 30,000-ton pride of the Cunard Line found she could not elude a submarine, despite her vaunted 25-knot speed. Of some 1,960 *on board, only 761 survived the sinking. The Lusitania had been doing 18 knots at the time, a wartime economy to save coal.

As with any disaster, some early reports had imprecise numbers of dead, etc. Figures have been left as in the original.

Prologue

The sinking of the Cunard passenger liner *RMS Lusitania*, on a voyage from New York to Liverpool in May 1915, was the first war atrocity to assault the senses of western opinion in modern times. The killing, without warning, of 1,198 civilians on a passenger vessel by a hidden submarine was almost incomprehensible, especially given the complacency that preceded the event:

German Threat Fails to Impress
London, Friday

No importance is attached in London shipping circles to the German threat to blockade Great Britain. It is regarded generally as a paper blockade made in Germany, intended to frighten. Similar views are held in Liverpool shipping circles.

(*The Kerryman*, 13 February 1915, p. 6)

Submarine or Battleship?

Last year, not many months before the outbreak of the war, the dovecotes of British navalism were grievously disturbed by a letter which appeared in the Times. *The letter was printed over the signature of Sir Percy Scott, a big figure in the British naval world, and it preached the seeming heresy that the proficiency and power which the submarines of the future might be expected to acquire and possess would revolutionise naval warfare and render all surface war vessels obsolete.*

Sir Percy Scott
Illustrated London News

Sir Percy Scott's letter started one of the most lively controversies within memory, and when the subject at last sank back again into the oblivion from which the letter to the Times *had momentarily reclaimed it, the verdict of the naval public had gone practically dead against Sir Percy.*

Many there were who supported his view, but those who believed it heretical were many more.

There is a certain plausibility about the prophecies … their forecasts will undoubtedly come true with time. But there is no reliable sign yet that the trident is soon to pass to the possession of the submarine commander.

(*Cork Free Press* Editorial, 14 April 1915)

German Threat to Atlantic Liners
New York, Sunday

The warning by the German Embassy published in all America's leading newspapers yesterday, declaring that a state of war exits between Germany and her allies and Great Britain and her allies, and that those sailing under the British flag or allied flags do so at their own risk, did not have any perceptible effect on the passengers sailing in the Lusitania yesterday. On the contrary, there were 1,258 passengers, a record number for the time of the year.

(*The Kerryman*, 8 May 1915, p. 6)

These are the early attacks off the Irish coast by the U-20, the submarine fated to destroy the *Lusitania*:

HUNS ON THE COAST
GERMAN SUBMARINE OFF THE FASTNET
FUTILE ATTACK ON LONDON STEAMER
QUEENSTOWN, THURSDAY

A Queenstown message says the London steamer *Cayo Romano*, from Cuba with sugar for the Clyde, has arrived there for coal. The captain reported that at 11 a.m. yesterday, when off the Fastnet, a German submarine with no letter or number visible, but painted a light colour, was sighted. The *Romano* put on full speed, and the submarine fired a torpedo which missed the stern of the steamer by a few feet.

It is supposed that this was the same submarine that sank the three-masted schooner *Earl of Latham* last evening off Kinsale. The weather on the coast today is foggy. It is reported that the submarine was seen this morning off Roche's Point.

(FROM OUR CORRESPONDENT)

BANTRY, THURSDAY NIGHT

The police authorities at Kilcrohane, Co. Cork, have reported here that a German submarine was seen off that coast in Dunmanus Bay soon after noon today.

The submarine came close to the shore, and having moved about on the surface for some time, apparently reconnoitring, dived, and was not again seen. It is thought that they mistook that bay for Bantry Bay. A close watch was kept for the enemy's reappearance, and all the stations were quickly apprised of the occurrence.

SUBMARINE OFF QUEENSTOWN
(FROM OUR CORRESPONDENT) QUEENSTOWN, THURSDAY

It has been persistently rumoured here all day that a German submarine was seen off Roche's Point, and again in the vicinity of Daunt's Rock in the early hours of this morning.

SINKING OF SCHOONER – CREW ARRIVES IN CORK
INTERVIEW WITH CAPTAIN

The Captain and four members of the crew of the three-masted schooner the *Earl of Latham*, which was sunk off the Old Head of Kinsale by a German submarine on the previous evening, arrived in Cork yesterday afternoon, and left by the mail train on the Great Southern and Western Railway at 3.30 o'clock for their homes in Carnarvonshire.

They did not appear to suffer much from the experience through which they had passed, but they felt hard the losses they had sustained as the result of the sinking of their vessel. They reached Albert Quay terminus at 2 o'clock, and attracted a good deal of attention as they proceeded to the offices of the agents, Messrs. Fitzpatrick and Sons.

The schooner was in charge of Captain Jones, Anglesea, and the crew was composed of Hugh Parry, Port Dinonwick, Carnarvonshire; Cook Edwards, Anglesea, and Seamen Wynne and Jones, Anglesea. After they had been attended to by the agents they partook of dinner, and left the city by the afternoon mail train for Carnarvonshire.

In response to the request of our representative, Captain Thomas Owen Jones gave an interview and stated that the schooner was a very smart and useful vessel of about 210 tons. They left Chester river about one o'clock on Monday morning on a voyage to Limerick with a cargo of fireclay goods. They experienced good weather, and made an excellent trip until off the coast at Kinsale.

When they were about eight miles south south-west of the Old Head of Kinsale, a submarine was noticed proceeding in their direction. The submarine was not flying any flag, and had no number, but as soon as it got within sight of the schooner it became apparent that it was a German submarine of the latest type. The colour of the submarine was light slate. It was about five o'clock when the submarine was noticed, and half an hour afterwards she reached the schooner.

When within a short distance of the schooner, the Commander of the submarine, in English, ordered them to lower their sails and to leave the schooner as quickly as possible, and bring her papers to him. The crew of the schooner behaved splendidly and not the slightest alarm was created.

Captain Jones added – 'We had of course no option but to comply with this order, and we proceeded to carry it out. I thought before the submarine approached us – at the time that she was proceeding towards us – that no such action would be taken, but we were soon made aware of the intentions of those in charge of the submarine. We lowered a small boat and entered it, and handed over our papers, and then the Germans proceeded to sink our vessel.

'They fired nine shots from a gun mounted abaft the conning tower, but their marksmanship was bad at first. I hoped it would continue to be bad all the time, and that our vessel would be safe, but it was not to be. Their first four shots missed, but they kept at it, and the fifth shot took away the mainsail, while the remaining four shots entered amidships, and the schooner quickly disappeared.

'We were left in our small boat, and the submarine proceeded over water in the direction from which she crossed to us. We watched her for a long time, and with her speed soon lost sight of her. We then took to the oars and rowed to the Old Head, but an hour later we were picked up by the steam drifter Daniel O'Connell, of Dublin, in charge of Capt. Jas Hogan, which was fishing off the coast, and were brought to Kinsale where we arrived about 8 o'clock in the evening.

'It was an exciting experience for us, but such things must be expected, and while we are glad to be returning home, we are sorry that our nice little vessel should have been sent to the bottom. We had to clear out of her at a moment's notice, and were not even given time to gather up our belongings, and that was very hard. We left as we were dressed at the time, and came away as you see us now, and that was the worst of our treatment. We intend to return to our homes in Carnarvonshire this afternoon'.

The members of the crew gave similar interviews, and one mentioned that the commander of the submarine spoke in a very 'gruff' voice when he ordered them to leave the schooner. The sea was calm at the time, and they would have reached the shore in the small boat, but the arrival of the steam drifter enabled them to reach the town of Kinsale much earlier than otherwise would have been the case. They were deeply grateful to Mr R. A. Williams, the agent for Lloyds at Kinsale, and also Mr Daly, Customs officer at Kinsale, for the kindness with which they attended to their wants during their stay in the town.

(CORK EXAMINER, FRIDAY 7 MAY 1915)

TWO HARRISON LINERS
SUNK OFF IRISH COAST
CREWS SAFELY LANDED

About midday on Thursday, the ss. Centurion, of Liverpool, one of the Harrison liners, which left Liverpool for Durban with 9,000 tons of general cargo on the previous day, was sunk by a German submarine in the smalls, in the Channel.

Captain Kerne and the crew of 44 hands arrived in Wexford from Rosslare yesterday morning. The men suffered keenly, having spent 12 hours in open boats, and many of them being only half clad.

Interviewed at Wexford, Albert Smythe, chief steward, said:

'We got no warning whatever. There was a thick fog at the time. We were at dinner when we felt a tremendous shock, and heavy sprays dashed over the ship. The men made a rush towards the deck, and were met by one of the officers coming off the bridge, who, with Captain Kerne, ordered

Sinking of the Earl of Latham *(from a painting by* Sphere *artist G. H. Davis)*

Centurion (courtesy Paddy O'Sullivan)

Candidate

all to take to the boats. We rowed off in two boats, not having time to take any belongings. When about 200 yards off, the vessel had sunk about 6 feet, and was evidently stationary.

'The Captain was about to order us to return when the submarine, the number of which we could not see in the fog, came up at the stern of the ship, and the officers shouted to us in good English to keep clear. They then fired another torpedo, and there was a loud explosion, after which the vessel suddenly disappeared.

'We rowed all day, and it was midnight before we reached the Barrel Lightship, on which we were taken and provided with food.

'The ss. Flemish, of Liverpool, was hailed at 4 o'clock this morning, and she brought us to Rosslare Pier'.

Mr W. W. H. McGuire, local representative of the Shipwrecked Mariners' Society, took charge of the men at Wexford, and provided food and clothing for them.

The Centurion was a ship of 5,860 tons, and traded to South African ports.

(DAILY EXPRESS, 8 MAY 1915, P. 6)

SECOND HARRISON LINER
SHELLED BY SUBMARINE

The crew of the steamer Candidate, sunk by a submarine off the Irish coast, landed at Milford Haven at 10.30 yesterday morning. Many of them, half naked, were clothed and sent home by train.

Their story is that at 8 a.m. on Thursday morning the Candidate was 45 miles south-west of Coningbeg Lightship when a large submarine rose on the starboard quarter, about fifty yards distant. Without warning of any kind, she commenced shelling the Candidate, which was going about nine knots.

The vessel was kept going, and the submarine followed, shelling all the time. She smashed two [life] boats, blew away the bridge, and one shell passed through the cabin.

The boats were ordered away, and the Germans deliberately shelled the men while launching them, and whenever the men got into a group. However not a single man was hit, save seaman Robert Owen, who was in one of the smashed boats, and had his hand injured slightly. Thirty or more shells were directed upon the ship, and finally a torpedo finished her.

One hour and twenty minutes elapsed from the time of sighting the submarine to the Candidate going down.

The crew of 43 were in the boats for six hours when they were picked up by the patrol drifter, Lord Allendale.

The Candidate was a steel screw steamer of 5,858 tons gross, built in 1906. She was bound from Liverpool to Jamaica.

Both the Centurion and the Candidate were owned by Messrs. T. and J. Harrison, Liverpool.

(DAILY EXPRESS, 8 MAY 1915, P. 6)

Introduction

The U-20 had already had a highly successful tour of duty. Two fine steamers had been sunk, along with the schooner, *Earl of Latham*. But the patrol was about to get even better, and the slate-grey submarine was primed for an immortal infamy.

Remember the Lusitania! Her name endures, the second most famous shipwreck in world history, and the most notorious ever created by the hand of man. Even had she not been sunk, the *Lusitania* was already a legend, a leviathan and a lodestone of maritime progress. Never had the blue riband for the fastest crossing of the Atlantic garlanded a more deserving bow.

Little is known today, in Ireland especially, of the immediate impact of the sinking. Yet it remains the single worst atrocity of Ireland's bloody history – an attack, less than twelve miles off the coast, accounting for *forty times* more deaths than any onshore event in twentieth century Ireland. This book is not about the *Lusitania* as the ship supreme of her day. The lavishness of her appointments can be well imagined, while her strength of line and technical specification, although outstanding, are somehow irrelevant in light of her fate. A tiny tinfish from a steel sheath filled with German submariners laid her ignominiously under. That much is known.

The *Lusitania* tragedy played an interesting part in the turbulent politics that unfolded afterwards in Ireland, and which continue to ripple in terms of nationalism and loyalty. The sinking may be said to have been a curtain-raiser to decades of travail, and in a curious way it touched on what was to happen later. One *Lusitania* survivor, nurse Nettie Mitchell, defied British soldiers in insurrectionist Dublin in 1916. Another escapee of the sinking, merchant Robert Mackenzie, refused the rebels the use of his premises – and was shot dead.

Ireland was on the cusp of dramatic change in May 1915, beginning the metamorphosis from a very British Ireland to an exclusively Irish one. That change would lead in turn to a certain amnesia about a gigantic harvest of death on Irish shores at the time of the Great War – a war that some in Ireland were then calling the king's war.

By the first anniversary of the *Lusitania*, the Easter Rising had wrecked Dublin. The destruction of the General Post Office also delayed the arrival of confirmation from Cunard to the authorities at Queenstown, now Cobh, that the company would indeed pay for wreaths to mark the first anniversary. The Sinn Féin Rebellion naturally diverted the course of Irish history thereafter. Yet some of those Irishmen in khaki 'caught offside' by events in Dublin in 1916 were fighting in France because of the *Lusitania* … having been recruited on the strength of her sinking.

Many argue about whether the sinking of the *Lusitania* brought America into the war. The question is never raised as to whether it might have done the same for Ireland. Yet concerted attempts were being made to influence a hesitant Irish manhood into enlistment from the war's very beginning until its eventual end.

There had been dire warnings of general conscription by early 1915, indicating that Ireland was not alone in wavering enthusiasm to join the colours. This was despite a speech soon after the war's outbreak by John Redmond of the Irish Parliamentary Party to the effect that Irishmen should be prepared to fight for the rights of small nations. Those of Belgium had been recently trampled on by the 'Hun', it was pointed out – although many horrors allegedly committed by invading Germans were later shown to be figments of propaganda and nothing more. Nonetheless, Redmond's listeners saw the analogy with the rights of little Ireland to her own nationhood, if not full sovereignty.

The speech at Woodenbridge, Co. Wicklow was undermined for many however by the fact that Britain had recently put Home Rule for Ireland back on the shelf for the duration of impending hostilities. This new disappointment came nearly 30 years after a Home Rule Bill had first been introduced, only to be struck down, like its successor, by fierce political opposition at Westminster. For Ireland to now do England's bidding – to prove herself so subservient as to deserve final independence – seemed ridiculous to the growing lobby that saw the Irish political situation as one of continuing manipulation of the weak by the strong.

Fighting for 'little Belgium' would be nothing of the sort, they said. It would instead be the actual opposite, akin to fighting for Goliath over David. It would leave Ireland a vassal state, permanently in thrall to Britain, draining her of lifeblood as well as her independence of thought and action.

So ran the arguments and counter-arguments. While some men took the shilling and donned uniform, others in the volunteer movement were drilling in the streets or going on route marches, determined to defend the notion of Irish nationhood. It was already being whispered that England's European difficulty was Ireland's opportunity. A number were already tearing down recruitment posters and predicting a German victory instead. While the Proclamation of Independence talked of Ireland's 'gallant allies in Europe' in 1916, there were many Irish a year earlier who were philosophically committed to the kaiser. Of course, aiding an enemy's enemy was all but impossible hundreds of miles from an embroiled continent. But still there were rumours – widely credited – of a network of coves and inlets, known to the Germans, where U-boats could put in to receive fresh food and supplies from Irish sympathisers.

By early 1915 the U-boats, with their February threat to blockade and strangle Britain, had become an object of fascination in Ireland – representing the nearest anyone at home might come to glimpsing a piece of the world crisis. Submarines were imagined to be seen from every headland and promontory. Few realised that Germany was able to deploy only two U-boats on station in Irish waters at the time.

Britain had an obvious self-interest in stoking the U-boat hysteria in Ireland. Notions of sex-starved members of the Kriegsmarine putting ashore in rowboats in the hours of darkness were encouraged, as if the Germans were latter day Vikings bent on rape and pillage. A corps of coast-watchers was put in place.

The drumbeat of propaganda was focused on recruitment through fear, but also through appeals to masculinity and patriotism, and even baser emotions such as shame and dis-honour. In March 1915, St Patrick's Day was turned to 'Shamrock Day', with one poster showing a nurse offering a sprig of the national trefoil to a male toddler dressed in army uniform. 'We Must Have More Men' ran the legend.

No stone was left unturned. Michael O'Leary, a Victoria Cross winner who clear-ed two German machine-gun nests single-handedly in February 1915 was returned to his native Cork and met by enthusiastic crowds. The reticent Irish guardsman, pro-moted to sergeant, was then whisked off on a promotional tour. At the same time, wives and sweethearts were encouraged to ask their men why they had not gone yet. The white feather was mentioned – as was a suggestion that the women of Ireland should withdraw the warmth of their affections until such

Recruitment poster

time as their menfolk saw the proper course. Pamphleteers went so far as to suggest, with little credibility, that it was Germany that had invaded Ireland and laid her waste in terrible days of yore. One such asked the public: 'Have you forgotten what the Germans did in Ireland once before – the Hessians in Wexford in '98, whose deeds were condemned by the British viceroy of the day?'

Few would have known of any Teutonic entanglement at Vinegar Hill. And even if the Hessians did run afoul of the British viceroy, as presumably was their purpose, the strained allusions eluded public comprehension.

Thus the *Lusitania* sinking – a few miles off the coast – came as a gift from God for the colour sergeants. At last the pamphleteers could discard their generalised focus on Catholic sensibilities through scandalised mention of alleged abominations in Louvain and other centres of the faith. They could go right to the meat of monstrosity within a few miles.

New leaflets accused the Germans of 'making war on Munster', although the appalled reaction in general hardly needed such sectoral targeting. Leaflet 41 told readers to re-member the *Lusitania*'s last message: *Send Out Soldiers!*

The recruitment boon of the sinking was a blow to those Irish people who fervently supported Germany, or who were merely perceived to be anti-English. The pendulum swung immediately and violently against nationalist Ireland, whose notions of 'ourselves alone' now seemed absurd in the face of total war.

Newspaper hostility to the Sinn Féiners was pronounced. Extreme nationalist arguments seemed undermined by the atrocity, and these 'extremists' were widely denounced from the pulpit. A Sinn Féin rally immediately afterwards in Limerick, which marched through an area in which almost every house had sent a son to the front, turned into a near-riot in which shots were fired before the forces of law and order prevailed.

Under a headline 'Sinn Féin Cowardice – the *Lusitania* Crime' the *New Ross Standard* reported a rally of 6,000 people who heard the preacher Rev. Fr Frank O'Hare insist that Ireland's message to every free man was that his place was in the great barricade:

'Pay no heed to the miserable handful of so-called Sinn Féiners [the reverend orator thundered to cheers from his audience]. Give no attention to those who preach the pale doctrine of neutrality.

'They are found skulking at corners in the shadows, willing to wound and yet afraid to strike! (cheers) When Ireland was together under great leaders for the purpose of binding up the nation's wounds and restoring her fallen fortunes, the only contribution they made to her forces was to sneer and criticise. Where they stood then, they stand now.

'They stood then in the path of Ireland's material progress, and today they would ask Ireland to sell her soul and go down in history in dishonour. More than that, some of them have had the insolent audacity, the unblushing cowardice, to approve of the murder of innocent men, women and children from the *Lusitania*.

'Kaiser Wilhelm will go down in history as Kaiser Cain, with the brand upon the brow because he planned the outrage. Those who executed it have shocked and anguished mankind, and retribution swift and fell will surely follow their steps.

'But what word of loathing and contempt can we coin strong enough to express our feelings towards those cowardly hearts, those venomous tongues, that would appraise the foul deed here? Ireland has no share in their dishonour.'

It was true that initial sentiment in some quarters had revelled in the sinking of a vessel designed to admiralty specifications and fulfilling the role of auxiliary heavy cruiser in time of war. But some in their glee had managed to overlook the vast roll of civilian casualties. Newspapers in Ireland were almost embarrassed to report that there had been celebrations in certain areas over the shock-filled sensation. But there were noisy parties in parts of Cork, Kerry, Limerick, Wexford and Dublin at least.

The *Cork Free Press* reported on 10 May: 'There are a few people in Limerick who glory in the piracy of the German Huns, and the awful crime has been gloried in by them. It is well that these people are few and far between'.

At the first meeting of the Cork Rural Council within days of the disaster, Councillor Wallace rose to second a motion expressing 'detestation of the unpardonable crime', but noted 'that in their own city at the present moment they had members of society who were gloating over, and congratulating themselves, on that tremendous disaster'. He had seen them with his own eyes.

Even in the council there were those who demurred from the general sentiment. Councillor Hayes dissented from the resolution of condemnation and was denounced as 'even worse than the Germans' for attacking those who attacked the perpetrators of the outrage.

The press in Ireland contented itself for the most part with reporting the worldwide outrage provoked by the sinking, while ignoring some isolated incidents of manifested support for the sinking in their own fiefdoms. They told instead how an Irishman had applied a punch to the jaw when pro-Germans had started to sing the *Wacht Am Rhein* in a crowd gathered at the offices of the *New York Herald* to read the billboards of the sinking. 'His act was generally approved', a newspaper noted.

'Humanity's Outlaw': The Irish Weekly Times *shows* Civilisation *refusing the excuses and explanations of the kaiser while* Lusitania *sinks in the background*

The Little Girl: WHO KNOCKED THE HEAD OFF THAT?
The Little Boy: S-S-SH! I'M NOT SURE—BUT—COOK IS GERMAN.

While there is no doubt that the universal tone of the domestic press was one of horror and anger, there was a marked divergence in the editorial attitude of Irish community newspapers in the USA as news of the sinking reverberated. These papers, heavily IRB-influenced and removed from the local impact of bodies washed ashore, continued to vigorously attack Britain, and to defend Germany. If there was a clear dichotomy with feeling at home, there was also in many cases a suspension of good journalism. The deaths of *Lusitania* victims from the local Irish-American community often went unreported in the midst of the diatribes directed at perfidious Albion. This was the syndrome later mocked as 'Deutschland go bragh'. The virulent Hibernian press in the USA suggested that Britain had invited the disaster through her own incompetence – yet they also held the view that the *Lusitania* had been a legitimate target by virtue of being crammed with contraband for the western front.

Back in Ireland, those who espoused such ideas had been vilified in the press, although deep-seated convictions still clashed in communities across the land. The *Lusitania* 'crime' or justifiable 'act of war' provoked interpersonal disputes everywhere.

Three days after the sinking Hugh Reilly was killed by Jim Foster in Killeshandra, Co. Cavan, in an argument about the Germans. The pair came to blows and Reilly succumbed to flurry of punches. 'When the news spread that a man had been killed outside the town, the police and many townspeople hurried to the place, and were horrified to see the unfortunate man lying dead along the roadside', the *Anglo-Celt* reported.

But while a Kinsale inquest jury would indict the

kaiser and Germany for the sinking of the *Lusitania*, the Cavan inquest jury was much more circumspect, finding that death was caused by a fall on the road, adding 'How this fall was caused we have not sufficient evidence to show'.

The tensions can also be glimpsed in a letter about 'pro-German youths' sent to the Sinn Féin-slating *New Ross Standard*, published on 14 May 1915:

> As an Irishman and Nationalist, I call on all fair-minded men to note those pro-Germans in our midst and leave them severely alone. Mark the conduct of those chaps having the effrontery of endeavouring by their vapouring nonsense to create disunion in this country at so critical a moment in her history, by endeavouring to cast discredit on men who have fought Ireland's battles over all the world, long before those newly-fledged worthies were born.
> I say the shopkeepers who allow those boys behind their counters to prattle their nonsense to their customers will soon find it to their loss, and some of them are feeling the pinch already.
> 'Labourer'.

Many a bar-room brawl might be sensed from the above, and it was not just boys who were 'prattling nonsense'. The fairer sex could be just as prominent in despatches. One vignette involves the obstreperous sister of Roger Casement, Alice Newman. She complained to the police in Newry that she had been abused in the most terrible terms by a soldier on a crowded train platform at Omeath. She wanted the man charged, if not court-martialled. It turned out that Miss Casement had first announced before all and sundry that the young recruit should be ashamed of himself for wearing the king's colours. The enlistee then replied with some choice observations about the *Lusitania* – and proceeded to be equally frank about Miss Casement's own appearance.

The police opted to take no action. The Casement family would later escalate its own involvement in such issues – with brother Roger being landed in Ireland by a German submarine less than a year later. Casement was carried to Banna Strand by a U-boat commander named Weisbach – the same officer who fired the fatal *Lusitania* torpedo from the U-20.

The *Ulster Guardian* meanwhile recalled that after the sinking of the *Titanic* the kaiser had telegraphed from Corfu to the White Star Company:

> Deeply grieved at the sad news of the terrible disaster which befell your line. I send expression of my deepest sympathy also to those who mourn the loss of relatives and friends.
> Wilhelm I. R.

The newspaper asked:

> Will the same Kaiser now pin the Emblem of the Cross to the breast of the assassin-commander of the U-boat who sent 1,457 people to their death?

The *Titanic* was a powerful emblem in Ireland after the loss of nearly 80 emigrants (as well as some 60 Irish crew) three years earlier. It was invoked in cross-sniping at the attitude of German newspapers – which were busy supported their government with the same vigour.

A Major McGillycuddy told a mass recruiting meeting in Cork on 12 May 1915 that the German newspapers, 'encouraged no doubt by their sovereign,' had expressed, 'desperate disappointment that in the murder of

Childkillers – 'whom the King delighteth to honour' (from *Life* magazine)

the people on the *Lusitania* they did not best the death roll of the *Titanic* disaster'. Naturally, nothing of the kind was ever printed in the German press, but the mere fact of the sinking of the *Lusitania* made anything credible. In fact the most notorious fiction of the entire war – the claim that a Canadian prisoner had been crucified on a barn door by his barbarous captors – slipped into the public prints within eight days of the sinking.

If propaganda was a war industry in itself, the destruction of the giant Cunarder certainly oiled the wheels. A total of 11,500 Irishmen were on the king's service abroad in 1915 – with the Royal Dublin Fusiliers and Royal Munsters heavily engaged in the Dardanelles landings – but it seems the early stream of enlistments had substantially thinned from the heady mood of the outbreak of the war.

Now, days after the sinking, Chairman Francis Lyons was able to tell a recruiting meeting at Cork that it had been 'left to their own shores to witness the crowning atrocity of the German barbarians. 1,200 human souls had been sent into eternity in cold blood'. The terrible outrage ought to appeal to all present and in particular to every inhabitant of Munster, he said. If the Germans should happen to reach their shores, they knew what would happen.

Other speakers summoned the same spectre, urging men to rally round the flag of freedom by joining their 'gallant Irish comrades in France and Belgium, who are saving Ireland from a fate which has already overtaken the brave Belgians'. A Colonel Barry had no difficulty in avowing the contradictory message that the men of Ireland had a duty to 'go and protect' their women and children by fighting at the front – because if the Germans reached their country no mercy would be shown to those same females and infants.

Yet there was no denying the simple stories of men who told their listeners of seeing large numbers of corpses brought in from the sea. The Hun was murdering their people in the very waters of Cork.

Now that the enemy had come to their very doors, Major McGillycuddy warned his listeners, they would realise that this was their immediate war, and they would lose their manhood if they did not come forward.

'It was an unspeakable thing that they should have to have to appeal to them in this way', the major admitted, knowing that the recruiting offices in London, Liverpool, Manchester and other centres had been besieged since the sinking. He did not believe that there was a decent woman in Ireland who did not look upon a young unmarried man with contempt if he did not now join the colours. He had been on a recruiting mission in his own county, and he was ashamed to say he had failed, as the people did not then see the necessity of recruiting, as they had since this diabolical outrage, the sinking of the *Lusitania* …

Did any of this tub-thumping work? It seems to have provided a far smaller lift in numbers than was seen in Britain. Despite the new proximity of the carnage, Irishmen remained reluctant. There is a stark contrast with the prolonged anti-German rioting that took place in British cities following the disaster, when hundreds of shops were looted and numbers of harmless enemy aliens killed and injured. In Ireland there were no such scenes.

A commentator in the *Sunday Freeman* of 16 May 1915 wrote: 'I am glad that Dublin has not been disgraced by anti-German riots this time. There was an outbreak soon after the war began, and in one case it was found that a victim was an Irishman, one who traded under a German name because before last August nobody believed that anybody but a German could properly run a pork shop'.

Certainly a mob gathered in front of the Queens Hotel in Queenstown, owned by a German, on the night of the sinking. But they dispersed on learning that survivors were being billeted there, and in any case the man in question, proprietor Otto Humbert, was nowhere to be found.

Perhaps public anger was vented on Sinn Féiners in the absence of a visible German emigré population in Ireland. Or it may be that Ireland on the whole remained unmoved to action. In this light, the later posters that cried out: 'Irishmen! Avenge the *Lusitania*!' might have been taken to suggest that Irishmen should fight the wars of others.

The overall failure of recruitment drives in Ireland that year was emphasised by full-page advertisements taken out in national and provincial newspapers throughout the country on 6 November 1915. These declared:

IRISHMEN!
You cannot permit your regiments to be kept up to strength by other than Ireland's sons!
It would be a deep disgrace to Ireland if all her regiments were not Irish to a man.

This call, aiming to put 50,000 Irishmen in khaki, guaranteed military service for the period of the war only, at shilling a day, together with pension and family support entitlements. Men were asked to join the Connaught Rangers, Royal Dublin Fusiliers, Royal Irish Fusiliers, Royal Munster Fusiliers, Royal Inniskillings, Royal Irish Regiment, Royal Irish Rifles and the Leinsters. But those who did join, whether for the shilling or shamrock, kith or king, could never have imagined how Ireland's situation would be transformed within a year – so that within half a decade the *Lusitania* would be something to forget, not remember.

The transformation can be seen in two separate inquest verdicts, each in the same language. The Kinsale inquest into the *Lusitania* returned an indictment of wilful murder against the kaiser and German government in May 1915. Less than five years later, in April 1920, a verdict of the same wilful murder was brought in by jurors empanelled over the political assassination at his home of the Lord Mayor of Cork, Alderman Thomas Mac-Curtain by masked gunmen. The jury laid that same charge of wilful murder against the Royal Irish Constabulary, 'officially directed by the British Government', and similarly accused David Lloyd George, Prime Minister of England. The irony was acute.

That same year too, the *Cork Examiner* carried its annual *Lusitania* graves memorial day photograph, but this time the caption named only the officiating clergy and omitted mention of any of the British admirals and officers standing in serried ranks. National selectivity of memory was already setting in. Unfortunately this choice has only served to erase the extraordinary rescue effort by Irish trawlers and lifeboats at the time of the sinking, the magnificent efforts to comfort those who lived, and the dignified manner in which the dead were conveyed to their last rest in Ireland.

The *Lusitania* when she rounded the Fastnet in the southern approaches was a seagoing boast of immense proportions, and a defiant diplomatic symbol of business as usual.

She was also crewed by a large number of Irishmen, with numerous Irish passengers walking her decks, some as they did so making jocular remarks about submarines.

At 1.20 p.m. local time, on 7 May 1915, Kapitänleutnant Walther Schweiger sighted four funnels and the masts of a passenger steamer directly in front of his command, at right angles to his course.

He gave immediate orders to dive, and *Unterseeboot 20* raced to the intercept. At 2.10 p.m., Schwieger's submarine fired a single torpedo.

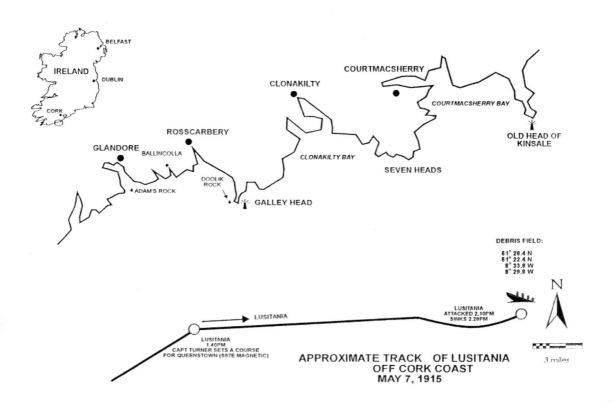

APPROXIMATE TRACK OF LUSITANIA
OFF CORK COAST
MAY 7, 1915

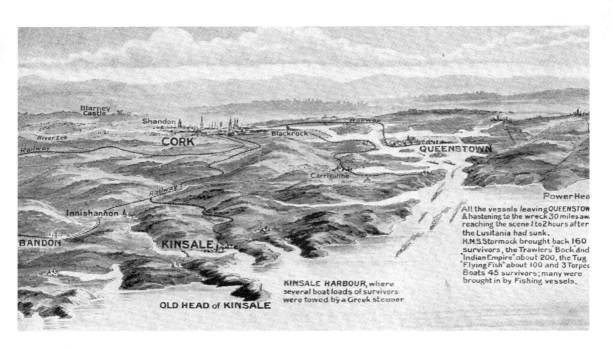

KINSALE HARBOUR, where several boat loads of survivors were towed by a Greek steamer

All the vessels leaving QUEENSTOWN & hastening to the wreck 30 miles away reaching the scene I to 2 hours after the Lusitania had sunk. H.M.S. Stormock brought back 160 survivors, the Trawlers Bock and Indian Empire about 200, the Tug 'Flying Fish' about 100 and 3 Torpedo Boats 45 survivors; many were brought in by Fishing vessels.

The Sinking

The gyro-torpedo struck to the forward of the *Lusitania*'s starboard side – where precisely is still the subject of argument. But there is no doubt about what came next – the vessel heeled sharply over, taking more water through the impact gash as the engines drove relentlessly on. Passengers who were in their cabins or just finishing dinner were flung off their feet and subjected to an immediate roulette of life and death.

The 790-ft vessel had only 18 minutes to live – if that.

One of her passengers, Oliver Bernard, later drew the sketches on p. 20 of the attack and sinking, originally published in the *Illustrated London News* on 15 May 1915:

> The sketches here reproduced in facsimile are of unique interest as being the work of probably the only man living able to draw them from this own first-hand experience.
>
> Oliver P. Bernard, the well-known resident scenic artist of Covent Garden Opera, happened to be among the saloon passengers on board the ill-fated *Lusitania*, and although unable to swim, he was saved.
>
> In these very vivid sketches he has reproduced the impressions of the great catastrophe as they struck his eye. He was one of the few people who were on deck (he had come up early from lunch) and actually saw the periscope of the German submarine, the track of the torpedo as it sped towards its mark, and the effect of the explosion on the liner.
>
> One woman who was saved was carried down one of the funnels in the water and then shot out again by the force of the steam generated when the water reached the furnaces.
>
> In describing his experiences (Mr Bernard) mentions that the torpedo appeared to him to enter the *Lusitania*'s side just about under the entrance to the saloon. Within about 18 minutes of the torpedo striking her, he says, the proud Cunarder had disappeared beneath the surface of the sea and there was left nothing but a mass of wreckage floating, and numbers of people struggling frantically in the water. The boat in which he himself escaped was nearly crushed by one of the funnels as the ship lurched over.

The LUSITANIA sinking on her starboard side in about 300 feet of water, and 8 miles South by West of the Old Head of Kinsale

Only two of the BOATS on this, the port, side could be launched owing to the list, but about 20 were got off from the other side

Where the second torpedo was reported to have penetrated

Where the first torpedo penetrated the Engine Room

TRACK OF THE TORPEDO

Position of the PIRATE SUBMARINE about 200 yards from the LUSITANIA, from which its cowardly GERMAN Crew were able to MURDER over 1400 innocent and defenceless people, without fear of retaliation

Oliver Bernard joined the British army as a result of his experience. He put his stage-design talents to use from 1916 as a camouflage officer on the western front, where he was wounded in the leg. He ended the war with the rank of captain, and died in 1939.

Oliver Bernard [left] gave a vivid account of scenes on board the Lusitania. Englishman Norman Albert Ratcliffe [middle], first-class, of Gillingham, Kent, and Christina McColm, second-class, from Ottawa, are also pictured outside the Westbourne Hotel in Westbourne Place, Queenstown. Ratcliffe was pulled to safety having clasped a floating chest for three hours in bitterly cold water

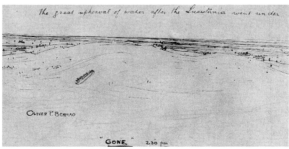

Irish Stories

Passengers

The *Lusitania*'s passenger manifest contained over 90 Irish men and women, more if one includes first-generation Irish from both Britain and the United States. The crew was even more Irish in character, strengthened by large numbers from an Irish background in communities such as 'Brutal Bootle', the Liverpool suburb famous for providing a steady supply of ship's firemen and other labourers.

While the following stories are not wholly exhaustive, they do provide a comprehensive commentary on the lives and experiences of the Irish aboard the *Lusitania*.

Thomas Agnew (27) Lost
Mrs Agnew (27) Lost
Third-class passengers
Ballylummin, Co. Antrim

MURDERED BY THE CREW OF A GERMAN SUBMARINE
MR AND MRS THOMAS AGNEW

Who were homeward bound on the Lusitania *when she was torpedoed by a German submarine. Mr and Mrs Agnew were resident in Monnessen, Pennsylvania, four years, and were returning to Ballylummin, Ahoghill. Tom Agnew, carpenter, was son of the late John Agnew, farmer, Ballylummin, who died in September last year. Walter Agnew, another brother, who had been a motor inspector in the States, and returned to this country six months ago to manage the farm, received a wire yesterday from the Cunard Company stating that the bodies of Mr and Mrs Agnew had not been recovered.*

(BALLYMENA OBSERVER, 21 MAY 1915, P. 4)

May Barrett (25) Saved
Second-class passenger
120 Barrack Street, Cork city

PLUCKY CORK LADIES
TERRIBLE EXPERIENCE
MIRACULOUS ESCAPE

Tragedies like that of the sinking of the Lusitania *always bear most harshly on the women and children. Yesterday our representative had a talk with two ladies, who travelled from New York on the ill-fated ship and were rescued at the last moment by almost a miracle. Their experience may be taken as a sample of what hundreds of other women had to endure on the fatal Friday afternoon.*

The young ladies were Miss Barrett and Miss MacDonald [actually McDonnell], both of Barrack Street, Cork. They were travelling together in the second cabin. Miss MacDonald was floating about for three-and-a-half hours before she was picked up, and yesterday morning she had hardly recovered from the effects of her terrible experience.

Miss Barrett carries a bold spirit in her slightly built frame, and she was able to give a perfectly connected and vivid account of what happened. 'We had just gone into the second saloon and were just finishing lunch. I heard a sound something like the smashing of big dishes.

'Then there came a second and louder crash. Miss MacDonald and I started to go up the stairs,

but we were thrown back by the crowd. Then the ship stopped and we managed to get up to the second deck where we found the sailors trying to lower the boats. There was no panic and the ship's officers and crew went about their work quietly and steadily. I went to get two lifebelts, but a gentleman standing by told us to remain where we were and he would fetch them for us.

'If you go into the cabin again,' he said, 'you will never get up again'.

'He brought two lifebelts and we put them on. By this time the ship was leaning right over on to the starboard, and we were both thrown down. We managed to scramble to the side of the ship, which was rapidly sinking. Just near us I saw a rope attached to one of the lifeboats which was floating near.

'I thought I could catch it. We murmured a few words, a prayer, and then jumped into the water. I missed the rope, but floated about on the water for some time. I did not lose consciousness, but the water got into my eyes and mouth and I began to lose hope of ever seeing my friend again.

'I could not see anybody near me, and I felt so lonely. Then I must have lost consciousness, for I remember nothing more until one of the Lusitania lifeboats came along. The crew was pulling on board another lady who was unconscious, and they shouted to me, 'You hold on a little longer'. After a time they lifted me out of the water. Then I remember nothing more for a time that seemed to be an age.

'In the meantime our boat had picked up twenty others and when I became conscious it was getting late in the evening. We were transferred to a trawler and taken to Queenstown. We got on the trawler at a quarter to six and it was half past nine when we reached Queenstown'.

(CORK FREE PRESS, 10 MAY 1915, P. 5)

Both May Barrett and Kitty McDonnell had emigrated to the USA on the White Star liner *Majestic* in April 1911. They stayed at the same address, 263 9th Avenue, New York City, and were returning together on holidays.

Josephine Burnside (49) Saved
Iris Burnside (20) Lost
First-class passengers
Cullybackey, Ballymena, Co. Antrim

Mr and Mrs Burnside, who are natives of the Cullybackey district of Ballymena, were on board the ill-fated Lusitania coming to Ireland for a short holiday from Toronto.

Mrs Burnside is a cousin of Mr David Barbour, hardware merchant, Broughshane Street, Ballymena. Her native name was Houston, and she appears in the list of survivors, but not that of her husband or children, about whose fate much anxiety is felt [She was travelling with a daughter – her husband and other children were not on board].

Mr Burnside was an engineer by profession and was employed by Ballyclare Paper Mills before he emigrated. A brother of Mrs Burnside holds an important appointment in the well-known firm of Eatons of Toronto.

(IRISH POST AND WEEKLY TELEGRAPH, 15 MAY 1915, P. 11)

Michael G. Byrne (47) Saved
First-class passenger
Paulstown, Co. Kilkenny

KILKENNY SURVIVOR

Michael G. Byrne, special deputy sheriff, New York, who is a native of Paulstown, Co. Kilkenny, and was coming on a visit to see his friends, has been saved and gave an account of his formidable experiences of the sinking of the Lusitania to our representative on Monday. He says: 'I was on the upper deck smoking a cigar at about two o'clock. We were sailing along nicely in beautiful weather and all on board seemed to be enjoying themselves. I saw away in the distance quite plainly the submarine, immediately I saw a peculiar-looking object coming from it along the water and straight in the direction of our ship.

'Several others saw it also and some of them remarked it was a torpedo fired from a German submarine; at the moment some of them got a little excited. Having heard so much about German submarines previous to my trip, I quickly proceeded to my bunk where I managed to get a few of my valuables and my lifesaving jacket as best I could.

'I hastened back, jostling passengers, till I got again on deck. The ship had been struck at this time and in an instant a thunderous roar, as if the skies opened, was heard from the bursting of the boilers. The ship reeled and staggered and passengers were thrown all over the place'.

Although Byrne said he could plainly see the submarine on the surface, the official report of the U-20 shows it was submerged throughout the attack. Some eyewitness accounts are lurid

Questioned as to the excitement of the passengers at this time, Mr Byrne replied – 'Well some of them appeared quite calm, extremely calm, while other were jumping frantically around everywhere, crying aloud "We are doomed". I heard an officer say it was a German submarine attack and the order for the lifeboats to be lowered was given and they were filled rapidly'.

In reply to a question, Mr Byrne said: 'I kept quite cool all this time, though fate looked certain and a sleep in a watery grave to be our end in a few minutes. At last when I saw no chance of a lifeboat, on the ship diving into the sea and many jumping out into the water, I then jumped into the sea as the ship was just going down.

'I swam about for two hours among dead and live bodies and floating wreckage'. Mr Byrne here remarked: 'I am a good swimmer. There was a boat about two hundred yards away and I swam to it, but it was overcrowded and I would not be taken in.

'I still swam to and fro, listening to drowning cries all around me of men, women and children. After some time I was picked up by another boat quite safe, and indeed I still think I see the struggling of the poor passengers in the water. Poor little children in the arms of their mothers tightly grasped in death floating on the surface of the sea.

'The dying cries are still in my ears and the sight of the struggle for life through the deep sea will remain forever in my memory. The hideous howl of the Lusitania as she was swallowed in the waves brings a dismal thrill all over me'.

Asked how things looked at Queenstown, Mr Byrne further stated – 'I managed to get to Queenstown in a weak and exhausted condition. All my trunks, etc., are gone down in the Lusitania. I was thankful to have my dear little life safe indeed. The scenes at Queenstown were also horrifying. Many had arrived in boats with life just in them, others dead. The ghastly look on the survivors' face as they met each other, many enquiring for lost friends'.

It was a sad landing port, through a few hours before bright and happy faces sighted the shores of Erin. Mr Byrne stated that he heard the warning of sinking the ship before leaving New York, but received no personal warning. He remembered well the farewell given by some Germans as they were about to start on their voyage – 'Goodbye, the worst is yet to come'. In fact the warning was not heeded by anyone.

Mr Byrne is married to a German girl and left Germany at the outbreak of the war.

(NEW ROSS STANDARD, 14 MAY 1915, P. 5)

In a letter from her husband, a survivor of the Lusitania, *made public last night by Mrs Michael G. Byrne, of No. 444 West Fiftieth Street, the sinking of the vessel and the activities of the submarine which sank her are described.*

A summary of the letter of fifty-four pages is given. Mr Byrne, a retired merchant, was a first-class passenger. He says he saw the periscope of the undersea fighter appear, and soon the wake of a torpedo approaching the ship. The letter continues:

'We were really led to slaughter. An officer ran about the decks, telling passengers there was no danger; that the ship would be beached, although several passengers questioned the statement, knowing the torpedo had struck near the engine room.

'I waited until the water was even with the main deck, then dived overboard. In the water, the sight of women with children and babies in their arms was terrible. Screams filled the air and mothers besought persons in boats to take their babies'.

Soon after the liner disappeared, he says:

'A ripple on the surface was increased to a wave as a conning tower appeared, followed by the hull of a submarine. It rested just even with the surface and a man looked about the surroundings and disappeared. The submarine quickly dropped out of sight'.

Mr Byrne was in the water two hours.

(NEW YORK WORLD, 25 MAY 1915)

Byrne occupied Stateroom B-64. He later complained that he lost property listed as one large steamer trunk, two dress suitcases, an umbrella, a silver-mounted rosewood cane, a silk American flag, a silk Irish flag, eleven pounds of Old Rover tobacco, and 300 cigars.

In June 1915, he wrote to the new US Secretary of State, Robert Lansing: 'When I asked the Cunard Co. about compensation for my personal effects, they said file the same claim with the Admiralty and at the termination of war they would collect it for me. In answer I said "I bought my ticket from the Cunard Co. and not from the Admiralty".

'I hope our Government will see to it that the Imperial Government of Germany make speed compensation for the destruction of all American citizens' property and effects destroyed by them while travelling on a merchant ship'.

Patrick Callan – Lost
Second-class passenger
Chicago, Illinois

Patrick was a 'big fair-haired young man', returning from Chicago to take over his father's business, according to authors Gus Smith and Des Hickey in *Seven Days to Disaster*. Pat made his money by supplying cattle to meat barons in Chicago. His address in Chicago was 3028 West Taylor Street, where he had received a letter from his father beseeching him to return to Ireland as he was in sharply declining health and wanted to review his affairs.

Married to Mary, Callan was the father of three children – Peter, Thomas and Catherine.

Callan enjoyed games of poker for high stakes on the *Lusitania*, but rose early on the morning of the sinking to recite a poem on the boat deck at dawn as the liner approached Ireland. It was *A Dream of Ireland* and contained the lines:

> I feel the touch of a Munster breeze,
> Thank God my exile has ended.

Fellow passenger Julia O'Sullivan saw Pat Callan enter one of the early lifeboats. It broke from the fall as it was lowered, throwing everyone out 'like apples'. His body was never recovered.

Margaret Canigan (28) Lost
Third-class passenger
Blacklion, Co. Cavan

Miss Canigan was buried in mass grave A in Queenstown on 10 May 1915. Her effects were sent to her brother Pat at Gubaveeny, Blacklion, on 7 June. Margaret, listed as body number 74, had been working as a domestic in Boston.

Patrick Carroll – Lost
Second-class passenger
Dundalk, Co. Louth

AN EXILE'S RETURN
DIES IN SIGHT OF HOME AFTER 30 YEARS
'LIKE MAN WHO SAW HEAVEN'

Robert Dyer, an American from Pittsburg, when interviewed by our special correspondent at Queenstown, said that he was taking a glass of beer in the lunch room and talking to Patrick Carroll of Dundalk when the ship was struck.

Pat Carroll was like a man who saw Heaven, Dyer said, from the moment he first sighted the Irish coast.

Pat was a bricklayer in Chicago, and was going home to see his father in Dundalk after an absence of 30 years. 'When the crash came, we were knocked off our feet, and one of our friends said, "That's these damnable German submarines, and I'll bet they have done for us at last".

'I saw that man from Dundalk afterwards, floating around dead'.

(IRISH INDEPENDENT, 10 MAY 1915, P. 6)

A contemporary postcard shows a leisurely scene at the lifeboats. Instead pandemonium reigned

Susan Coleman – Saved
Second-class passenger
Cootehill, Co. Cavan

ON THE LUSITANIA

Miss Coleman, of the Cootehill district, whose safety is a matter of rejoicing among friends and neighbours, lost £100 worth of property.

(IRISH POST AND WEEKLY TELEGRAPH, 15 MAY 1915, P. 3)

That on Monday, a Miss Coleman, of Cootehill district, passed through by train, and on being interviewed by him, said she was one of the survivors of the Lusitania, *and had just got so far on her way home from Queenstown. She looked in no way upset after her thrilling experience, and expressed her thanks at getting away from the agonising scenes of disaster. She lost over £100 of property in the ill-fated vessel.*

(BALLYBAY CORRESPONDENT, ANGLO-CELT, 15 MAY 1915, P. 1)

Second-class passenger Brigid Lee (*qv*) mentions encountering Miss Coleman on the *Lusitania*, and afterwards in Queenstown.

John Coughlan (40) Lost
Catherine Coughlan (40) Saved
Children
John (3) Saved
Magaret (2½) Lost
Jeremiah Bernard (11 mo.) Saved
Third-class passengers
Goleen, Co Cork

WIFE AND TWO CHILDREN SAVED FROM LUSITANIA
TRAGIC FATE OF HUSBAND AND CHILD
SKIBBEREEN, WEDNESDAY

Mrs John Coughlan, of Corranmore, Goleen, who with her husband and three children were passengers on the ill-fated Lusitania, *passed here last night.*

Her husband is not accounted for, and it is feared he is lost. She had with her two young children, and a third who was picked up dead at sea and conveyed to Queenstown, was brought to Goleen today for interment.*

The family were coming home form America to take up the farm which was the ancestral home. A large number of bodies were seen floating off Glandore by fishermen who communicated through the police with the Admiralty and the Cunard Co.

(CORK EXAMINER, 11 MAY 1915)

On Wednesday a pathetic sight was witnessed at the Railway Station, Skibbereen, when the body of an infant passed through on the way to the burial ground of his ancestors at Goleen. The little coffin with the body was sent on by rail from Queenstown with a label addressed to Mrs John Coughlan, Corran, Goleen.

The mother, with two of her children, survivors of the disaster, travelled by the 4.15 p.m. train from Cork to Skibbereen on Tuesday. Of her husband who sailed with her and the three children on the Lusitania *from America, there is no account.*

The little coffin reached Schull at 2.30 o'clock on Wednesday and was taken by road to Goleen where interment was made.

(CORK COUNTY EAGLE, 15 MAY 1915, P. 10)

26 ◆ LUSITANIA

* The body of two-and-a-half year old Margaret Coughlan [body 62] was not buried in Goleen. It lies in mass grave Common B in the Old Church Cemetery in Cobh.

The family gave an address in Butte, Montana, USA, when returning home. Their US hometown newspaper, the *Butte Independent*, heavily centred on the Irish community, made no mention of the family in subsequent coverage, but had these front page headlines a week later:

ANGLO-MANIAC AMERICAN PRESS WOULD PLUNGE COUNTRY INTO WAR ON ENGLAND'S SIDE

A crusade of sloppy sentiment and hysteria, combined with vile innuendo and abuse of all who differ from the maniacs, is vigorously pushed in the daily press since the sinking of the Lusitania *with its contraband cargo of war munitions a week ago.*

(BUTTE INDEPENDENT, 15 MAY 1915)

John Coughlan – 20 December 1915. Administration granted at Dublin to Kate M. Coughlan, widow, in the amount of 89 pounds and nine shillings. Deceased a miner by profession, late of Butte, Montana. Died at sea 7 May 1915 (Irish index records of wills and administrations).

THE LUSITANIA DISASTER
UNSUCCESSFUL PLEA OF NEGLIGENCE

Judgement was given at Liverpool yesterday in the action for damages brought by Mrs Coughlan, widow of an Irish farmer who went down on the Lusitania *against the Cunard Company on the ground of negligence.*

Mr Justice Bray submitted the following questions to the Special Jury:

Did the deceased know that the writing on the ticket contained conditions relating to the terms of the contract to carry him? – Yes.

Did the defendants do what was reasonably sufficient to give the deceased notice of the conditions? – Yes.

Was Captain Turner guilty of negligence? – No.

Was such negligence the cause of the sinking of the Lusitania? – No.

Was such negligence the cause of the death of the deceased? – No.

His Lordship entered judgement for the Cunard Company.

(THE TIMES, 11 FEBRUARY 1920. P. 13)

Margaret Cox (27) Saved
Son Desmond Francis (17 mo.) Saved
Second-class passengers
Winnipeg, Canada

DUBLIN LADY'S STORY
PITEOUS CRIES FOR HELP

Mrs Cox, Winnipeg, who is a native of Dublin, and was coming with her seventeen months old baby son on a visit to her friend, Mrs Hobcroft, Dalkey, has been saved, and gave an account of her dreadful experience to our representative last evening. She said:

'*I was at lunch when there was an explosion right under us, and everyone jumped to their feet. We made for the door, but the steward told me to go back – that it was only a panic and that there was plenty of time. I went back, but when I saw the staircase crowded with people I went to another steward and asked him what was I to do, that I had to get my baby away, and he said I had better go on deck.*

'I was at the high side of the ship, where men were working at the boats. A man named Mr Ward of Bundoran, who was coming from Pittsburgh – I don't think he has been saved – gave me a hand to a boat that was on the deck. Where I was standing there was a crowd of others. I was holding up a delicate lady, who had two children, with one arm whilst I held my baby with the other. We were told to go to the lower side of the ship, that the boats on the high side could not be worked, and I was parted from the lady I was holding. Owing to the fearful list, I was unable to hold my feet, and the baby was knocked out of my arms several times.

'There was a young man of about twenty-three years – I hope he has been saved – every time I lost the baby he got it back for me, and he led me to where the men were working at the boats on the lower side. I was turned away from the first boat, because I think there were too many in it, and I was sent to a second boat. They told me there to go back to the first, but I said I would not go. I said "You will have to take the baby, and I will be all right". Then someone took the baby and put it into the boat.

'A Mrs Wilson, who was also saved, caught the baby. I don't know how I got in. I think I was thrown in. The boat was swinging from the davits, and the men had to cut the ropes to get it away. I think that the first boat was broken up. When we got away, our boat went right in under the funnels, and we were afraid of being drawn in with the suction.

'There were 85 people in our boat and she was near turning over, when two or three people jumped into the water. One lady was drawn down the funnel, and she was shot up and was saved. The men worked hard with the oars to get away from the ship. I saw the water closing over her. It was terrible.

'Though there was some excitement, I did not hear much crying. My baby then became hysterical. We were rowed to a small boat, which contained only one man, and some of the people in our boat were transferred into it.

'Mrs Burdon of Newcastle told me that she saw the submarine, and a man on it hoisting a flag, and that the submarine cruised about among the boats. The women were wonderful, they were so calm. They kept their heads; I could never have believed it; it was a credit to them.

'The only thing I cannot forget was the piteous cry of the people in the water appealing to be taken into our boat, which was over-crowded. I had to place my hands on my ears. Some Americans told me that the Germans would never torpedo a ship in which they were. They know differently now'.

Mrs Cox spoke very highly of the kind treatment they received in Queenstown.

(DAILY EXPRESS, 10 MAY 1915, P. 6)

Hannah Cunniffe (30) Lost
Third-class passenger
Ballyhaunis, Co. Mayo

A Miss Cunniffe, of the same parish, [Aughamore, Ballyhaunis, Co. Mayo], has also gone down
with the vessel.

(MAYO NEWS, 15 MAY 1915, P. 8)

A cousin who travelled with Miss [Delia] Kilkenny has, it is presumed, gone down, as no tidings have been forthcoming of her since the disaster.

(MAYO NEWS, 15 MAY 1915, P. 8)

Hannah lived in New York and had travelled home with her friend and neighbour Delia Kilkenny. Her body, like the large majority, was never recovered.

William Dale (31) Lost
Second-class passenger
Tullinsky, Castledawson, Co. Derry.

Mr Dale had booked his passage to come home by the ill-fated Empress of Ireland when that ship went down, but he was then saved from the sad fate which has now befallen him by being prevented from sailing at the last moment.

The late Mr Dale, who was little over 30 years of age, was a graduate of Galway College, where he took his civil engineering degree, and from whence he proceeded to the important managerial position in Toronto which he held since.

Accompanying him on the Lusitania was an invalid friend, a Mr Thompson, who, alas, is also among the lost.

The lost engineer was a man of the kindest and most generous disposition, and though in the forefront of his profession in Canada, was unobtrusive to a degree. The family in Tullinsky are naturally prostrate with grief, and the sympathy of the district goes out to them, especially in this dire calamity.

(MID-ULSTER MAIL, 15 MAY 1915, P. 6)

* The *Empress of Ireland* sank in 14 minutes having collided with the collier *Storstad* in the St Lawrence seaway off Father Point, Quebec, on 29 May 1914. Over 1,100 were lost.

Deep sympathy has been extended throughout the locality to Mr John Dale on the tragic death of his brother, Mr William Dale, who it is to be presumed, went down with the Lusitania. Mr Dale, who was a civil engineer and connected with a prominent firm of engineers in Toronto, was a second-class passenger on the vessel, and as his name is not to be found amongst the list of survivors, it is concluded that he is amongst the many victims of the German atrocity. Mr Dale's main object in visiting his friends at this time was to see a sister who is stricken with a serious illness.

(TOOMEBRIDGE CORRESPONDENT, LARNE TIMES, 15 MAY 1915, P. 4)

Mary Delaney (34) Saved
Third-class passenger
Shannow, Co. Cavan

CAVAN LADY'S RESCUE
PICKED UP UNCONSCIOUS

One of the survivors is Miss Mary Delaney, whose home is at Shannow, Co. Cavan. Miss Delaney, who has been 12 years in America,* is on her way home, and stayed last night at the Athlone Hotel, Upper Dominick Street.

Describing her experiences, she said that when the first torpedo struck the vessel, there was no panic, but the passengers made for the lifeboats in an orderly manner. They were, however, she said, led to understand by the officers that there was no danger, and apparently there was then the hope of making the shore.

One learning this, Miss Delaney stepped out of the lifeboat in which she had got a place, onto the deck. However, on the second torpedo striking the ship,• the same people again made for the lifeboats and Miss Delaney again got into one. Some accident occurred to it, however, and she was thrown into the water.

She became unconscious, and the next thing she knew was that she was safely on board a trawler. It appears that she was pulled into a lifeboat by a man she afterwards met in Queenstown, and who told her that she came up by the side of the boat and clutched on to the side. She does not remember that.

Miss Delaney spoke appreciatively of the treatment she received at Queenstown. The guests in the hotels, she said, gave up their beds, and stayed up all night attending to the survivors.

(DAILY EXPRESS, 11 MAY 1915, P. 6)

* Mary Delaney had emigrated to Hartford, Connecticut, in 1904 on the *Oceanic*.
• There was no second torpedo fired by the U-boat, yet there was a secondary explosion aboard the sinking *Lusitania*, the cause of which is hotly disputed to this day. In my opinion it is most likely to have been a boiler detonation.

Catherine Dingley (38) Lost
Second-class passenger
Clones, Co. Monaghan

Dingley – Drowned in the Lusitania *disaster, Mrs Catherine, a native of Clones, late of 242 West 142nd Street, New York City. Interred at Queenstown on Monday (10 May). American papers please copy.*

(CORK EXAMINER, 11 MAY 1915)

Amongst those interred was Mrs Catherine Dingley, a native of Clones, Co. Monaghan. Née Glenn.

(IBID.)

Catherine's husband, a machinist, could not afford to ship the body (number 70 on the official list) back to the United States. Mrs Dingley is buried in grave 591 in the Old Church Cemetery in Cobh. The inscription, which spells her Christian name with a K instead of a C, reads as follows:

Drowned on the *Lusitania*
7 May 1915
Katherine S. Glenn
Of Taunton, Mass, USA
Beloved wife of Howard Dingley
Aged 38 years.

Annie Doyle (24) Lost
Third-class passenger
Mullingar, Co. Westmeath

FEARED LOSS OF MULLINGAR GIRL IN LUSITANIA SINKING

We deeply sympathise with Mr Tom Doyle (employee in Mr P. J. Casey's) on the sad fact that he has reason to believe that his daughter, Miss Annie Doyle, is one of the victims of the latest German crime, by which hundreds of innocent creatures were recently sent to their deaths.

Mr Doyle received news that his daughter was a passenger on the Lusitania, *and within an hour of learning this ominous intelligence, he learned that his son, who is in the fighting line in France or Flanders, had been admitted to hospital suffering seriously from the effects of that cowardly weapon, poisonous gases.*

All enquiries regarding Miss Doyle have brought no good news, and the worst is feared.

(WESTMEATH EXAMINER, 22 MAY 1915, P. 6)

Annie had been working in New York as a domestic servant.

Michael Doyle (31) Saved
Third-class passenger
Main Street, Kenmare, Co. Kerry

KERRY MAN'S ESCAPE

Michael Doyle (harness-maker) of Kenmare, Co. Kerry, was … wearing a stoker's jacket at the time which was supplied to him by one of those on board the patrol boat. 'Hallo,' he told our representative, 'Don't you know me? We were often together before I thought of going to America'.

I at once recognised an old friend in Mick Doyle, and needless to say I heartily congratulated him on his escape. 'I am coming back to Kerry again,' he said, 'and I was one of the last to leave the deck. You know of old I am a good swimmer, and I can tell you I swam for a long time today. Of course, I had a lifebelt on, but I am as fit as a fiddle now. Why, it is grand to meet one you know here, and it makes me forget the trying time I passed through this afternoon'.

(CORK FREE PRESS, 8 MAY 1915, P. 5)

Doyle was rescued by the steam patrol boat No. 85 and landed at Kinsale.

Michael Doyle of Kenmare, who had been a third-class passenger on the Lusitania *and who had been nearly two years in America,* said he had been standing near the Master-at-Arms [Peter Smith, Lost] when the latter suddenly said 'Here comes the submarine as sure as hell. She will get us'.*

He saw nothing himself, but he saw a streak made on the water and almost immediately he heard an explosion in the ship. After the vessel went down he swam around for two hours before he was picked up.

A juror – 'You're a brave man'.

(WEEKLY IRISH TIMES, 15 MAY 1915, P. 1)

* On 1 June 1913, Doyle landed in the USA from the Cunard liner *Caronia*. He had left his wife Bridget at home in Kerry while he sought his fortune. He remained living in Kenmare and working as a harness maker for more than half a century and is buried in Old Kenmare graveyard.

Kate Duplex (35) Lost
Third-class passenger
Mountmellick, Co. Laois

Dark-haired Kate was a Quaker, from the village of Fannins, Queens County (Co. Laois). She had first arrived in the United States a year earlier, on 2 May 1914, on a sailing by the White Star Line's *Baltic*, from Liverpool. She lived and worked in Long Island, New York, and was heading home for a summer holiday.

A snap taken during the sinking of the Vestris *in 1928, in which 115 died [compare to p. 25]*

Teresa Feeley (34) Lost
Joseph Feeley (29) Lost
Third-class passengers
Kilmallock, Co. Limerick

The body of Teresa Feeley was recovered, unlike that of her husband, and interred on 10 May in mass grave Common A in the Old Church Cemetery. But the estate Teresa left behind was to lead to an unseemly wrangle. Her grief-stricken father, Michael Clery, a farmer in Kilmallock, Co. Limerick, was soon shocked to learn that Joseph Feeley's parents were seeking possession of his daughter's residual finances. The young couple, based in New York, had been childless.

Both sets of in-laws felt there was a point of principle at issue and could not conceive of the other side being so insensitive as to insist on their own entitlement. The matter went to law – and then to wigs on the green. A High Court case was held before the Lord Chief Justice himself, sitting in the High Court at the Four Courts in Dublin, on 5 October 1915. Both sides had expensively engaged senior counsel. Points of succession law were rehearsed. The judge heard counsel Mr Marnan for Anne Feeley, and then Mr Comyn, KC, for Teresa's father, Michael D. Clery. There were disputed documents and statutes. In the end it came down to a decision as to who had died first.

Eventually the learned judge decided to treat the case as if it were one of intestacy. He granted administration of the estate in favour of Mr Clery, of Ballyquinnan, Bulgadden, allowing him the costs of the action.

Mr Clery had deposed that his daughter died intestate, 'she and her husband having been passengers in the steam ship *Lusitania* when said ship was torpedoed and sunk off the coast of Cork on the 7 May 1915, and both having been drowned in the sinking of said ship, and there is no reason to believe the said Joseph Feeley survived the said Teresa Feeley.

'The said Teresa Feeley left no lawful husband, no lawful children or other more remote lawful issue her surviving, but left me this deponent, her lawful father and sole next of kin her surviving'.

The court agreed. Teresa's effects were forwarded to Mr Clery's solicitors, Fox & Co. of Kilmallock, in November 1915.

John Ferrick (26) Lost
Margaret Ferrick (22) Lost
Third-class passengers
Ballinrobe, Co. Mayo

Grave fears are entertained for the safety of Mr Ferrick, Boxboro, Ballinrobe, who, with his sister, Miss Ferrick, was a passenger on the Lusitania.

The brother and sister were about ten years in the States, and were at the time of the calamity on a visit home to their friends. The sister is reported as saved [error], *but so far there has been no trace of the brother.*

(CONNAUGHT TELEGRAPH, 22 MAY 22 1915, P. 4)

* John Ferrick from Ballinrobe first sailed to New York on the *Baltic* from Queenstown on 3 April 1910, at the age of 21. The Cunard manifest lists Margaret as 'Mrs Ferrick', but she and John were sister and brother. [People often lied about their ages when entering the United States.]

Margaret Galligan (28) – Saved
Second-class passenger
Ardlogher, Co. Cavan

SAVED FROM LUSITANIA
CAVAN PASSENGERS' EXPERIENCE

Amongst the 777 passengers of the Cunard liner Lusitania who were saved out of a total of 1,960, after the great vessel had been torpedoed by a German submarine off Kinsale Head on Friday last, are two Co. Cavan ladies who were interviewed by an Anglo-Celt representative on Tuesday, at the residence of Mr Francis Smith, Killycannon, Cavan, a brother-in-law of Miss Bridget Lee, who said she was accompanied on the trip over by her niece, Miss Maggie Galligan, formerly of Ardlogher.

She had been a resident of New York for 25 years, during which time she has crossed the Atlantic several times. Miss Galligan went to the United States about five years ago.

They had their passages booked on the Carmania [actually Cameronia], but were with a large number of other Irish people transferred to the ill-fated Lusitania at the last moment, the Anchor Line boats having been requisitioned by the British Government to convey troops from Canada for the front.

Miss Lee, who looked none the worse of the terrible ordeal through which she had passed, continuing, said that she was at lunch when the first shock was felt, the general topic at the table being the submarines. Everyone rushed out of the dining-room, but the stewards and waiters assured them that there was no cause for uneasiness. Miss Lee and her niece then returned to their seats, and when the second shock came it was with difficulty that they made their way out.

They were supplied with lifebelts, as owing to the suddenness of the attack, there was a delay in the launching of the lifeboats. The scene was a terrible one. She and her niece clasped each other's arms, and then suddenly the vessel went down, and they went with it, praying fervently to God for mercy.

She could not tell anything that happened then, but she next found herself, still clasping her niece, on the surface of the water, and seeing a deck chair floating, they caught hold of it, as did a gentleman who was also in the water. In this terrifying state they held on for two hours, desperately clinging to the frail support, until they were picked up by a lifeboat in which there were twenty other passengers.

They were then transferred to a tug-boat and taken to Queenstown, where they remained until Monday morning. Miss Lee said that the spectacle of dead bodies floating on all sides was one never to be forgotten. She added that the only Cavan people she had come into personal contact with on the boat were a lady from Cootehill district, and Mr Ernest Moore, of Lisdarn, who was returning home after a two years sojourn in the United States.

She had been speaking to Mr Moore on the morning of the disaster, and that was the last she saw of him. She was most anxious to know if he had been saved. The Cootehill lady was amongst the survivors, Miss Lee having met her in Queenstown before leaving. All their luggage was lost. Had they been allowed to sail in the Anchor line steamship in which they booked, they would have been saved their desperate ordeal.

(ANGLO-CELT, 15 MAY 1915, P. 1)

Christopher Garry (51) Lost
Second-class passenger
Oldcastle, Co. Meath

Mr Christopher Garry, Lower Fennor, Oldcastle, a second-class passenger, is also reported as a survivor. [Error – actually lost]

(DROGHEDA INDEPENDENT, 15 MAY 1915, P. 6)

Mr Garry had become a wealthy businessman over a couple of decades in America. He owned substantial property in Cleveland, Ohio.

Catherine Gilhooly – Saved
Second-class passenger
Co. Leitrim

SURVIVOR'S STORY

Miss Gilhooly … and Miss McClintock went at once to the starboard side of the vessel to get into a lifeboat, but they saw the first of the lifeboats lowered break apart, many people being thrown into the water. She was advised to get to the port side, and this she did, although not without much difficulty owing to the list of the vessel.

She managed to get into a boat and got clear just in time, thanks to the plucky work of a pantryman, who pushed them off with an oar.

One of the ladies in the lifeboat drew the attention of a male passenger to the liner as she was sinking, but he refused to turn his head, declaring that he could not look at such a spectacle.

Later the party were picked up by a Government boat and landed at Queenstown about 9.30 on Friday evening.

(ULSTER GUARDIAN, 15 MAY 1915, P. 6)

Joseph Glancy (43) Saved
Second-class passenger
Clones, Co. Monaghan

THE CHOKING LIFEBELT

Mr Joseph Glancy, another survivor, a native of Clones, and now at 12 Camden Street, Belfast, in which city he was formerly employed, told an interviewer that after putting on a lifebelt he slid down the side of the ship until within 12 feet of the water, and then dropped in.

He got his leg and arm injured with pieces of wreckage. He sank, and on coming to the surface saw that the liner had disappeared. His lifebelt was practically choking him by this time. He afterwards became unconscious, and knew nothing more until he found himself in a broken lifeboat with other people, the party being brought safely to Queenstown.

(IRISH INDEPENDENT, 13 MAY 1915, P. 7)

An interesting narrative was related by Mr Joseph Glancy, a survivor of the terrible tragedy which befell the Lusitania. Mr Glancy, who is at present residing at 12 Camden Street, Belfast, is a native of Clones, which he left when he was nine years of age, and came to Belfast.

Prior to going to Canada about a year and eight months ago, he held the position of secretary of the Catch-My-Pal Union in Belfast, and was formerly employed in the law stationery department of the firm of Messrs W. & G. Baird, Limited. While in Canada, Mr Glancy was engaged in Eaton's stores in Toronto and was returning to Belfast to take up a position.

In an interview with our representative, Mr Glancy said he was not aware of the warnings that had been given by the German officials in America regarding the intended torpedoing of the Lusitania. Nothing of incident occurred during the passage until they were in sight of the Irish coast.

SHOOK FROM STEM TO STERN

The first thing that attracted his attention was that the vessel was sailing round in a semi-circular course, and he came to the conclusion that there was some danger in the vicinity. In about three minutes she was struck by a torpedo. The ship shook and quivered from stem to stern, and then there was a terrific explosion.

Attempting to get away from the starboard side of the Lusitania. An image by the acclaimed artist Fortunino Matania, who also illustrated Titanic scenes and later the Tarzan books. Published in The Sphere, 15 May 1915. A note to this front cover image by the magazine said it was drawn with the assistance of eyewitnesses

Joseph Glancy

He immediately ran down to his berth, and got hold of his lifebelt. He then made for the deck, where he put on the lifebelt, and assisted another man to put on his. At that time the vessel to all appearances seemed to be stationary. One man came up to the deck and said that all were safe, that the watertight compartments were closed, but he (Mr Glancy) saw that the ship was gradually going down. A large number of the passengers were on the deck at that time, but were without lifebelts.

Mr Glancy slid down the side of the ship until he was within twelve feet of the water, when he dropped in. He got his leg and arm injured with pieces of wreckage. He sank after he got in the water, but came to the surface shortly afterwards, and the liner had then disappeared.

He saw around him numbers of men, women and children struggling in the water, most of them without lifebelts. His own lifebelt was at this time getting very heavy and was practically choking him. He became unconscious after being about three quarters of an hour in the water, and remembered nothing further until he subsequently found himself with fourteen others in a broken lifeboat.

They were afterwards picked up by the steam trawler Brock *and landed at Queenstown, where they received every kindness, both from the people and the officials of the Cunard Company.*

(LARNE TIMES, 15 MAY 1915, P. 9)

Patrick Hanly – Saved
Third-class passenger
Lisnagry, Co. Limerick

LIMERICK MAN SAVED
THRILLING EXPERIENCES

Mr Patrick Hanly, son of Mr Michael Hanly, Mountshannon, Lisnagry, Limerick, was a traveller on the ill-fated Cunarder, but fortunately he was rescued. In an interview with a Limerick Leader representative, he stated that at about 2.10 p.m., when in sight of land, a German submarine appeared some 700 or 800 yards away and launched a torpedo with deadly accuracy into the ship. He immediately rushed, with a number of other men, into his cabin and put on his lifebelt (which article he now treasures in his home) and some minutes later, in company with his companions, jumped from the port side into the water some fifty feet below.

He was unable to swim, but the life preserver kept him afloat, and he lay on his back and used his hands to get clear of the giant leviathan and the flying wreckage which was caused by the discharge of a second torpedo into the ship's side.

The scene was, he said, pitiable. Women and children were screaming and floundering in the water, while others had been killed by the fall of the decks, and were floating on the surface of the calm sea. He drifted about for over half an hour when he came up with an overturned boat, which he mounted and clung onto. He assisted some women and men on board the craft, and there they remained for over two hours before they were picked up by a cutter from a torpedo boat.

On arrival in Queenstown they were taken in charge by the company's officials and placed in the Rob Roy Hotel, where all the necessary comforts were given them after their trying experience. Mr Hanly appears nothing the worse for his cruel experience at the hands of the ruthless German savages, but he stated that he cannot sleep very well, the nerve-wracking experience he has undergone making him start from his slumbers every few minutes. He has been the recipient of numerous congratulations from his friends and neighbours, who all speak with great indignation of the murder of innocent non-combatants.

(LIMERICK LEADER, 10 MAY 1915, P. 3)

Bessie Hare (27) Lost
Second-class passenger
Tuam, Co. Galway

Bessie lived with her brother Daniel at 204 West 78th Street, New York. Her parents and another brother lived on the Dublin Road in Tuam, Co. Galway. Daniel went to the Cunard offices in Manhattan in the wake of the tragedy, and told the *New York Times* that his sister had journeyed home to see the rest of the family, and in particular her severely ailing father, William.

Bessie's remains were recovered and labelled body 95. She was identified by her sister, Mrs Julia Stewart, who travelled to Queenstown with Willie Hare, Jr, on learning of her death. They took possession of her effects.

Bessie lies buried in private grave 622 (Row 19, No. 12) at the Old Church Cemetery in Cobh, her father's grave illness being cited as the reason why the remains were not brought at the time to the family plot in Tuam New Cemetery. An attempt by the family to secure permission to exhume the body in December 1915, after Bessie's father's death, proved unsuccessful.

In 1924, Bessie's brother Willie wrote to the Department of State in Washington to prefer a claim for compensation for the loss of his sister. He was referred to the Cunard Company, who prevaricated, telling him that reparations paid to Americans 'are not in any way connected with the claims dealt with by the British Government'. It referred him to the Foreign Office reparations department, saying that compensation for wartime fatalities was 'entirely a matter to be dealt with by the claimant and the Government'.

Mr Hare received no reply from the Foreign Office, and thereupon involved a TD, Tom O'Connell, who agitated on his behalf and involved the Department of External Affairs. The family had originally sought financial relief for their loss as early as May 1916 and they had waited a year without result.

In 1925, after a fruitless year spent pursuing the issue for a second time, the Hares abandoned the attempt, having never secured any financial acknowledgement for the loss of their sister.

Margaret Hastings (40) Lost
Second-class passenger
Lisburn, Co. Antrim

Mrs David Hastings' Fate

It is, we regret to say, almost beyond a doubt that Mrs D. Hastings lost her life in the terrible disaster. A letter was received from her a short time ago, stating that she was leaving New York on 1st inst., and hoped to arrive on Sunday. She did not mention the name of the steamer by which she intended travelling, but her relatives presumed it was the Lusitania.

Not being positive, they delayed going to Queenstown until they became definitely assured on Sunday by seeing her name in the published list of second-class passengers who had booked at New York. On Monday morning, as no further information could be obtained, Mr Robert Gardiner (her brother), accompanied by Mr Samuel Chambers, stationer, Castle Street, proceeded by the first train from Lisburn, arriving in Queenstown at 2 o'clock a.m. on Tuesday.

They at once instituted enquiries, calling first at the Cunard office, where lists of survivors and bodies recovered were examined, but her name was missing. A visit to the hospital and morgue was likewise fruitless. Then they went to the police station, where they had a conversation with a con-

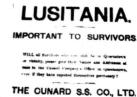

LUSITANIA.

IMPORTANT TO SURVIVORS

WILL all Survivors who are still to be in Queenstown or vicinity, please give their Names and Addresses at once to the Cunard Company's Office in Queenstown, even if they have reported themselves previously?

THE CUNARD S.S. CO., LTD.

Confusion reigned when some survivors failed to register their names – Cork Constitution

stable to whom they handed a photograph of Mrs Hastings.

He at once showed some excitement, but strange to say, instead of making any reply, he transferred the card to a woman who was present and speedily left the barracks and was not seen again by Mr Gardiner or Mr Chambers. The woman, however, declared positively that she had seen a body which corresponded to the likeness.

Subsequently the same photo was shown to five different persons, at different times and places, and each of them identified it with the body of a woman they had seen brought ashore. Two of the persons were fishermen, who were agreed without the shadow of a doubt that the first body that they recovered from the water tallied exactly with the photograph, and the description they gave was practically convincing.

It appeared that the body was interred on the previous day. The belongings of the dead were afterwards inspected, but nothing could be identified as the property of the deceased. Messrs Gardiner and Chambers returned from their melancholy quest, satisfied in their mind that Mrs Hastings' remains rested in Queenstown.

The late Mrs Hastings was a daughter of the late Mr Patrick Gardiner, Ballantine, who died a short time ago. She served her time at sales in Messrs George Duncan & Sons. Some time after the completion of her apprenticeship, she was married to Mr David Hastings, flesher, Lisburn Road, by whom she had five children.

On the death of Mr Hastings, she returned to Lisburn and took over the stationery and fancy goods business of Mr Bertie Gillespie, Market Square. About five years ago she went to the United States, settling down at New Rochdale (sic) near New York, where she had the companionship of her eldest boy Jack. Her daughter Florrie resides with her grandmother Hastings in Belfast, while her three youngest children reside in Lisburn – David with his uncle Robert at Ballantine, Fred and Robbie with Mr Chambers. Very deep sympathy is felt for the bereaved family in their irreparable and lamentable loss.

(LISBURN HERALD, 15 MAY 1915, P. 5)

*Margaret lived at New Rochelle, New York. If Mrs Hastings was indeed buried in Queenstown, her body remains officially unidentified. See further for descriptions of the unidentified dead at the Old Church Cemetery.

Catherine Henry (24) Saved
Third-class passenger
Swinford, Co. Mayo

MAYO GIRLS WHO CAME THROUGH ALL

On Tuesday morning last our reporter interviewed Mrs John Henry at her parents' residence, Cloonconna, Swinford, she being one of the survivors of the Lusitania disaster. She arrived in Swinford on Monday evening, travelling from Queenstown that morning, and, as our reporter informs us, apart from a discoloured left eye and a scratched chin, she appears not the worse for her awful experience.

She emigrated to the States in May, 1908, at the age of 16, and settled down in New York City, where she married John Henry in November last. She sailed upon the ill-fated liner on May 1st on her first trip home for seven years.

She was in her cabin when the first torpedo struck the vessel at a distance of about 30 yards. She remained on the ship until that portion of the deck on which she was standing was submerged and then she was carried away by the water, where, with her lifebelt on, she remained for two long hours, when she was taken on top of an upturned boat on which there were 35 already, excluding her.

On this they remained until a Greek trawler came along and picked them up. Hundreds of dead bodies with heads above the water, kept there by means of the lifebelts, were observed by her all round, and the cries of others, especially mothers, was heartrending.

The loss of goods, jewellery, etc., to her amounted to over £100.

(MAYO NEWS, 15 MAY 1915, P. 8)

On Monday evening, Mrs Henry, of Cloonacanna, Swinford, who was also rescued, passed through Claremorris on her way home. She bore some marks of her frightful experience. Her face was bruised and her eye blackened.

She was for two hours in the water, clinging to a raft, before she was picked up. She states that all the men and crew behaved gallantly and heroically and cleared the way for women and children. Mrs Henry was only married last November, her father being Mr John Ruane of Cloonacanna.

(WESTERN PEOPLE, 15 MAY 1915, P. 6)

While Mrs Henry claimed to have emigrated at age 16, and was listed on the *Lusitania* manifest as 24, Ellis Island records show that she was aged 27 when she left Queenstown on the *Campania* at the end of April, 1908.

The 'Greek trawler' was the *Katarina [Caterina]*, a disguised British freighter flying the neutral Greek flag, which illustrates German complaints about her enemy's flouting of the rules of engagement.

Jane Hogan (39) Saved
Third-class passenger
Derreen, Mullagh, Miltown Malbay, Co. Clare

LUSITANIA SURVIVOR FROM WEST CLARE

Miss Jane Hogan, Derreen, Mullagh, Miltown Malbay, one of the saved from the Lusitania, has arrived home. In the course of a conversation with our representative, she relates that on the fateful day, about 2 o'clock, she heard a crash and then saw men fall on the deck at her feet.

She ran as fast as she could to the first cabin, and a gentleman there placed a lifebelt on her, while the crew were ordering the passengers into the boats. It struck her when she saw the men fall that there was something wrong with the section that prevented the boats from being lowered.

After a short time the vessel went down and she with it. She says she was about five hours in the water and not a stitch of clothes were left her.

'All were in my box,' said she, 'and valued at 300 dollars. The Company suggested to me that they would procure clothes, but I declined the offer. The clothes I have now on me belong to my sister. I have been twenty years in America. You can see my left arm is all black, and my legs and feet were all swollen.

'I am at present under Dr Hillery's care, and Nurse Hogan's. All these marks that you can see were received from floating wreckage coming into contact with me in the sea. The first time I went into the water my pocket book was swept out of my hand.

'All my belongings but my money have been lost. It would have been about seven o'clock when I was picked up and brought to the hospital at Queenstown. I can still fancy the awful scenes and surroundings during those fatal moments and it makes me shudder to think of them! How good Almighty God has been to me when I consider how all my comrades were lost'.

She can remember six of her women comrades having a hold of each other, clinging to each other, all of whom went down under her eyes. This occurred during the lowering of the boats, and she fancied she would be the next to go down.

One of the second-class passengers appended another lifebelt to her until the boat came along and picked them up. Fortunately she had all her money secured, it being stitched on to the inside of her corset.

(CLARE JOURNAL, 17 MAY 1915, P. 3)

Jane was returning from New York.

Miss Jane Hogan, Derreen, Mullagh, near Miltown Malbay, one of the survivors who has reached home after an absence in America of 20 years, said she must have been 7 hours in the water before she was picked up. She is still under medical treatment.*

(IRISH INDEPENDENT, 18 MAY 1915, P. 5)

* Jane also had a sprained ankle as a result of the evacuation.

Frank Houston (27) Lost
Third-class passenger
Carnmoney Road, Belfast, Co. Antrim

Mr Frank Houston, a victim of the Lusitania disaster. Deceased was the only son of Mr and Mrs Houston, Fernbrook Cottage, Carnmoney Road, Belfast.

(LARNE TIMES, 26 JUNE 1915, P. 8)

Mary Agnes Hume – Lost
Second-class passenger
Belfast, Co. Antrim

A PATHETIC CASE

Amongst those who it is feared have been lost is Mrs Mary A. Hume, of New York (formerly Miss Elliott of Belfast), who is a relative of Mr W. S. Patton, 34 Yarrow Street, and a niece of Miss Fleming of Doagh, Co. Antrim.

Four years ago she proceeded to New York to be married, and was on her way home to pay a surprise visit to her friends, who only knew that she was a passenger on the Lusitania when a pathetic telegram from the husband reached them on Sunday morning asking to be informed if she was amongst the saved.

(IRISH POST AND WEEKLY TELEGRAPH, 15 MAY 1915, P. 11)

Mrs Hume and her husband Samuel lived in Harrison, New Jersey. They married in 1910.

Edmond Ireton (36) Lost
Third-class passenger
From Co. Clare

INFORMATION WANTED

Edmond Ireton, passenger on the Lusitania, whose named appeared on the Daily Papers as being amongst the survivors, has not yet been heard of.

Height 5ft. 11ins., fair moustache, brown eyes.

Any information will be thankfully received by his brother, Henry Ireton, Leasana, Quin, Co. Clare.

(ADVERTISEMENT IN THE CORK EXAMINER, 15 MAY 1915, P. 10)

Mr Ireton had an address at New York.

Francis Cranston Kellett – Lost

First-class passenger
Bailieboro, Co. Cavan

No news has been received concerning the fate of Mr F. C. Kellett, a member of a family well-known in the Dublin drapery trade, who was a saloon passenger. Mr Kellett was proprietor of an important drapery business in New York, and is understood to have been on his way to the London markets. Prior to his going to the States, he was a superintendent in Messrs Switzers.

(IRISH INDEPENDENT, 11 MAY 1915, P. 5)

A telegram from Bailieboro inform us that Mr Frank Kellett, a native of that town, and son of the late Mr Edward Kellett, draper, was drowned in the Lusitania. *He was in Messrs Arnotts, Dublin, about 20 years ago.*

(ANGLO-CELT, 15 MAY 1915, P. 1)

Mr Kellett had an address in Tuckahoe, New York. Another passenger, Joseph Myers, later related how he was walking on the starboard side of the boat deck with Kellett when he saw the torpedo strike. He grabbed Kellett's arm: 'My God, Frank, we're lost!'

One man grabbing another by the arm to point out the torpedo wake
– The Sphere, 15 May 1915

Annie Kelly (19) Lost

Deported third-class passenger
New Bridge, Mountbellew, Co. Galway

Annie Kelly was one of seven children living with a widowed mother at New Bridge, Mountbellew, Co. Galway. She gave her age as 18 and her occupation as a housekeeper when she arrived in New York on the *Lusitania* on an earlier sailing which docked on 24 April 1915.

Annie's boyfriend, William Murphy, had earlier emigrated earlier to America and Annie planned to marry him soon after arrival. Initially she intended to stay with her Uncle Patrick at 116 Greenville Street, Roxbury, Massachusetts. She did not have the $50 in her possession required by law before she could land. Annie hoped this could be overlooked, as it often was. As an immigrant, she was obliged to undergo a medical examination at Ellis Island, and ship surgeons were also required to examine steerage passengers *en route*.

Lusitania surgeon James McDermott discovered that she had a valvular disorder of the heart and as a result, Annie was detained on the 'Isle of Tears' without formally entering America. Since the defect would limit her ability to earn a living and make her likely to end up as a 'public charge', Annie was told she would be sent back.

When Annie's brother Thomas, already in America, learned of her plight he took steps to seek an exemption. He went to the mayor in Boston, where he lived, petitioning him on the basis that he would personally assume all responsibility for Annie in the event of bad health preventing her from working. Having encountered one frustrating delay after another, he was eventually granted the exemption he sought.

Thomas rushed back to New York but when he arrived at Pier 54, the *Lusitania's* berth, the great liner had departed on her fatal voyage, taking a deported Annie Kelly far from the Manhattan skyline and a married future with the man she loved.

A notation on the original arrival manifest notes that Annie was deported on the vessel's next sailing, by which time she had turned nineteen. The deportation trip ended in a torpedo, and both Annie and the surgeon who had examined her lost their lives.

1911 Census
New Bridge, New Grove, Mountbellew.
Head of Household – Margaret Kelly, 57, widow. Farmer.
Children: Thomas, 34, Mary, 20, Bridget 18, **Annie**, 16, Patrick, 14, Sarah, 12, James, 11.
All in the household could read and write, and speak both English and Irish.

Marie Kelly (32) Lost
Third-class passenger
Kinvara, Co. Galway

Marie Annie Kelly was working in Boston and was home to visit her father, Patrick Kelly, of Cloosh, Kinvara.

Body number 87 was identified as that of Marie, and she was buried in pit Common C in the Old Church Cemetery in Queenstown.

On 9 June 1915, her paltry effects were sent to the Corless Hotel in Kinvara, where Mr Kelly was told he could call to collect them.

Margaret Kenny (31) Lost
Mary Bridget Kenny, daughter (2) Lost
Second-class passengers
44A Park Street, Charlestown, Massachusetts

Margaret was born in Ireland in 1884, and emigrated to Boston in 1907 at the age of 23. She married Peter Kenny in that city in 1911, with their only daughter born late the following year. Margaret was a widow by 1913. She earned a living by helping relatives to run a boarding-house.

Margaret Kenny – of 44A Park Street, Charlestown, Mass. 13 October 1915, administration of estate granted at Dublin to Thomas Kenny, farmer, in the amount of £287 18s 6d. Died at sea 7 May 1915.

Also her infant Mary Bridget Kenny, same address, died at sea 7 May 1915 (Irish index records of wills and administrations).

Delia Kilkenny (33) Saved
Third-class passenger
Ballyhaunis, Co. Mayo

Miss Delia Kilkenny, of Aughamore, Ballyhaunis, who was amongst the rescued passengers of the Lusitania, *arrived home safely on Saturday night. A cousin of hers from the same locality, who was accompanying her home on a holiday, is missing.**

(CONNAUGHT TELEGRAPH, 15 MAY 1915, P. 4)

* Her first cousin was Hannah Cunniffe (*qv*).

Miss Delia Kilkenny, Aughamore, Ballyhaunis, is another survivor of the disaster. She arrived here on Saturday night, bringing with her the lifebelt which saved her from a watery grave.

(MAYO NEWS, 15 MAY 1915, P. 8)

One girl was coming home to see her dying mother in Mayo. She had been in two boats, both of which had turned turtle. As she was going down she thought of her poor mother, and thinking that the end was near she began to pray. After a desperate struggle she caught hold of another woman's heel and someone else caught hers, and together they all rose to the surface and were taken on some boats.

(CORK FREE PRESS, 10 MAY 1915, P. 7)

According to her grandson, Delia was on her way home to visit her ill father, having worked for seven years in Boston. It had been her intention to return to the States, but after the terrible experience she remained in Ireland for the rest of her life.

Her cousin, who on the point of boarding the lifeboat, decided to go back for some personal belongings, and Delia never saw her again.

On Easter Monday 1916 – the day of the Rising in Dublin – Delia married Edward Brennan of Pollagh, Kiltimagh, Co. Mayo. They had one child, a girl.

A rug given to Delia by a kindly man as she climbed into a lifeboat has been donated by the family to Kiltimagh Museum at the former railway station in the town.

Sir Hugh Lane (40) Lost
First-class passenger
Dublin

Medium Hester Dowden was holding a séance in Dublin on the night of 7 May 1915, when her pencil began 'automatic writing'. It was a message from Sir Hugh Lane, stating he had been on board the *Lusitania*, but had fallen into the sea from a lifeboat full of people. Sir Hugh wanted to give messages to several friends. Neither the medium nor other sitters present supposedly knew that Sir Hugh was on board the vessel torpedoed that afternoon. Several times during later sessions, Dowden's pencil wrote alleged messages from Lane.

One of then said that he was worried about the disposal of his pictures and wished that they were exhibited in Dublin. 'These pictures must return to Dublin,' said the script. 'I can't rest until this affair is at an end. It tortures me'.

This reference was to 39 impressionist paintings, then on display in the Tate Gallery, which Lane, in an unsigned codicil to his will, had wanted returned to Ireland. The issue led to a prolonged dispute between London and Dublin.

No account has been received yet concerning Sir Hugh Lane, one of the honorary directors of the Dublin Municipal Art Gallery. He as 40 years of age, son of the late Rev. J. W. Lane, MA, Co. Cork, his mother being a member of the well-known Persse family of Rosborough, Galway.

(IRISH INDEPENDENT, 11 MAY 1915, P. 5)

MR G. B. SHAW AND THE LUSITANIA TRAGEDY

Interviewed in Birr on his way from Galway, Mr G. B. Shaw, as regards the loss of the Lusitania, *said, 'It is a terrible affair', and that the scenes at Queenstown must have been awful. He was much concerned as to the fate of Sir H. Lane, who he said was a nephew of Lady Gregory, who had been his hostess in Galway.*

'Sir Hugh,' he remarked, 'was one of the best fellows I ever met, and Lady Gregory and all his relatives and friends are terribly distressed about him'.

(DAILY EXPRESS, 14 MAY 1915, P. 6)

Sir Hugh Lane – An Appreciation
(By Thomas Bodkin)

Sir Hugh Lane has not been saved from the wreck of the Lusitania. *There is no hope of that now. He was a man with singularly admirable qualities, both of mind and spirit. The grief which has come through this most foul and wanton murder, to those who knew him well, is so sudden and so bitter that a calm estimate of the loss his death involves is an impossibility at present.*

He was not quite forty when he died; he had started life with no material advantages, and for nearly ten years his taste and knowledge in matters of art, coupled with his indomitable generosity, had made him famous in three Continents.

Reckoning the number and importance of those lost and forgotten masterpieces which he recovered and restored to mankind, we realise that here was one who did more practical work for civilisation than many of the most celebrated creative artists.

The unimaginative were often pleased to attribute Lane's triumphs to chance. When he detected in a dark canvas at Christie's the great Titian of Lorenzo de Medici – which sold later for £25,000 – and bought it, before the eyes of the big dealers, for £2,000, his discernment was described as 'Lane's luck'.

If it was luck, that luck was so persistent as to seem a habit. One day he would find in an old curiosity shop, amid a heap of ancient daubs, a Mancini, painted, possibly, only three or four years before. Such a find hangs on his staircase at this moment. Next day he would buy at auction, for what was seemingly a fantastic price, something that looked like a clever work of the school of Lawrence.

The high light on a lip, the sweep of an eyebrow, had shown him that below the upper layer of paint which had lain there undisturbed for a hundred years, he would see a superlative Romney, worth full twenty times the money the critics had thought squandered …

I remember once, when in his house at Chelsea, admiring the brush work of the magnificent imperial crown that Philip II of Spain wears in the Titian portrait. Lane himself told me how this crown had come to light. The picture had been for many years in the important collection of the German painter, Lenbach. Its ownership could be traced back to Titian himself.

'When I first saw it', he said, 'the King wore what looked like a cap of maintenance. I had always thought there was repainting in that, but no one would believe me till Lenbach died, and then I bought the picture, cleared off the old paint, and proved myself right'. These incidents are selected haphazard from hundreds like them.

Lane's permanent memorial is to be found in the collections he got together, the galleries he supervised, and in the magnificent gifts he constantly made to an unappreciative public …

Lane began early. His first big exhibition was of Old Masters in Dublin, and was organised and opened when he was twenty-nine years of age. Others came in quick succession. In 1904 he took charge of the thirteenth annual Exhibition in the London Guildhall, confined it to works by Irish artists, and made it a record success.

In the same year he held in Dublin the Exhibition of the Staats Forbes pictures, from which he desired to form the nucleus of a Gallery of Modern Art for Ireland, to be second to none. At the Franco-British Exhibition in 1908, the Irish Art Gallery was his idea and his triumph. It was characteristic of the man that when the Minister of Fine Arts in France refused him the loan of a Lavery he coveted from the Luxembourg, he went across at once to Paris, persuaded the Minister, and returned with the picture by the next boat.

In 1911 he inaugurated the Johannesburg Gallery of Modern Art. The pictures for it were shown in London before going out to South Africa, and created by their worth a real sensation in art circles. He was then the first Director of that Gallery, but resigned almost immediately, because, as he wrote to me, 'I find that one cannot buy for two galleries (the same sort of thing), and I want all the bargains for Dublin' …

Lane's first thoughts were always for Dublin. His project for the establishment of a Municipal

Gallery was his dearest ambition. He made many sacrifices to attain it, and the failure of his schemes proved cruelly disappointing. His appointment to the Directorship of the National Gallery last year gave his generosity a new outlet.

The city was already deeply indebted to him for many wonderful gifts, both to the Gallery in Harcourt Street and the one in Leinster Lawn. After his appointment, his desire to benefit became unbridled. Last year alone he gave us pictures of immense value and significance by, amongst others, Beerstratin, Desportes, Espinosa, Gainsborough (two), El Greco, Magnasco, Piazzetta, Bassari, Romney, and Nanine Vallain.

He was never adequately thanked. His motives were constantly maligned by men who did not imagine that generosity and patriotism could be so independent of profit. But he bore no malice. He made no taunts. His thoughts were too much taken up by plans of increasing benefactions for the future, to leave leisure for rancour.

It is inexpressibly painful to try to write about his lovable personal qualities. All intimate memories of him must be most precious and tender, for he was a charming companion and a loyal, kindly friend. He could show inflexible decision in acquiring, no matter at what price, such beautiful things, from jewels to pictures, as pleased his exquisite taste.

But his manner was invariably amiable and pliant, and his triumphs and his talents left him amazingly modest. I never heard him speak of any opponent with more than a touch of careless scorn. He was instantly responsive to sympathy, wherever it came from, and was tolerant of every prejudice and ignorance that was sincere.

Meanness and commonness in any form were utterly repugnant to his instincts. We have not heard definitely the manner of his dying, but we can be sure, from what we know of him, that he was unselfish and noble to the end.

(IRISH TIMES, 10 MAY 1915, P. 9)

SIR HUGH LANE'S PROPERTY
PICTURES VALUED AT ABOUT £100,000

Mr Justice Younger, in the Chancery Division, London, yesterday heard an application for the appointment of a receiver to protect the assets of Sir Hugh Lane, the art expert, who went down on the Lusitania and who bequeathed the bulk of his estate, consisting mainly of pictures, said to be of the value of nearly £100,000 to public galleries in London and Dublin.

The application was a friendly one, and Mrs Shine, a sister of Sir Hugh, was appointed receiver until such time as probate could be granted. Mr Ernest E. Bird, Mrs Shine's solicitor, undertook to be accountable for her receipts.

(IRISH TIMES, 22 MAY 1915, P. 7)

LOST ON THE LUSITANIA

Sir Hugh Lane.

Sir Hugh was shipping a crate of 27 masterpieces across the Atlantic from New York on the *Lusitania*, and the vessel's original manifest establishes the point. The cache was said to include works by Monet, Rubens and Titian, but specific claims about the canvasses were undermined when it was discovered that one alleged to be aboard – *Man with a Hawk* by Titian – was safe and well in a private collection.

In January 1995, a British diving team claimed it had seen lead cylinders in the debris field of the *Lusitania* and speculated that these might have contained the art works. It was common to seal canvasses in lead when consigned by ship because of the danger of fire.

The allegations about sealed containers suggested the possi-

A flyer distributed in Queenstown aimed at recovering Lane's body. It mentions that he was of very slight build, wore a pearl tie pin, had cellular undergarments marked 'H. Lane', and had a hairy chest

bility that some works might have survived decades-long immersion in seawater, although this assumption must be doubtful at best. Nonetheless the opportunity for rediscovery is believed to have played a major part in the Irish government decision of that year to designate the *Lusitania* as a protected national monument.

It was finally agreed to share the 'Lane paintings' in dispute (because of the unsigned codicil to the will) between London and Dublin, although Britain did not surrender ownership. The matter had been forced to negotiation in 1956, after two Irish students stole one of the works, *Jour d'Eté* by Berthe Morisot, removing it from the Tate Gallery in broad daylight. The painting was later recovered in Ireland and returned.

Bridget Lee – Saved
Second-class passenger
Denn, Co. Cavan

When the news of the Lusitania disaster was received in Cavan much anxiety was felt in their native parish of Denn as to the fate of Miss Bridget Lee and her niece, Miss [Margaret] Galligan, who were passengers on the ill-fated ship, but on enquiries being made it was learned that they had been saved, and they arrived in Cavan during the week little the worse for the trying and terrible experiences which they had gone through.

Both ladies were coming across from New York to pay a visit to their friends in Denn, and like the majority of the other passengers, paid but little attention to the sinister warning issued from the German Embassy prior to the sailing of the ship, never for a moment dreaming that the Lusitania, carrying innocent passengers, many of them women and children, would be the victim of a fiendish attack.

On the voyage they thought little of the warning, but when nearing the Irish coast its full import was brought suddenly and forcibly to their minds when the periscope of a submarine was observed, and a few moments afterwards they heard a sound like a shot.

They were at dinner at the time, and realising that the ship had been struck, rushed to the deck, whether they were told that there was no danger. Then the second torpedo found its mark; the ship listed dangerously, and in but a few minutes settled.

They went down with the vessel, and after struggling in the water for almost two hours were picked up by a boat and brought to Queenstown, where they were provided with dry clothing, and subsequently proceeded to Cavan. The scenes as the ship went down were heartrending, and left a lasting impression in their memory.

Miss Lee had been 25 years in America.

(IRISH POST AND WEEKLY TELEGRAPH, 15 MAY 1915, P. 3)

John MacEneaney (23) Lost
Third-class passenger
Clones, Co. Monaghan

Mr John MacEneaney, son of Mr Peter MacEneaney, fowl dealer, Clones, was a passenger on the Lusitania, intending to pay a visit to his relatives, and as his name does not appear on the list of survivors, and inquiries have failed to trace him, it is feared that he is amongst the victims. He had been in the United States for some years and held a good position.

(CLONES CORRESPONDENT, DAILY EXPRESS, 12 MAY 1915, P. 6)

Mr MacEneaney was normally resident in New York.

Robert Anderson Mackenzie (40) Saved
Third-class passenger
Cavendish Row, Dublin

A DUBLIN MAN'S EXPERIENCES

Mr Robert A. Mackenzie, fish and poultry merchant, of 3 Cavendish Row, Dublin, arrived home on Saturday evening after a tour of 12,000 miles. He was absent for about three months, and having transacted business in New Orleans, he made a round tour visiting Meridian, Birmingham, Chattanooga, Cincinnati, Chicago, Detroit, Niagara Falls, Toronto, Buffalo, Syracuse, and back to New York.

He travelled out by the Lusitania and arranged his trip to return by the same vessel. He said he was in his stateroom of the second cabin when the torpedo struck the ship. The first intimation he received was the dull thud with which the torpedo struck the side, and there seemed to be an explosion in the hold, though there was very little noise and the shock was slight where he was standing.

He at once made his way to the first cabin deck, which at the time was practically deserted except for a few stewards. There was no panic, and the stewards seemed quite confident that the vessel would reach the shore, towards which she was headed.

It was just after lunch, and most of the first-class passengers were either in the smoke rooms or their own berths, and the second lot of second cabin passengers were at lunch at the time. There was an unusual number of those on board, as after the Lusitania had left the slips in New York she was recalled to embark the first and second-class passengers of a vessel which was being diverted to another port for a different cargo.

This over-taxed the capacity of the Lusitania, so that the second-class passengers had to be dined in two lots. It also threw an extra burden on the crew, especially the stewards, and the impression of the passengers was that the vessel was very short-handed.

They travelled at the average speed of about 20 knots, and their best day's run was 501 miles. There was a heavy haze over the Irish coast all Friday morning, and the foghorn was continually sounded and bearings taken. They only sighted the Irish coast about a half hour before the vessel was struck, and when the torpedo was fired they were travelling at about 15 knots. He did not see the submarine at all.

The vessel began to settle down almost immediately after the first torpedo struck her, and within a few minutes there was a heavy list to starboard, which rendered it almost impossible to launch the boats from that side. Most of the boats had been hung out on their davits at boat drill on the Thursday morning, and left there ready for lowering.

Had it not been for this, it is extremely doubtful if so many passengers would have been saved, as a large number of the crew were at the time involved in the transfer of the mails and luggage from the holds to the main decks prior to the disembarkation at Liverpool. By the time these men reached the decks, the vessel had well settled down, and it was too late to get many of the boats off, and those at the starboard side could not be launched as the vessel was almost on her side.

He saw a good many boats get off on the port side, but many of them were at once swamped. He and other passengers helped launch some of the boats, and one of these got swamped by a funnel as the vessel was heeling over. He jumped six feet into the last boat, and before it got clear it was entangled in the wireless [lines], but they were able to get free before the vessel finally went down.

They escaped between two funnels and rescued some women and children who were clinging to the bottoms of two overturned collapsible boats. They rowed some distance to a fishing smack, which was becalmed at the time, and so unable

Lifeboat getting away from the Lusitania's port side

to render any assistance. They were put aboard the drifter, and the crew rowed back to the scene of the calamity to pick up any survivors.

They were taken off the drifter by a tug boat about 7 o'clock, and brought to Queenstown. The Lusitania went down almost straight on her bow.

Amongst those in the boat which he got off by was the wireless operator [Robert Leith]. He learned that when the torpedo exploded, the main apparatus was put out of order, as was also the emergency apparatus used for sending the messages for help.

(IRISH TIMES, 10 MAY 1915, P. 8)

Mr Mackenzie later wrote of his experiences in *The Grocer* magazine, in which he claimed to be 'absolutely the last man to leave the ship'. He added: 'There were hundreds down below on the lower decks who were drowned long before the ship finally sank and who never got on deck at all'.

DUBLIN REBELLION

A provision merchant named Mackenzie, who refused the rebels the use of his premises and provisions, was at once shot dead. He was a passenger on board the Lusitania when she was torpedoed.

(THE TIMES, 4 MAY 1916, P. 6)

Martin Mannion – Saved
Second-class passenger
Kildare, Co. Kildare

BOUND FOR THE CURRAGH

Martin Mannion, a jockey of Irish parentage, was coming to take an engagement at the Curragh. He does not know how he was saved. He believes that the vessel would have reached port, had not a second torpedo been launched, or that at the worst all the passengers could have been saved.

'It was,' he said, 'an awful sight. When I came to the surface, I saw a bunch of at least 200 men and women clutching and clinging to each other, and crying for help. They were all drowned. I was lucky to have kept clear of that lot'.

(IRISH INDEPENDENT, 11 MAY 1915, P. 5)

CURRAGH JOCKEY SAVED FROM THE LUSITANIA
FOUR HOURS IN THE WATER
DUBLIN, THURSDAY

A press representative had a very interesting talk at Kildare with Mr Martin Mannion, who had the experience of going down in the ship when the Lusitania was torpedoed, and after four hours' swimming was able to climb onto a raft, eventually arriving safely home.

Mr Mannion will be remembered to many sporting friends in the County Kildare, as before he left for the United States, he was attached to the stables of the popular Curragh trainer, Mr Michael Dawson.

Second-class smoking room

Mr Mannion said he left the Curragh and went to the United States in 1911, sailing on the Laurentic – 'The ship which, by the by,' said Mr Mannion, 'brought Dr Crippen from Canada at the time of his dramatic arrest.

'I was in the smoke room of the Lusitania, speaking to Mr Turpin, of Maryborough, when the disaster occurred. The cry immediately arose that the ship had been torpedoed; but I said I had no *chance when asked to move for the boats as unfortunately I had been severely injured in an accident a few weeks previously in America, and was then wearing an artificial leg.*

'*I told Mr Turpin also at that time, that I would stand no chance. The scenes on the ship I will not attempt to describe, but when the final turn and the list of the Lusitania came, I found myself in the water, and even before I realised the plunge, I was swimming.*

'*I have fortunately always been a good swimmer. I went down with the ship, but thank God I am saved. After going down with the Lusitania I had to continue for about four hours struggle in the water, and you can understand what it means – the swimming in the open sea for such a long time. But I can always remember the experience as a sorrowful in every way, and one which will be (no matter how long my life may be) always with me*'.

(CORK EXAMINER, 21 MAY 1915, P. 6)

Mannion, who had an address in Albany, New York, found himself quoted in the *New York Tribune* of 10 May as saying that he had been playing poker when the torpedo struck and that all his fellow players had deserted him. He then supposedly made his way to the bar and offered to play dice with its attendant, who told him to 'go to Hell' and fled. Whereupon Mannion helped himself to a bottle of beer and sat down to drink it. This would appear to be a typical piece of yellow journalism.

Fr Basil Maturin (67) Lost
First-class passenger
Grangegorman, Dublin

A DISTINGUISHED IRISH PRIEST

The world-famed preacher Father Basil Maturin, who was lost on the Lusitania, *was at one time in Anglican orders. He was born in Ireland in 1847, the son of the Vicar of All Saints, Grangegorman. His family came of old Huguenot stock.*

Father Maturin graduated at Trinity College, Dublin. After entering into Holy Orders, he went to Peterstow to become a curate with his father's great friend, Dr Jebb, in 1870. He remained there for three years, and then he joined the Cowley Fathers at Cowley St John, and on their behalf went to take charge of St Clement's parish, Philadelphia, in 1876.

It was not long ere his popularity as a preacher rivalled that of Bishop Phillips Brooks in America. It was in 1897 that he was received into the Church by Father Pope, SJ, at Beaumont, and in the following year Cardinal Vaughan ordained him a priest.

It is not generally known that Father Maturin had at one time the ardent desire to embrace monastic life, and therefore he entered for a time Downside Abbey, the Benedictine Monastery, but being convinced that his vocation was not there, he left Downside.

Fr Herbert Vaughan's Catholic Missionary Society was the next scene of his labours, and he worked at Warwick Street, London, the then headquarters of the Mission (later removed to Brondesbury) until 1913. In that year he was appointed Chaplain to the Catholic undergraduates at Oxford, and he lived there ever since.

It was while returning to Oxford from America (where he had been preaching) to resume his duties that he lost his life in the Lusitania, no details up to the time of writing being forthcoming as to his last moments.

At Oxford, Fr Maturin, although not living in a House, was constantly in touch with those under his spiritual care, and he arranged meetings at which he spoke to them on matters connected with their religion, and in fact he looked after them generally.

It is hard to realise that he will be seen no more or heard no more in London pulpits.

(*WATERFORD NEWS*, 14 MAY 1915, P. 7)

Additional details of the manner, worthy of the best traditions of the Irish priesthood, in which he employed his last moments on the Lusitania are given in the Westminster Gazette on the authority of a friend of Father Maturin. 'We have heard,' he says, 'that after the ship was torpedoed he exerted a quieting influence on those about him. He endeavoured to calm the women and children and to help them into the boats.

'The last that was seen of him was after he had been carrying a child who was separated from its parents, and at the time also when he assisted a lady into one of the boats. 'Take this, little one,' he said to her, handing in the child, 'you may be able to find the parents to whom it belongs'.

'Father Maturin's act probably saved the child's life, for later on the mother was found and the child restored to her. He was always a great lover of children, and when with them was seen at his best'.

(*WATERFORD NEWS*, 21 MAY 1915, P. 5)

Fr Maturin's body was recovered eight miles south-west of the Fastnet rock by a patrol boat and landed at Crookhaven. From there it was removed, with four others, to Queenstown by the tender *Flying Fish*. It was taken to the railway station for the journey to London and interment followed Solemn Requiem Mass at Westminster Cathedral. The procession to the station included the clerk and members of Queenstown Urban Council, the local clergy, and a large number of local residents.

Thomas McAfee (28) Lost
Third-class passenger
42 Summer Street, Belfast, Co. Antrim

LOST IN THE LUSITANIA
MR THOMAS MCAFEE

of Toronto, who was coming home to see friends and also to enlist, was lost on the ill-fated Lusitania. Previous to going to Canada, he had been twelve years in the York Street Spinning Company, and has two sisters residing at 42 Summer Street, Belfast. He put off booking his passage by an earlier steamer to wait for his friend, Mr R. G. McCready [qv], who was also drowned.

(*IRISH POST AND WEEKLY TELEGRAPH*, 5 JUNE 1915, P. 10)

* A pocket-book with letters and papers belonging to Mr McAfee was found floating in the sea in the wake of the disaster. It was forwarded to his sister at the Summer Street address on 30 August 1915.

Samuel McClemond (32) Saved
Third-class passenger
Moyvore, Mullingar, Co. Westmeath

A Moyvore survivor in Mullingar
Thrilling Story

Much sympathetic interest was aroused on Sunday in Mullingar when it became known that Samuel McClemond, one of the survivors from the ill-starred Lusitania, had arrived in the town on his way to his home in Forgrey district, near Moyvore, about ten miles from Mullingar.

McClemond, who is about 30 years of age, appears considerably shaken by his terrible experience and was naturally rather nervous, but otherwise he appeared not much the worse for the wear – at least he had not suffered any injury.

In the course of an interview, he said:

'It was a terrible shock. I was eating at the time, and when I heard the first crash I knew at once that it was a torpedo had struck the ship. I was a third-class passenger. I believe most of the first-class must have perished. I rushed for a lifebelt, but found there were some hundreds of women and children looking for belts, and other means of escape, and I needn't say they, like us all, were suffering from wild anxiety and terror, though there was no disorder.

'When I saw the women and children, I of course waited until they were provided with lifebelts, and then, having secured one for myself, made for one side of the ship and slid down to the water by a rope. I attempted to get into a lifeboat but failed; indeed in order to escape being pinned between the lifeboat and the vessel's side I have to dive under the lifeboat.

'I came up all right on the other side and after about twenty minutes in the water I was picked up by a submarine chaser'.

Mr McClemond also said he had been seven months in America. He added that when the ship was struck, one of the funnels was projected up about 90 or 100 feet in the air.

He had personally received no warning before embarking of the risk of the ship being torpedoed, but was aware that several passengers had received some such intimation.

(Westmeath Examiner, 15 May 1915, p. 6)

Margaret McClintock – Saved
Second-class passenger
Mountpottinger, Belfast, Co. Antrim

Miss M. McClintock, who has been in New York for three years, despite the German threats of which she was fully aware, had no fear in regard to crossing the Atlantic, in coming to visit her sister at 3, George's Terrace, Castlereagh Street, Belfast.

She was thrown from her seat when the torpedo struck, and subsequently she went through a terrible ordeal in getting to safety, but emerged little the worse of her terrifying experience.

(Irish Independent, 11 May 1915, p. 5)

Local Lady Survivor

Amongst the Belfast survivors who underwent a thrilling ordeal was Miss Margaret McClintock, who was on a visit to her sister, who carried on a business as a dressmaker at 3, George's Terrace, Castlereagh Street.

In the course of an interview, Miss McClintock said she heard a terrific noise and was thrown from her seat at the lunch table. She realised immediately that the Lusitania had been torpedoed. She succeeded in getting into a lifeboat which carried over 60 persons. After two and a half hours had elapsed, they were transferred to a trawler, and subsequently to a Government boat, being

AN IRISH TRAGEDY ♦ 51

eventually landed at Queenstown. The crew, according to Miss McClintock, did everything possible for the passengers.

(Northern Whig, 11 May 1915, p. 8)

Thomas McCormick (30) Saved
Third-class passenger
Robertstown, Co. Kildare

Amongst the survivors is Mr Thomas McCormick of Robertstown, Co. Kildare, who is little the worse for his terrible experience. He told an Irish Independent *reporter that seeing there was no hope for the vessel he plunged into the water and swam for about two hours, when he picked up a lifebelt.*

With this he continued swimming about amongst the dead bodies until rescued at 6 o'clock by the trawler Indian Empire *and taken to Queenstown.*

(Irish Independent, 12 May 1915, p. 5)

Mr McCormick had an address in Nashua, New Hampshire.

ROBERTSTOWN MAN ON THE LUSITANIA
STORY OF HIS EXPERIENCES
A FORTY FEET JUMP FOR LIFE

Amongst the survivors of the Lusitania *disaster was a young man named Thomas McCormack [sic] , a native of Robertstown, who arrived at Cooleragh, near Blackwood last week, where he now resides with his relatives, and is showing little sign of the terrible ordeal he had passed through. When I called on him to hear his story on Tuesday, writes our representative, I found him engaged in carting turf from the bog of his uncle.*

Starting with his narrative, Mr McCormack [sic] said he had been about two years in the United States and decided to come home, booking on the Lusitania, *as in ordinary times. Before leaving he was not aware of any threat on the part of the Germans to sink the ship. He saw no placards in New York, and although he had seen the daily papers for a week before he left, he noticed no published warning.*

The first he heard of submarines was on the Wednesday preceding the disaster, when he saw the ship's lifeboats hung over the side. He inquired of a sailor the reason for this and was told it was done so as to be prepared for attacks coming near England, and also that there was no cause for alarm as it was done on all trips then.

Coming to the eventful day, he said they sighted land about 11 a.m., and they were beginning to consider themselves safe. He was walking on the main deck about 2 o'clock when he heard the two bangs. They were not very much, he added, and he did not know what was wrong till he noticed the ship keeling over to starboard and saw a bit of a panic with people tumbling over one another running for lifebelts.

He also went to procure his belt, but as he was travelling third-class, his berth was situated three flights of stairs below, and before he had descended more than halfway he found himself knee-deep in water. He returned to the deck to find the ship was almost on its side, with the bow dipped low and the stern high in the air.

The boats were being lowered and large numbers of people were standing around. No life belt was available, but he decided to jump. Jumping from the side on which the deck was nearest the water, he said, meant certain death, because it was becoming a howling mass of human beings clinging to one another in groups, 'and you know', he added. 'If a drowning person catches hold of you and you have no lifebelt, it is all up.' Continuing, he said he had no friend or chum with him. He knew no one on board, and made no acquaintances. It was merely up to him to devise a plan to save his own life, and he was powerless to do more.

He scrambled up towards the stern, the deck being now almost perpendicular, with the stern towering upwards of 40 feet in the air. Divesting himself of coat, vest and boots, he made the fateful jump, diving to an awful depth. On rising to the surface he started swimming away from the ship, and got to a distance of about four or five perches when she disappeared. Then came the explosion, which was dreadful, water and wreckage being hurled high in the air.

After a short time he came upon something like a trunk, but this capsized and was near drowning him. He kept afloat for about an hour and a quarter, when he saw about half a dozen lifebelts floating about, and donning one of these survived the ordeal till rescued about 6 p.m. by a trawler, called, he thought, the Indian Empire.

He pulled himself on to the trawler by means of a rope, his hands still showing traces of the ijuries thus received. On reaching the deck he fell, having temporarily lost the power of his legs. This boat, he said, picked up a large number of people wearing lifebelts, but many of them died before reaching Queenstown. While in the water he also saw many dead bodies of children floating about.

On arriving at Queenstown, he said, the survivors were very kindly treated. Questioned, he said he learned to swim when a child in the canal, and then spent most of his time in the water in the summer months. While employed as a boatman later with the Canal Co. he once succeeded in swimming across the Shannon. As to his loss, he said, £75 in notes and all his belongings, including a new suit of clothes and a valuable watch, went to the bottom of the sea.

He had saved a good sum while working on the canal before emigrating, that which he had lost representing a portion of his total savings, the remainder being safely banked in Boston. An interesting fact which transpired in further conversation with Mr McCormack [sic] was that he was one of the crew of the string of boats off one of which a Robertstown man named Weir lost his life in the Shannon a few years ago, the boats drifting 40 perches before they could be stopped. He also stated that on the trip from America he saw people throwing wreaths and flowers into the sea, and on asking the reason was told that they were passing over the Titanic.

(Kildare Observer, 29 May 1915)

Robert McCready (28) Lost
Third-class passenger
Oldpark Road, Belfast, Co. Antrim

Mr Robert McCready, who was one of the victims of the Lusitania horror, was the son of Mr W. J. McCready, Oldpark Road, Belfast. He was about 27 years of age, was a photographer by profession, and had made a very successful tour of business in the United States, and was returning home when he met his fate.

There was no better known young man in the Oldpark Road locality than 'Bob' McCready, and his untimely death is much lamented by his many friends and the friends of his bereaved parents.

(Larne Times, 15 May 1915, p. 4)

Prior to leaving Belfast for Canada a couple of years ago, deceased was twelve years in the employment of Messrs Charles and Russell, photographers, Royal Avenue. He was the second son of Mr William J. McCready, 43 Oldpark Road, Belfast.

(Larne Times, 29 May 1915, p. 8)

Survivor Ralph Mecredy (no relation) told the Cork Examiner that 'another thing I noticed before the ship sank was a steward who was busy taking photographs of the doomed ship; no doubt he had a good idea of the value of war photographs. His dead

THE SINKING OF THE LUSITANIA.

£10,000 FOR PHOTOGRAPHS

ONE PICTURE CAN WIN £700.

The *Daily Sketch* is offering £10,000 for the best photographs illustrating incidents in the great war.

One picture can win a fortune—even if it is only a snapshot with a five-shilling camera.

Films or plates will be developed free at the *Daily Sketch* offices, Shoe-lane, London, E.C.

Remember that a news picture loses value with every moment of delay.

Despite newspaper hunger, no authentic photographs of the last scenes aboard the Lusitania ever materialised

body was brought ashore afterwards with two cameras strapped round his waist'.

Kate McDonnell (25) Saved
Second-class passenger
25 Prosperity Square, Cork City

Miss MacDonald (sic) told me how she floated about for nearly an hour and was in a dazed state. She had little remembrance of what passed until a boat passed near her. 'I heard somebody say "Oh, the poor girl is dead", and they began to pull away from me. I had just strength enough to raise my hand, and they returned and pulled me on board. It was nearly midnight when we got to Queenstown'.

(CORK FREE PRESS, 10 MAY 1915, P. 5)

ALL-FOR-IRELAND CLUB
VOTE OF CONDOLENCE TO LUSITANIA SURVIVOR

After some routine business had been transacted, on the motion of Mr J. Penny, seconded by Mr English, a sincere vote of congratulation was passed to Miss Barrett, 120 Barrack Street, and Miss McDonnell, Prosperity Square, on their providential escape from the Lusitania disaster.

(CORK FREE PRESS, 21 MAY 1915, P. 5)

Kate, known as Kitty, was travelling with her friend May Barrett (*qv*), with whom she had originally emigrated to New York four years earlier. Kitty stood 5'4" tall and had blue eyes that sparkled when she was reunited with her father Eugene, himself mightily relieved that the 'poor dead girl' had returned to him.

Henry McEvoy – Saved
Second-class passenger
Donacloney, Co. Antrim

DONACLONEY MAN SAVED

Amongst the very few survivors of the Lusitania who arrived home yesterday was Mr Henry McEvoy, a son of Mr Wm John McEvoy, Donacloney, who is employed in the New York house of Messrs Wm Liddell and Sons, Ltd. Mr McEvoy's parents were fortunately unaware that he had sailed on the Lusitania, and therefore they had no anxiety on his account, the first intimation that he was one of the passengers and had been saved coming from Mr R. M. Liddell, JP.

Mr McEvoy was having his luncheon when the liner was struck by the torpedo, and in company with his fellow passengers he rushed on deck, and after a delay of fifteen minutes, recognising that the vessel was doomed, and clad as he was, he jumped overboard, and none too soon, as within a few minutes she sank.

Mr McEvoy was drawn underneath the water by the suction for what he computed to be five minutes. When he regained the surface he swam about for twenty minutes until he and some others succeeded in mounting an upturned boat, on which they remained until rescued by a Queenstown liner some three hours later.

(LARNE TIMES, 15 MAY 1915, P. 4)

Patrick Vincent McGinley (32) *Saved*
Second-class passenger
233 Albert Bridge Road, Belfast, Co. Antrim

An interesting reunion of brother and sister occurred in the lace shop of Mrs Aherne, on the Beach, Queenstown. Mrs Murray, while making purchases in the shop, saw her brother Mr McGinley enter the same establishment. Both belonged to New York, and each thought the other drowned. The brother had given 5,000 dollars to the purser to place in the ship's safe.
(Cork Free Press, 10 May 1915, p. 7)

Belfast Man Sees Torpedo Fired

Mr P. V. McGinley, of Belfast, claims to have seen the first torpedo actually fired. 'My sister,' he said, 'was with me, when we got separated, and I thought her lost, but met her today in Queenstown. The submarine was about 400 yards from us. I saw the periscope first and then the turret, and then it disappeared quickly and we were struck by the torpedo.

'When we got to the lifeboats first, I took a child with me – just grabbed it as I went. We were ordered out of the lifeboat and told everything was safe. A few minutes after we were hit by the second torpedo. I sank with the ship, clinging to the wreckage, and was picked up after two hours by the trawler Caterina [sic]. The people were flinging themselves off from the ship in all directions as she was breaking up and sinking'.

(Irish Times, 10 May 1915, p. 8)

McGinley previously sailed to the USA aboard the *Lusitania* in March 1910. His occupation was given as schoolteacher, and he stayed with a friend in the naval training academy in Newport, Rhode Island. He was originally from Strabane, Co. Tyrone.

In November 1915, McGinley wrote a letter in reply to relatives of a victim of the disaster seeking information about their son. He was unable to help, except to say that the man's face, from a photo supplied, was familiar to both him and his sister.

In the course of the letter he declared: 'I was picked up with about forty others, after being four hours in the water, by an old tramp steamer called the *Caterina* [sic], which was flying the Greek flag and was bound from Havana, Cuba, to Liverpool with a cargo of sugar. She was really a British ship, assumed the name *Katrina* and flew the Greek flag in order to evade the submarines.

'I had the satisfaction of saving several lives, including Lady Allan, who unfortunately lost her two beautiful daughters, and Miss Rita Jolivet – principal or leading lady in Seymour Hicks' Company'.

Archibald McIlroy (55) *Lost*
Second-class passenger
Drumbo, Co. Down

Well-known Author on Board

Amongst the passengers believed to have been lost was a well-known Ulsterman in the person of Mr Archibald McIlroy, JP, who resided near Drumbo, Co. Down, and was known all over Ulster, and indeed over a much wider area, as a man of high literary tastes and accomplishments.

His well-known book, When Lint Was in the Bell, *created quite a furore on its publication, and commanded a very extensive sale. It was generally regarded as one of the best and most typical pictures of Ulster life that has ever been sketched.*

He was a man who took a very keen interest in public affairs, and was intimately associated with many activities, notably the Land Reform crusade. About two years ago he proceeded to Canada to enter upon pioneer work there on behalf of the Presbyterian Church in various districts throughout the Dominion.

His labours were eminently successful, and were highly appreciated. In a letter home to some friends three weeks ago he mentioned that he had offered his services, and hoped to be permitted to proceed for work at the front. It was doubtless to carry this intention into effect that he was on his way back to England.

He was one of the most popular of men, for his genial good nature made him a favourite everywhere, and his death under such tragic circumstances will be widely and sincerely mourned.

(IRISH POST AND WEEKLY TELEGRAPH, 15 MAY 1915, P. 11)

Deep regret has been felt throughout Ballyclare and district by the loss of Mr Archibald McIlroy, who went down on the ill-fated Lusitania. Mr McIlroy was born and brought up at Kyln Park, Ballyclare, and received his early education at the Old School, now used as the council chamber.

When as a young man he entered the service of the Ulster Bank, he spent the weekends at his father's house. His well-known book The Auld Meetin' House Green, depicts scenes and people well known about town.

(LARNE TIMES, 15 MAY 1915, P. 3)

Mr McIlroy had been staying in Edmonton, Alberta.

Patrick McLoughlin (35) Saved
Third-class passenger
Tully, Calry, Co. Sligo

HANGING BY THE ROPES

Mr P. L. McLoughlin, son of the Mr John McLoughlin, JP, Tully, Calry, Co. Sligo, had a marvellous escape. His attention was directed to a 'ripple on the water', and a couple of minutes later the torpedo struck the ship. A coal trimmer ran on deck exclaiming: 'It's all up with us now'. The vessel, when struck, trembled all over, and began to list to starboard.

As it was thought the watertight compartments would keep the liner afloat until help could be received, no boat was lowered. When the second torpedo struck, the vessel began to list over more and more. Mr McLoughlin went to the stern.

When the boats were lowered he saw some of them topple over, and they were dashed to pieces against the side of the Lusitania. People were clutching and hanging by the ropes. A Sligo lady whom he knew appealed to Mr McLoughlin to save her. He got her a lifebelt and went for one himself, but when he returned she had disappeared.

He could then see no one on the ship and he jumped into the water. Another man jumped on the top of him. He was stunned and driven under the water. Rising to the top he found the surface covered with dead bodies. He got such 'a knock' through the suction that he remembered nothing for a considerable time. He recalled an explosion which drove him away from the side of the ship.

Coming to an upturned boat, he managed to crawl on top. While there he succeeded in rescuing a lady whom he took up beside him. About an hour afterwards, he and his companions saw the smoke of a steamer in the distance, but they were disappointed that she passed away instead of coming towards them.* Later about five vessels came up and by 7.30 all who were alive were rescued.

(IRISH INDEPENDENT, 11 MAY 1915, P. 5)

* Two steamers, the City of Exeter and the Narragansett, initially responded to the Lusitania's distress calls, but they thought they detected a continuing submarine presence in the area and rapidly steamed away instead.

Mr McLoughlin had an address in Hartford, Connecticut, where he was a waiter in a hotel. He was returning home to his wife and four children.

Stephen McNulty (27) Lost
Third-class passenger
Jonesborough, Co. Armagh

Mr McNulty had an address in New York. His father was a Bernard McNulty of Flurry-bridge, Jonesborough, Co. Armagh. Body number 19 was identified as his. It was buried in mass grave Common C in the Old Church Cemetery, Queenstown, on 10 May 1915.

Dr Ralph Mecredy – Saved
Second-class passenger
Bray, Co. Wicklow

DUBLIN DOCTOR'S GRAPHIC ACCOUNT
SCENES ON SINKING SHIP

An Evening Mail representative says: I had the pleasure of lunching today with Dr Ralph Mecredy, son of Mr R. J. Mecredy, who is so well known in connection with the Irish motor and cycling world. Dr Mecredy was a passenger on the ill-fated Lusitania, and when I saw him today, except that he was a little pale, a little hoarse, and had his fingers bound up in bandages, he did not appear to be a great deal the worse for the terrible experiences through which he had passed.

Dr Mecredy was kind enough to tell me his experiences, always with the proviso that it is not very easy in an emergency of the kind through which he has passed to preserve clear and collected memories of everything that happened. There was a great deal of confusion, a great deal of excite-

ment, and a series of dramatic pictures that have burned themselves into his mind.

'It was fortunate for me,' he said, 'that I happened to be on deck when the torpedo struck us. It took me quite unawares, and I am not amongst those who say that they saw the track of the torpedo coming straight to the ship.'

I asked Dr Mecredy if he could tell me what the sensation is like when a big liner is struck by a torpedo? 'I cannot very well describe it,' he said, 'but it was as though the ship was suddenly checked by a gigantic and invisible hand. It was though the ship was pulled back once, went on again a bit, and was pulled back again.

'Then there was an explosion, and everything seemed to turn black. Huge spouts of water, apparently black, came up all around us, and then washed down over the decks. There was a lady standing by the rail just under where the torpedo struck. A huge water-spout rose beside her, fell on her, and knocked her down, but I do not think she was seriously injured'.

'What happened after the shock?' I asked. 'Well,' he said, 'I remember walking along the deck realising what had happened and wondering in my own mind whether the ship would sink. I cannot say that there was any panic, which is a relative term, but there was a great deal of confusion.

'The first thing that I noticed was that an order was issued that the women and children should go at once to the boat deck. Another thing I noticed – although whether then or subsequently I am not quite clear – was that when a large number of passengers were going to one of the stairs, followed by a number of seamen and stokers, some children fell. There was no attempt to rush over them. They were carefully picked up and set on their feet again.

'It was after walking around the deck for a few minutes that I made up my mind that the vessel was going to sink. I did so because she was sinking by the head and listing to one side. I think it was at this moment that I saw that one of the boats had been swung out and had caught on one of the davits.

'There were people still in her, and then I saw some people in the sea a little distance away, and I remember wondering how they got there, and realising afterwards that they must have fallen out of the boat. Then I decided that if the ship was going to sink I should be safer in the water.

'I had an idea that I would be better to strip and jump in at once, and that the sea would be safer than the ship at that moment. But as she was still travelling, I realised that if I jumped in I would soon be left far behind and perhaps out of sight. And there were no rescue ships in sight, not a sail nor a smoke track in the horizon.

'Then I had to make up my mind to drop into the sea over the stern of the ship, or to go for'ard to the bow where she was sinking, and where her deck rails were awash. I thought that if I tried the for'ard plunge she might do down at that moment and perhaps roll over onto me, or that in any case if she went down I should be sucked under with her, and perhaps be struck as I came up with some of the floating wreckage. It was while I was pondering this matter that it occurred to me that I ought to go down below and get a lifebelt.

'I found no great difficulty in going down below and getting a lifebelt, though I am sorry to say I did not know exactly how to put it on. However I took off everything except my trousers and shirt, and got into the lifebelt as best I could. Then I tackled again the problem as to whether I should get into the sea from the stern or the bow.

'Just as I came on deck, the vessel gave a lurch, which knocked a lot of people down, and it occurred to me that it was time to move. I decided that I would go aft and see what I could do there.

'I went aft as far as I could go, but the dive which I saw from there was too much for me. I never was much of a high diver, and with the stern of the Lusitania sticking out of the water, it was a murderous-looking jump. I noticed the log rope hanging over the side, and I decided that I would take the risk of going down by that.

'I climbed over and began to lower myself hand over hand, and using my bare feet to steady myself. But I found the rope soon tailed off into a wire rope, and when I looked up I found a couple of stokers were coming down on top of me, and that I had to hurry.

'I proceeded to slide down, and that is why my fingers are in bandages. It tore the flesh off them, although I did not feel it at the time, or indeed, until the next day. When I was in the water I think they soon got numb. When I reached the water I must have gone down a few feet and when I came to the surface I was bumped into by the stoker who was coming down the rope after me, and I was driven under the surface again.

'I immediately struck out with the idea of getting as far as I could from the sinking ship. I swam around for a bit, trying to collect my wits, and to decide what was the best thing to do. Presently I saw a ship's boat, and although she was pretty full, I thought the best thing I could do was to go after her'.

'Were you invited in?' I asked. 'Well,' he said, 'to tell you the truth I was not. But I did not think it an occasion to stand upon ceremony, or rather to swim upon ceremony. I came up behind the stern of the boat, and simply climbed in.

'Perhaps I forgot to tell you that one of the most trying moments was when I was attempting to get upstairs after getting my lifebelt. The stairway in the interval had become packed with a struggling mass of humanity pushing their way down, and against whom I could have had no chance of making my way up. I swung my leg over the banister, and crawled up on the outside, hand over hand, without interfering with the crowd. I dare say if I had had to wait for them to pass by I should have been too late.

'But I was telling you how I got into the boat. It was pretty full, with women and children, and some of the crew, seamen, stokers and stewards. There did not seem to be anybody able to take charge, and we were rowing with two oars on one side and four on the other. There was a good deal of excitement. Somebody suggested that there was no plug in the bottom of the boat, merely because there was a little water in her, and somebody else suggested that we should probably be torpedoed.

'As soon as I took a look around however I was satisfied that things were all right for the present, and I at once turned round to see what I could of the Lusitania. She was sinking rapidly by the head, and her stern was getting higher and higher out of the water. There were boats dotted about here and there, and a number of people clinging to wreckage.

'Then she gave a great lurch, and went right under. I cannot say whether there was much suction. I don't think there was any explosion, but I could not be sure of that, because I do not think that in a moment of intense excitement the memory registers sound.

'The sea was churned up into a froth over the place where the liner had been and air bubbles came bursting up. Then wreckage began to come up and float around, and you found it almost incredible to believe that the great liner had been there so short a while ago.

'I suppose it may have been an hour before we saw the first sign of rescue ships. We saw a smoke track on the horizon, a little while afterwards another, and in a short while help could be seen coming from all points of the compass. We were picked up by a trawler, but some of my fellow passengers declined to go on board the trawler as they feared that she might be torpedoed.

Churned up into a froth … Another survivor told an artist he saw 'a large white mound' after the sinking, the centre having 'globes of immaculate white water'. The ever-widening ripples swept through floating wreckage

A French propaganda postcard of the time with drowning children asking 'Why?'

'The Irish coast was by this time in sight, and we were taken to Queenstown. There we were taken in charge by the Cunard Company, and I was quartered in the Rob Roy Hotel, and given food and clothing. We were not given any money, and I had left everything behind on the ship.

'I was given a pass from Queenstown to Dublin, and I was fortunate enough to be able to induce the Cunard Company to advance me one shilling, which represented my fare from Dublin to Bray'.

Dr Mecredy smiled over the recollection of the financial embarrassment, surely the least troublesome thing in an experience of this kind. 'It is hard,' he said, 'to give you a connected narrative where so many things come crowding into your mind. For example I believe I saw the German submarine.

'I thought I saw an upturned boat some distance away with men walking up and down upon her. A lady who was saved told me the same thing, and that she recognised it as a German submarine because it flew a German flag. Another thing I noticed before the ship sank was a steward taking photographs of the doomed ship; no doubt he had a good idea of the value of such war photographs.

'His dead body was brought ashore afterwards with two cameras strapped round his waist'.

(CORK EXAMINER, 11 MAY 1915)

Young Mr Mecredy had been in the States for the past two years, studying American methods at Battle Creek Sanatorium, where the principles of the simple life are inculcated into the hundreds of American millionaires who patronise this world-known establishment.

On taking his degree at Trinity College, where he had a most distinguished university career, Dr Mecredy determined to devote himself for a few years to special study before taking up practice in Dublin, and though he had an offer of a most lucrative appointment in India, he preferred to spend some time in America before going into immediate practice.

As was quite to be expected of the eldest son of one who has made such a mark on the Irish sporting world as Mr R. J. Mecredy, the young medico took considerable interest in cycling and athletic matters during his university career. While he did not attain the same eminence on the road or track as did his father, he put several important records to his credit, including the Irish 24 hours bicycle record.

He was the first man to cover 300 miles on the road in Ireland in a day unpaced, and as those who follow this branch of the sport are aware, this performance was accomplished quite unaided, and without the help of pacemakers.

Dr Mecredy while at Trinity College has the unique distinction of winning both athletic and cycling races on the same day – a feat for which we believe the history of the college races does not afford a parallel.

(IRISH POST AND WEEKLY TELEGRAPH, 22 MAY1915, P. 3)

Dr Mecredy, who is a gentleman of a very humorous character, in conversation with a prominent member of the Oldcastle Board of Guardians when discussing the accident which befell the Titanic, declared that if he was on board the great ocean 'King' at the time, in order to get safe he would have divested himself of his coat and vest and procured a lifebelt, which he said would be the best possible chance of escape.

True to his plans of escape, when the Lusitania was struck, he took off his coat and vest, and procuring a lifebelt, narrowly eschewed a watery doom.

(DROGHEDA INDEPENDENT, 15 MAY 1915, P. 6)

Walter Dawson Mitchell (26) Lost
Jeanette M. Mitchell (28) Saved
Infant son Walter (9 mo.) Lost
Second-class passengers
Ballylesson, Co. Down

The Mitchells had been childhood sweethearts. In December 1912, Walter was offered a job in New Jersey and decided to take it. He immediately proposed to his girlfriend, 'Nettie' Moore and they moved to live at 177 Broad Street, Newark.

Walter junior was born in August 1914, and photographs of the 'cherub' were regularly sent home to Ireland, according to a family memoir. One showed him in his basket on the kitchen floor, with the poignant caption on the back: 'Rowing for shore, aged 4½ months'.

In spring 1915, Walter was asked to come back to Lisburn and they sailed on the *Lusitania*. Nettie noted that when they came close to where the *Titanic* had gone down, some passengers threw wreaths into the sea. After their own sinking, they found themselves clinging to a capsized lifeboat in the sea, with Walter holding the baby. Nettie said they soon knew he was dead because his skin went a dark, bruised colour and he had froth at his mouth. As Walter slipped into unconsciousness, his last words were: 'I can't hold on any more Nettie'.

When pulled out of the water by fishermen, Nettie was just alive and remembered the sensation of being dragged by her feet, with her head bumping along the deck.

The next day, her brother John, also a survivor (*qv*), brought her to buy clothes. A group of sailors in one shop were talking of the disaster and one described a beautiful baby he had taken out of the water. Nettie rushed over, insisted it was hers, and begged him to tell what he had done with the body. The sailor replied: 'Listen, love, where your baby is now, there is nothing more you can do for him'.

ULSTER VICTIMS
LISBURN MAN AND CHILD

Amongst the passengers on the Lusitania *were Mr W. D. Mitchell of New Jersey, his wife and baby, and Mr John Moore, Connecticut, brother of Mrs Mitchell, who were returning to Ireland on a visit to their parents at Drumbo, Lisburn.*

Mr Mitchell was the second son of Rev. G. P. Mitchell, rector of Drumbo, and grand-nephew of Canon Pounden, Lisburn.

On Saturday evening, Rev. Mr Mitchell received a brief wire stating that his daughter-in-law and her brother were saved, but that his son and the baby were lost.

A second telegram announced that the survivors and the remains of Walter would arrive at Lisburn by the midnight train from Dublin.

Rev. Mr Mitchell and Mr Moore [Jeanette's father] attended at the railway station, and when the train came in there was a very pathetic scene when young Mr Moore and his grief-stricken sister alighted.

Both bore the appearance of having passed through a terrible ordeal, and were suffering from the effects of shock. Consequently they were unable to give any connected account of their awful experience.

Mr Moore stated that there were an exceedingly large number of passengers – he believed about 600 second-class.

Along with Mr and Mrs Mitchell he had just finished lunch, and Mrs Mitchell had gone to the cabin to see after the baby, when there was a great crash. On reaching the deck he found the passengers rushing for the boats. Some of them had lifebelts but he had none, and he managed to get into one of the boats, which, however, was overturned.

He then got hold of a rope which was hanging over the ship's side, and while clinging to this he

Nettie and Walter Mitchell and their baby son Walter junior. They jocularly dubbed his picture below 'Rowing for shore'

got bruised by numbers of men jumping from the deck in their frantic efforts to save their lives. Getting tossed into the water he was able to reach one of the upturned boats, and clung to the keel till rescued by a minesweeper.

Soon afterwards he saw his sister and her husband brought on board. Mr Mitchell appeared to be unconscious, and efforts were made to resuscitate him both on the ship and ashore, but without avail. The baby, nine months old, was lost.

The remains of Mr Mitchell were enclosed in an oak coffin, the breastplate of which bore the simple inscription:

W. D. Mitchell

Died May 8, 1915.

The late Mr Mitchell served his apprenticeship to the mill managing business in the Island Spinning Co.'s works, Lisburn, and went to New Jersey to take up an appointment with Messrs Marshall & Co. He was twenty-seven years of age, and married two years ago.

Mr Moore served his time with Messrs McGowan & Ingram, Belfast, and had been in Connecticut for the past four years.

(Irish Post and Weekly Telegraph, 15 May 1915, p. 11)

Administration of the estate of Walter Dawson Mitchell was granted at Belfast to his widow, in the amount of £640 13s 4d

The remains of baby Walter Mitchell, later recovered, were buried in the Old Church Cemetery, Cobh, in mass grave Common C.

Perhaps because of the shattering loss of her own infant, Nettie resolved to help other mothers and went to work as a nurse at the Rotunda Maternity Hospital in Dublin, and was there during the 1916 Rising. The area was cordoned off for days, as a deadly hail of rifle and machine-gun fire rattled outside, yet babies continued to be born. Nettie said she was alone on duty one night when there was a commotion in the corridor outside her ward. She found British soldiers searching the hospital for gunmen. She told them not to dare disturb her ladies – and of course there were no rebels in such a place.

Nettie remarried in 1920, and had two sons. She now lies in the same cemetery as her first husband, both of them many miles from the grave of her first born.

Margaret Molloy – Lost
Second-class passenger
New York

Margaret lived at 4329 West 47th Street, New York, right next door to the rooming house of her brother, Michael.

Michael went to the Cunard offices after learning of the calamity, where he told a New York Times reporter that his sister had travelled home to Ireland immediately on receiving a cablegram telling of the serious illness of their father.

(NEW YORK TIMES, 10 MAY 1915, P. 6)

Practical-minded Margaret selected the *Lusitania* because it was known to be the quickest steamship on the Atlantic run. She sailed on Saturday 1 May. The following Monday, 3 May, Michael received a fresh cable conveying the news that their father had passed away.

Martha Moody (70) Lost
Meta Moody (38) Saved

Second-class passengers
Limavady, Co. Derry

Mrs Moody, of Limavady, and her daughter, were passengers. The latter is safe, but it is feared Mrs Moody has been drowned. They were on a visit to California.

(IRISH INDEPENDENT, 10 MAY 1915, P. 6)

Among those reported lost is Mrs M. Moody, sister of the Rev. John Hemphill of Los Gatos, formerly pastor of the Calvary Presbyterian Church. Miss Meta Moody, her daughter, who became a great favourite among the smart set of San Francisco while here, is reported saved.

Mrs Moody and her daughter were returning to their home in Londonderry, Ireland, after a visit of three months in San Francisco. While here they extensively entertained and also received at their suite in the Loring apartments, 2400 Van Ness Avenue.

The Rev. Hemphill yesterday expressed grave apprehension for the safety of his sister, who is 70 years old. 'I thank God,' said the Rev. Mr Hemphill, 'my niece has been saved, and I pray that my sister, Mrs Moody, may yet be numbered among the saved. I am anxious for more details and hope my sister has been spared'.

(SAN FRANCISCO EXAMINER, 9 MAY 1915)

Administration of the estate of Martha Moody – (369) – Granted 8 June at Dublin to John H. Moody, effects £1,443 10s 3d. Deceased late of Limavady, Co. Derry. Died at sea 7 May 1915.

Ernest Moore – Lost

Second-class passenger
Lisdarn, Co. Cavan

CAVAN MAN A VICTIM OF LUSITANIA DISASTER

Returning to his native country after an absence of three years, Mr Ernest Moore, of Lisdarn, Cavan, was one of the victims of the Lusitania *disaster, and despite the fact that every effort has been made to find the body, the remains have not yet been discovered, although it is proved conclusively that he was on the vessel when she was torpedoed.*

The first intimation that he was on board was received from two Cavan ladies – Miss Lee and Miss Galligan, from the Denn district – who were amongst the survivors, and on learning the news his sister, Miss Jennie Moore, immediately cabled to the people with whom he had been stopping in America to learn if he had taken passage on the ill-fated vessel, and the reply, anxiously awaited, confirmed her worst fears. He had sailed on the Lusitania, *and his name was not amongst the list of survivors.*

On Sunday Miss Moore left for Queenstown in the hope of being able to find the body of her brother, but her mission was unsuccessful, as no trace of him could be found. A steward on the vessel with whom she had a conversation in the course of her search recognised a photo of Mr Moore as being one of the passengers.

Mr Moore was a prosperous farmer and a successful exhibitor each year at the agricultural shows in the county. Owing to ill-health he was obliged to take a trip to America, and crossed about the same time as the Titanic *disaster.*

He had been greatly improved in health, and was probably intending to give his sister a surprise visit, as no definite information had been received that he was returning. It is sad to think that when within such a short distance of his native land he should have met with such a sudden death. To his grief stricken sister the greatest sympathy is extended.

(IRISH POST AND WEEKLY TELEGRAPH, 22 MAY 1915, P. 7)

Mr Moore gave an address in Moose Jaw, Saskatchewan, on the *Lusitania* passenger manifest.

LOST ON THE LUSITANIA

The first intimation Miss Moore, Lisdarn, Cavan, had of the loss of her only brother, Mr Ernest Moore, by the sinking of the Lusitania, was when she read the announcement that he had been one of the passengers in the Anglo-Celt on last Friday morning. She did not know of the return of her brother, who, in order to pay her a surprise visit, had not intimated his intention of coming back. Subsequently she proceeded to Queenstown on the melancholy errand of identifying the remains.

(ANGLO-CELT, 22 MAY 1915, P. 7)

John Moore (24) Saved
Second-class passenger
Ballylesson, Co. Down

Two of John's brothers, Bobby and Archie, had enlisted to fight at the front, and John was of a like mind.

He was travelling home from Connecticut with his sister Nettie, her husband Walter Mitchell (*qv*), and their baby.

John was still in the *Lusitania*'s dining-room when the Mitchells finished their lunch and left the table to go down to their cabin to see the baby. Moments later, John told the *Lisburn Standard*:

> There was a great crash, which shook the ship. In a moment the passengers were rushing on deck to ascertain what had happened. When he got there the vessel had listed, lifeboats were being swung out from the lower side, and lifebelts handed out. He did not get a lifepreserver, but managed to get into a boat, which on reaching the water overturned.
>
> Luckily he got hold of a rope which was hanging over the ship's side and held on for a little time, during which the passengers were jumping down in crowds, many of them striking him on the way down and bruising his body. Subsequently he found himself struggling in the water and just managed to clutch the keel of one of the upturned boats until he was rescued by what he thought was a minesweeper.
>
> He could not describe the awfulness of the scene. He had lost sight of his sister and her husband, and was despairing of ever seeing them again when he observed them being taken out of the sea and brought aboard a trawler.

When John got to Queenstown, he searched for the Mitchells. He found the two adults among corpses laid out on the harbour steps. He thought he saw his sister's eyelids move, realised she was alive, and managed to resuscitate her. The *Lisburn Standard* reported that it was 'chiefly due to his presence of mind that his sister did not share the same fate as her husband … As to the search for some trace of the baby and the heartrending scenes he witnessed, Mr Moore could not trust himself to speak; and we could only wring his hand in silence as a token of the great sympathy we felt for him in his overwhelming grief'.

John Moore died 31 years after the disaster, in May 1946.

Mrs Rose Ellen Murray (30) Saved
Second-class passenger
New York and Belfast

Mrs Murray was travelling home to Belfast with her brother Patrick McGinley (*qv*). Neither realised that the other had been saved and both feared the worst.

Mr McGinley later wrote in a letter: 'My sister, Mrs C. Murray, was picked up unconscious whilst clinging to an oar by one of the ship's lifeboats after being one hour in the water.

'Each of us thought the other was lost until we met on the street next morning in Queenstown. Needless to say it was a joyful meeting'.

Thomas O'Brien Butler – Lost
Second-class passenger
Kilmashogue, Rathfarnham, Dublin

IRISH COMPOSER MISSING.

Mr T. O'Brien Butler, the well-known Irish musical composer, was amongst the passengers on the Lusitania, *and as his name does not appear in the list of survivors, it is feared that he has been lost.*

Mr O'Brien Butler is a Kerryman, and the scene of his chief musical composition, the Irish opera Murgheis, *was laid in Iveragh. The music of the opera was composed while the author was living in Kashmir, Northern India.*

Though composed so far away from Ireland, the music was characteristically Irish, the author having from childhood been steeped in the traditional music of his native country. He used to say himself that he owed much of his inspiration to the haunting Irish airs which he heard an old Irish-speaking nurse sing when he was a child.

One of the most delightful melodies in the opera was the fairy chorus, which was arranged for four voices. The arrangement for chorus and orchestra were the work of Mr O'Brien Butler himself, and he conducted the orchestra when the opera was performed some years ago in the Theatre Royal, Dublin.

At different times since the first production the author has been in negotiation with American managers, and it is believed that his recent visit to America was connected with the staging of the opera in the States. Mr O'Brien Butler also composed a number of songs which in recent years have often been set as test pieces at the Feis Ceoil. His Cincoragh *was the test piece at the Feis Ceoil today in the Irish Soprano Singing competition.*

His death would be a great loss to distinctive Irish music. Mr O'Brien Butler lived at Rathfarnham, and his brother, who also lives in Dublin, has gone to Queenstown to make enquiries.

(CORK EXAMINER, 11 MAY 1915)

On 25 June 1915 administration of the estate granted at Dublin to Pierce Butler in the amount of £206 9s 6d.

Patrick O'Donnell (28) Saved
Second-class passenger
Morameelon, Dungloe, Co. Donegal

THE CAPTAIN'S ESCAPE

A passenger named Patrick O'Donnell, a native of Dungloe, County Donegal, stated that he saw Captain Turner wearing a lifebelt, standing on the bridge as the Lusitania *sank. He thought he had* surely perished, but was greatly surprised and delighted to find the captain three hours later amongst the rescued party on board the boat that had taken himself out of the water.

(<small>IRISH TIMES</small>, 10 MAY 1915, P. 8)

A farmhand, Patrick originally emigrated to the USA at age 23, aboard the *Furnessia* from Glasgow in April, 1910. He stayed with his sister Mary in Avenue A, Bayonne, New Jersey. At the time of the *Lusitania* sinking, he had an address in Hoboken.

DONEGAL MAN'S EXPERIENCES

A graphic narrative of the disaster was furnished by Mr Patrick O'Donnell, of Dungloe, Co. Donegal, to a representative of the Daily Express.

Mr O'Donnell, who is a merchant in New York, said the first he heard of the disaster was a grating noise, followed by a big cloud of smoke and steam. He did not know at that time what had happened, but for safety ran to his state apartment to get a lifebelt. He got on one of the lifeboats, but it capsized. He said he was prepared to die, and thought death was inevitable.

'Women and children were clasped in each other's arms,' he said. 'The cries and shrieks of the women were terrible to hear. I was three hours in the water before I was rescued. I was then brought to the Sailors' Home in Queenstown, and everything possible done for me. The shrieks of the women were loud and piteous – so loud you could have heard them from the mainland. A great many people would not wait for the lifeboats but jumped overboard, and most of these were lost.

'I saw several stewards rushing from the deck with blood gushing from their ears and mouth. I saw the Captain going down in the suction, but he came up again, and was taken to Queenstown in the same boat I was'.

(<small>DAILY EXPRESS</small>, 10 MAY 1915, P. 5)

Florence O'Sullivan (26) Saved
Third-class passenger
Kilgarvan, Co. Kerry

A KILGARVAN MAN'S STORY

Amongst those travelling to Kinsale on Saturday by the 5.45 p.m. train from Cork was Mr O'Sullivan of Kilgarvan, whose wife is amongst the survivors landed at Kinsale and who himself was taken to Queenstown. In the course of a talk with our representative he said he was on deck with his wife when the Lusitania *was torpedoed.*

'I saw it happen,' he said. 'I saw the ripples along the water – it was like a fish. It came from the land side. Then I heard a crash, something like the sound of glass broken with a hammer. When I found things were wrong I rushed down to the cabin for lifebelts and when I returned, after an absence of ten or eleven minutes, I found the deck awash.

'The gangways were inclined, and children were clambering up; but they were being shoved on one side. I then went to the stern portion of the ship, and saw a boat being lowered by a man from Clifton (Clifden). He was doing it nice and quietly. The boat was full of passengers. Another man cut the rope, and the whole lot of the occupants were thrown into the water.

'Another boat was just being launched at that time, and I wanted my wife to go in it, but she would not go. This boat was broken off the side of the ship. We both remained standing on the deck for a few minutes, and just before we were thrown into the water we both shook hands, and I gave my wife all the money I had – about three hundred dollars. Of course, if she were saved, it would be useful to her.

'I could do something for myself. I did not see my wife after we got into the water. When I reached the water the mast broke and sent me under, but I rose again and caught some floating wreckage. A stewardess rose form the water just at the same moment and caught me by the arm.

Here are the marks', he said, raising up his sleeve and showing the finger prints on his arm.

Continuing the narrative he said: 'After a time I went down again, and when I rose next the stewardess was gone. I again clutched some floating wreckage and hung on to it. I have also a locket', he said, putting his hand in his pocket and producing it. It contained the photograph of a woman and a boy, 'that a lady passenger threw to me as she was going down. She tore it off her neck.

'I believe it was about twenty minutes past six when I was picked up. I was in a dazed condition then and can only just remember a man standing over me. I don't remember any more until I recovered at Queenstown. But when I did come to again I came out and remained on the wharf at Queenstown all night looking amongst the bodies for my wife.

'I thought she was drowned till I saw the morning papers, which contained the pleasant news that she was landed safely at Kinsale'.

Asked as to the behaviour of those on board when it became known that the liner was doomed, he said: 'I saw no officer at all, nor did I hear any commands the whole time,' and added, 'it is only the strong horse got through'.

(CORK FREE PRESS, 10 MAY 1915, P. 6)

… In the meantime, her husband, Mr F. Sullivan, who had been rescued and brought to Queens-town, came along to Kinsale, but his wife had left before he arrived. He told our representative that he and Mrs Sullivan had been some years in the States and having made some money, they came back to reside in their old home.

When the attack was made on the liner, his wife had about £100 in gold and notes in her possession, and she had a draft for £200. This he gave to Mrs Sullivan to keep, so that if she was saved – she could swim, whereas he could not – she would have some means of livelihood for the future. As things turned out, all their money was lost, 'but,' he added fervently, 'thank God we were both saved'.

WENT DOWN WITH THE SHIP

When the vessel was torpedoed, he said, 'I rushed below to my stateroom to get a lifebelt, previous to which I lashed my wife to the ship's rails. I came back to her and saw the boats being lowered. They were full of people, but many of them overturned. In a minute hundreds of people were in the sea struggling for life. I thought the boats unsafe, and did not get into them, but went down with the ship. When I came to the surface I could not see a sign of my wife.

'I saw a large empty box in the water, and I struck out for that. There were about ten people clinging onto it. A lady in the water held up her hands in which there was a bag and said – 'This is my purse. It contains nothing but money, and I will give it to anyone who saves me'. A man clinging to the box answered 'I will'. She threw the purse at him and he grabbed at it. In doing so, he upturned the box and the persons clinging to it all went down again'.

When he once more rose, he found near to him what he described as a large tin vessel or box which floated like a buoy. To this he clung, but owing to the size and shape, he was barely able to keep his head above water. The sensations of the sinking of the vessel

The speed of the Lusitania's sinking, coupled with her acute angle, killed many aboard before they had even reached the water. O'Sullivan bumped into many bodies on finally entering the sea

and his terrible predicament after he came to the surface, he said, were something awful, and couldn't be described. While he was floating around, many bodies, numbers apparently lifeless, struck against him.

WAILS OF THE DYING

The cries and lamentations of the women and children and the shouting of men were something dreadful. In a little while he was suddenly grabbed by the right forearm by a woman whom he recognised as Miss Jones, a stewardess. He had divested himself of his coat and put on a lifebelt before the ship sank. When Miss Jones caught him by the arm she held on so tightly – so dreadful was her fright – that she left deep marks on his flesh.

A young man, well-built and evidently of great strength of body and mind, he clung tenaciously to the tin vessel with his left hand, and with his right arm continued to support the unhappy stewardess, who was soon in a terrible state of collapse. Thus they drifted about in the sea, frequently encountering other hapless victims, and striking up against dead bodies. It seemed to him that they were two hours in this awful predicament. As time passed and they were tossed from wave to wave with no boats in sight, Miss Jones began to lose strength. Her condition was most pitiable, and time and again she appealingly asked if there was any boat in sight.

A TERRIBLE TRAGEDY

A terrible and pathetic tragedy was now happening. He saw the unfortunate girl growing weaker and weaker, but owing to his own helpless position he could do no more for her. Her cries were heartrending. Her strength was spent, and as he saw a boat in the distance, the poor girl died, and, losing her hold, disappeared for ever.*

Half an hour later, as far as he could judge, he himself was picked up. That was about 6 p.m., the rescuing vessel being the destroyer O. 10.

'During all this terrible experience,' Mr Sullivan said, 'I fortunately never lost my head, nor did my strength fail me, but the moment I was taken on the destroyer I completely collapsed, so dreadful was the strain of all those hours in the sea'.

Mr Sullivan added that one of the first boats that was launched from the Lusitania broke in two, with the consequence that its large human freight was thrown into the sea. This and the terrible noise created by the sinking of the ship and the indescribable scenes that followed were all most horrible and dreadful to see, while the drowning cries and shrieks of the women and children were appalling to hear.

(IRISH INDEPENDENT, 10 MAY 1915, P. 6)

* The body of 43-year-old stewardess Mary Elizabeth Jones was recovered and is buried in mass grave Common C in the Old Church Cemetery in Cobh.

Florence O'Sullivan died on 7 July 1941, at the age of 55. He is interred with his wife at Kilgarvan burial ground.

Julia O'Sullivan (25) Saved
Third-class passenger
Kilgarvan, Kenmare, Co. Kerry

Mrs Florence O'Sullivan, of Kilgarvan, Kenmare, who is in a delicate condition, was very distressed. She was coming to Kerry with her husband, and did not know whether he had been saved or not. She had a lifebelt on when thrown into the water and managed to hold onto some wreckage until she was rescued. 'It was simply awful,' she said, 'to hear the hundreds of drowning men, women and children shouting and crying for help.'

Fred Bottomley of Brighouse Yorkshire, said he was in the water for three-quarters of an hour. 'I had the hell of a time', he said, 'and so had the others. The lady (Mrs O'Sullivan) was very ill when *she was picked up, and almost dead, but the un-remitting attention of the crew of the trawler brought her round again'.*

(CORK FREE PRESS, 8 MAY 1915, P. 6)

EXILED KERRY COUPLE RETURNING HOME, LOST ALL, BUT ARE SAFE

Mrs F. O'Sullivan, who was the only lady survivor brought into Kinsale, a native of Kilgarvan, Kerry, had a frightful experience. Getting separated from her husband, she spent four hours on a raft in the water, and went through great tortures. When rescued by a small boat she was unconscious and had not regained consciousness at the time of her arrival in Kinsale, but she was promptly attended to by Dr Corcoran, Military Hospital, and had considerably recovered by Saturday morning.

> A woman resembling Julia O'Sullivan is helped through the streets of Queenstown. Julia was landed in Kinsale while her husband went to Queenstown. It is not clear where they were finally reunited

She became very happy and joyous when a telegram was received by her announcing the glad news that her husband had been rescued and safely landed at Queenstown.

Mr and Mrs O'Sullivan were in possession of a large sum of money at the time of the disaster – in fact they were returning to the old country with all their savings after an absence of a number of years, and with the intention of starting business in their native district.

Prior to jumping from the Lusitania, Mrs O'Sullivan placed £100 in her lifebelt, but while being taken into the trawler that rescued her, it became necessary to cut the belt, and the money, as well as larger sums in her trunk, went to the bottom of the sea.* Happily she was able to leave Kinsale last evening for her old home.

(IRISH INDEPENDENT, 10 MAY 1915, P. 5)

* Not quite. The bag, containing a bank draft, notes and gold, was found washed up in September 1915, and forwarded to Florence at her home. See Appendix: *Property handed in at Queenstown.*

DRIVEN HOME BY MOTOR

Mrs F. O'Sullivan, one of the survivors landed at Kinsale, was motored to her home near Rosscarbery in a car kindly lent by Mr R. C. Pratt. She was accompanied on the journey by Miss Heard and a military nursing sister. She has now quite recovered from her trying experience.

(CORK EXAMINER, 11 MAY 1915)

Julia O'Sullivan, *née* O'Neill, grew up in Rosscarbery, Co. Cork and moved to Kerry when she married. Despite surviving the *Lusitania*, she was to suffer the loss of her own daughter as a result of German bombing. Nellie, aged 20, was a nurse in the children's ward at St Paul's Hospital in London when it was bombed by the Luftwaffe during the Blitz. She was killed by falling masonry.

Another daughter, Mary, died on New Year's Day, 1941, at the age of 21, having been struck by a mystery illness.

Julia herself died on 18 October 1948, and is buried with her husband and daughters in Kilgarvan cemetery.

Edwin Perkins – Lost
First-class passenger
Belfast, Co. Antrim

The Belfast victims include Mr E. Perkins, a Director of Messrs W. R. McCall and Co. Ltd, linen merchants.

(IRISH INDEPENDENT, 12 MAY 1915, P. 6)

Annie Ruane (29) Saved
Third-class passenger
Cloonacannan, Swinford, Co. Mayo

Miss Annie Ruane, Cloonacannan, Swinford, one of the Lusitania survivors, has arrived home. In the terrible scramble for life, she says, she was thrown into the water but clung to a raft, to which other women and several men were clinging. She was two hours in the water before being rescued. 'It was like a horrible nightmare', she declares.

The men throughout behaved heroically in making way for the women and children going to the boats. Miss Ruane sustained some injury to her face. She lost all her belongings.

(IRISH INDEPENDENT, 13 MAY 1915, P. 7)

Miss Ruane had been living in Chicago.

George Scott – Saved
Second-class passenger
Bellevue, Clontarf, Dublin

CLONTARF MAN RESCUED

George Scott, a young Dublin man, who was a passenger on the Lusitania, and who had a terrible struggle for life, reached Dublin on Saturday afternoon, arriving at Kingsbridge about six o'clock. Interviewed by a press representative at his home, Bellevue, Clontarf, Mr Scott, who looked little the worse for his awful ordeal, gave a vivid account of his experiences. Mr Scott has spent two years in Toronto, and was returning to Dublin on a holiday trip.

At the time the Lusitania was torpedoed, Mr Scott, with about 200 others, was lunching in one of the dining apartments. 'When we were about halfway through our lunch,' he said, 'we heard a terrible crash. The vessel trembled first and then listed to one side. Everyone jumped from their seats and rushed on deck. The women and children shrieked wildly, and when we got on deck there was a great deal of panic.

'Men, women and children rushed about on all sides. We were not sure at the time if the disaster had been caused by a floating mine or a submarine, and indeed, the only concern uppermost in our mind was what our fate was to be. It was evident at this time that the vessel must perish, for she was sinking fast by the head.

'Two young ladies approached me, appealing for help. I got them two lifepreserving jackets and did all I could to see them securely in one of the lifeboats. I remained on board till the water was almost washing the deck, and rendered what assistance I could to the women and children, who were crying piteously for help.'

Mr Scott next went on to describe his own struggle for life. He explained that, having procured a lifebelt, he climbed the railings of the vessel and plunged into the water. 'I was in the water only a short while when the Lusitania sank, and the suction of the vessel brought me down. I don't know how long I was under the water, but it seemed to me to be something like an hour.

'On coming to the surface I felt very much exhausted, and was tangled up in a mass of wreckage. I struggled there for a few minutes, and an upturned boat drifted towards me. I got onto it with the assistance of an oar, which was thrown out by one of the men. About ten minutes after,

we were taken into another boat.

'Several others – men and women – were taken into our boat, which was taken in tow by a fishing smack about a half-hour afterwards. Later we were taken onto a trawler, and started the voyage to Queenstown, where we arrived at eight o'clock.

'The scene was a terrible one,' exclaimed Mr Scott in tones of deep emotion. 'The whole thing appears to me now as a terrible nightmare. The cries of the hundreds struggling with death in the sea were distressing beyond all description, and I shall never forget the awful scenes I witnessed'.

(IRISH TIMES, 10 MAY 1915, P. 8)

George Scott lived for a further 46 years, passing away on 2 June 1961.

Patrick Sheedy (30) Lost
Third-class passenger
Bansha, Ennis, Co. Clare

Sheedy had been denied permission to land in the United States and was deported to Ireland on the *Lusitania*.

Buried in mass grave A in Queenstown's Old Church cemetery on 10 May, it is perhaps notable that the man who was unluckily sent back by the US authorities was officially designated number thirteen in the lists!

His property, such as it was, was sent on to his mother, Honora Sheedy, at Bansha, Darragh, as late as 1 December 1915.

Patrick Slattery (27) Saved
Second-class passenger
Tipperary

'I was delighted to find that my messmate, a young man named Patrick Slattery, from Tipperary, had also been saved. He could not swim, and although he had his overcoat and boots on him, his lifebelt kept him afloat until he was picked up.'

(FELLOW SECOND-CLASS PASSENGER JOHN SWEENEY IN AN INTERVIEW WITH THE WESTERN PEOPLE, 15 MAY 1915)

John Sweeney – Saved
Second-class passenger
Ballina, Co. Mayo

THE SINKING OF THE LUSITANIA
BALLINA MAN'S THRILLING EXPERIENCE
HIS MIRACULOUS ESCAPE
TWO HOURS IN THE WATER

Mr John Sweeney, brother in law of Mr James Murphy, vice-chairman Ballina Urban Council, was one of the lucky passengers saved from the ill-fated Lusitania. He is at present at home in Ballina suffering from nothing worse than slight nervous prostration and a nightmare of (as he described it) two hours suspension between life and death.

Seen by our representative a few evenings ago, Mr Sweeney gave a graphic description of the terrible experiences he underwent. 'I intended sailing on the 3rd of April,' he said, 'but circumstances intervened, and I had to take passage by the Lusitania.

'There was nothing unusual in the departure of the Lusitania from New York. I was utterly unaware of any warnings having been given. The only remark I heard made, and which in the light of later events might be construed into a warning, was an observation by some person on the shore to 'cheer up, the worst is to come yet'.

'I was travelling second-class, and the gaiety of the life on the ship and the prospect of returning to old Ireland after thirteen years' exile made me forget the terrors of the sea. Of course there were rumours for some time before the ship left that she would be attacked by German submarines, but the passengers did not pay any heed to them.

'We had a splendid time of it coming over with concerts, etc., and the ship's orchestra entertained us with beautiful music. On the fateful Friday, coming from the dining saloon on to the deck at about 2 o'clock p.m., I went to the port side of the ship and gazed at the Irish coast with longing hopes. The ship was going slowly – I would say about 15 knots an hour, and the sea was beautifully calm, but the sky was rather hazy. I think I never felt so happy as at that particular moment, but my happiness and thoughts were soon to be turned into a struggle for life and against an awful death.

'The ship was suddenly struck by a torpedo on the starboard side. It appeared to be like a smothered explosion beneath the bow of the mighty vessel. Immediately there was a great commotion and excitement amongst the passengers. It could not be described as a panic, because the most remote idea from our minds was that the ship could be sunk at all. I asked a sailor what was the position of the ship, and he told me we were about 25 miles from Queenstown and eight miles from Old Kinsale Head.

'After the ship was struck, I ran down to the dining saloon to find out exactly what had happened, and while there I heard another and a louder crash, and the ship gave a tremendous lurch. I then fully realised all. The first thought that struck me was to run to my bunk and get a lifebelt, but my sleeping quarters were at the bow of the ship, and I would have to go down three flights of stairs. I decided not to risk going down and I went to the crew's apartment and asked one of the sailors to give me a lifebelt.

'By this time the ship's lights had been extinguished, and it was with some difficulty the sailor got me the belt, owing to the darkness. As soon as I got it, I ran to the port side, and from there saw two lifeboats smashed into pieces, one at the bow and the other at the stern of the boat.

'The ship had by now listed heavily, and the women on board seemed to have lost their heads completely. I saw several of them fling themselves over the side of the ship. It appeared to me that they were very slow in getting the lifeboats from the davits.

The location of the torpedo strike is crucial to determining the cause of an internal explosion soon afterwards. Most witnesses placed it as shown here. The cargo was stored in the bow, where Sweeney had the impression of a 'smothered explosion'

'Several of the boats when lowered immediately capsized. A Church of Ireland clergyman asked me to help him to affix his lifebelt for him, and I did so. I did not notice that clergyman amongst the survivors in Queenstown. By this time the ship was almost lying on her side, and knowing how to swim, I decided to make a jump for it.

'I got into the water and started to swim towards a lifeboat. Luckily I was carried way from the ship by the current. I tried to get as far away as I could from the doomed vessel, in order not to be drawn in by suction when she went down. Shortly afterwards I saw the ship tumble over on her starboard side.

'Some of the lifeboats left on her broke loose as the giant vessel lay writhing in her death agony. The bow of the ship then disappeared, and the stern shot into the air, and in two or three minutes afterwards, with a tumbling noise, something like a groan, she sank beneath the waves.

'I was carried back toward the vessel by the suction, but I managed to keep on the surface. I afterwards got hold of a piece of wreckage and swam towards an upturned collapsible boat, to which some of the crew and a number of the passengers were clinging, among them a woman with her head partly submerged. I pulled her onto the boat. She died in the same position in which I laid her in the boat, mouth downwards.

'We subsequently managed to rescue a few babies who were floating about on the water. There were two other lifeboats quite near to us, and we succeeded in attaching the three boats together by a rope so as to form a raft. There was another boat about 20 feet away and it was waterlogged.

'It overturned several times, throwing its occupants into the water. They shouted to us to stand by, but we were unable, unfortunately, to go to their assistance, as we had no oars. However they eventually drifted towards us, and we managed to get them onto our raft'.

Proceeding, Mr Sweeney said that when the ship went down the air was filled with the heart-rending shriek of women and children. 'I saw the living persons,' said Mr Sweeney, 'hanging to floating dead bodies. While swimming dead bodies bobbed against me several times. It was the most terrifying sight I ever witnessed, and the recollection of it – the dying shrieks, wild yells, and muttered prayers, all intermingled – will never be effaced from my memory.

'About two hours after the ship went down we sighted the smoke of three steamers, but they did not see us and did not come to our assistance. Three fishing smacks subsequently came on the scene, and rescued a number of people. Five or six other vessels afterwards hove in sight, filling us with happy emotions and causing some of the men on the raft to burst out into It's a long way to Tipperary.

'We were picked up by the Indian Empire, a patrol boat mounted with one gun. Personally I did not suffer any great physical hardship. I did not feel cold while in the water, but when I got on to the patrol boat a reaction set in and I could hardly move hand or foot.

'There were six women and three babies dead on our boat when we arrived at Queenstown. The large crowd at the landing stage received us with cheers. Every kindness and hospitality was shown to us, and we were supplied by the agent of the Cunard Company with prepaid telegraphic forms to communicate with our friends.

'I was delighted to find that my messmate, a young man named Patrick Slattery, from Tipperary, had also been saved. He could not swim, and although he had his overcoat and boots on him, his lifebelt kept him afloat until he was picked up.'

Concluding the interview, Mr Sweeney said he hoped President Wilson would 'wake up' and let the Germans see that they could not murder American citizens on the high seas with impunity.

(WESTERN PEOPLE, 15 MAY 1915, P. 8)

Mr Sweeney had an address in Watertown, New York.

Albert Thompson (37) Lost
Second-class passenger
Clogher, Co. Antrim

Another Donacloney man on the sunken boat was Mr Albert Thompson of Clogher, whose fate is yet uncertain.

(LARNE TIMES, 15 MAY 1915, P. 4)

Mr Thompson lived in Toronto, Canada. He was travelling with his friend William Dale, who was also lost. Dale may have tried to save his companion, who was reportedly an invalid.

Thomas Turpin – Saved
Maud Turpin – Saved
Second-class passengers
Portlaoise, Co. Laois

A REMARKABLE COINCIDENCE

Mr Freeman, manager of the Hotel Imperial, received telegrams last night from the Head Constables of Kinsale and Clonakilty to the effect that some of the passengers and crew of the Lusitania

had been landed at Kinsale or Clonakilty, but he traced a survivor in a way that showed an extraordinary coincidence.

A lady named Mrs Turpin, of Maryborough, telephoned to Mr Freeman from Killarney asking if he could obtain tidings of her son or his wife, who had been returning to Ireland on the Lusitania.

Mr Freeman rung up on the telephone the Cunard Office, and in reply to his query, he was informed that Mr Turpin was in the office at the moment, but so far there were no tidings of his wife.

(CORK CONSTITUTION, 8 MAY 1915, P. 6)

BOILER EXPLOSIONS

Mr T. Turpin, son of Mr H. Turpin, solicitor, Maryborough, who, with his wife, was returning from Victoria, B.C, said the vessel listed to starboard on being first struck, and remained in that position for about ten minutes, so that the passengers were disposed to think there was not much danger.

The striking of the torpedo was like 'a bottle being thrown into a basket of other bottles', and was accompanied by very little sound. He knew nothing of a second torpedo. The deck became to them, as it were, 'the side-wall of a house', going deeper and deeper, and the boilers began to explode as she sank by the bow, still retaining the list to starboard.

He was anxious to go below for lifebelts, but yielded to his wife's entreaties that he should not do so. They got two deck-chairs and held on to them. A man tried to take the lady's chair from her, but Mr Turpin prevented him. There was a good deal of panic in their part of the vessel, and they knew nothing more until, following a boiler explosion, they found themselves in the water.

Struck on the forehead by some object, Mr Turpin went down.

Survivor Thomas Turpin in Queenstown. He fought a man to secure a deck-chair to help his wife float

When he came up, his wife was nowhere to be seen. His deck-chair was gone.

After swimming about for ten minutes or so, he reached an upturned boat, on the keel of which several people were astride. With their assistance he managed to get up on the keel of the boat, where they all remained for four hours until rescued by a tug-boat and brought to Queenstown. While he was afloat on the upturned boat, people on a similar boat about 200 yards away hailed him and told him his wife was safe.

Mrs Turpin only recollects that after being thrown into the sea, she went under twice, and when she came up the second time she found herself near an upturned boat and was dragged onto the keel by one of the parties upon it.

She, with the others, was rescued by a trawler and brought to Queenstown, arriving some time after the tug which brought in her husband. She is still suffering from the effects of her awful experience. Mr Turpin looks none the worse of all that he went through, but he complains that he cannot sleep. 'The cries of the drowning were heartrending, and they are still in my ears', he says.

(IRISH INDEPENDENT, 11 MAY 1915, P. 5)

Mr and Mrs Turpin gave their address on the passenger manifest as Victoria, British Columbia, Canada. Mr Turpin's descriptions of his experiences on the upturned boat formed the basis of an *Illustrated London News* double-page illustration of the post-sinking scene, published in its 15 May issue.

Michael Ward – Saved
Second-class passenger
Bundoran, Co. Donegal

I was at the high side of the ship, where men were working at the boats. A man named Mr Ward of Bundoran, who was coming from Pittsburgh – I don't think he has been saved – gave me a hand to a boat that was on the deck [Joseph Ward, third class, lost].

(MARGARET COX, SECOND-CLASS PASSENGER, IRISH INDEPENDENT, 10 MAY 1915, P. 5)

William H. Winter (28) Lost
First-class passenger
Mountpleasant Square, Ranelagh, Dublin

Winter – 7 May 1915, drowned by the sinking of the Lusitania, *William Henry Winter, aged 28, only son of the late W. H. Winter, Coleraine, and Mrs Daly, 7 Mountpleasant Square, Dublin.*

(DAILY EXPRESS, 17 MAY 1915, P. 1)

Mr Winter was travelling in first-class in his role as a culinary consultant to Cunard, and was actually designated as an assistant superintendent caterer for the voyage, which might arguably have put him on the ship's articles as a member of crew.

His body, number 228, was recovered. He was initially reported to be 'a ship's official named Daly' because his corpse held a letter addressed to Mrs Daly in Dublin, beginning 'My own dear Mother …' (she had remarried). Winter's remains were forwarded to Dublin for burial on 25 May 1915.

He left a widow.

Irish Stories

Crew

James Battle – Saved
AB Seaman
Sligo

James Battle of Sligo, an A. B. on the Lusitania, *whose left foot and leg were badly injured, said to our reporter:*

'At the moment we were hit I was in my bunk below, smoking. The force of the first explosion threw me out on the floor, and I said to a chum: "That's a torpedo". We ran on deck, as the ship was heeling over heavily.

'The port boats were flung in on our decks, and the starboard boats were swinging away some feet beyond the vessel's side.

'We got some of them away, and after an hour in the water myself and three or four other men got on to three upturned boats. We lashed them together and made a raft. There were boats enough on board to save twice as many people as we had if we had time to launch them, but the submarine didn't give us a second's warning and after sinking us slinked away and left us to drown. It was wholesale wilful murder.

'We picked up 69 people. Nobody could know the horror of that time. I was on the end of the keel, helping to keep a woman and some others afloat. A man was clinging to my legs with one hand. His other hand and arm from above the elbow was hanging off.

'We pulled him on top of the boat. His arm was only hanging by a thin strip of muscle, and an Italian doctor who was also on the craft cut off the arm and bandaged the stump with a piece of another passenger's shirt.

'We were on that raft, drifting about, 69 of us, each helping the other as well as we could to keep a grip. We were that way from 2.30 until 6.30, when the trawler Caterina [sic] picked us up and brought us to Queenstown'.

(Irish Independent, 10 May 1915, p. 5)

Albert Bestic (24) Saved
Junior third officer
Dublin

Albert Arthur Bestic was born in Dublin on 26 August 1890. He had been at sea for seven years when he obtained his first berth as an officer with the Cunard Line – aboard the RMS *Lusitania* on her final, fatal voyage.

Bestic survived, and died aged 72 in Bray, Co. Wicklow, on 20 December 1962. A few months earlier, on 8 May 1962, he had written a piece for the *Irish Independent* on his emotions about a television documentary marking the forty-seventh anniversary of the disaster:

A. A. BESTIC A SURVIVING OFFICER OF THIS ONCE-FAMOUS SHIP, WRITES
SO I SHALL SEE THE LUSITANIA AGAIN
WRECK IS NOW ON FILM

The first time I saw the Lusitania *was when she was on her trials in the River Clyde. The next time, years later, it was from the deck of a sailing ship in mid-Atlantic: she sped past us in a welter of foam.*

The third time was when I joined her, and the last time was when she sank. Now I am going to see her again on television. The mystery which so puzzled people in Kinsale and elsewhere last year is at last explained. Who were these strangers who refused to talk, and, having chartered a trawler, paid frequent visits to the famous wreck?

Doubtless interest would have waned considerably had it become known that they were only taking photographs, and not, as was romantically speculated, hunting for treasure.

When recently visiting the BBC studios in connection with a Lusitania film programme which they hope to transmit early this month, I met the chief diver, Mr Lagos, who had been in charge of the underwater photography off Kinsale.

He told me that the divers had actually swum down the 300 feet to the wreck, with nothing on but a breathing apparatus and thick underclothing. They were able not only to walk along the Lusitania's decks, but to take photographs.

What tremendous strides deep sea diving has made since the days of the rubber suits, or even the metal ones, when there was always the danger of the diver's tube or wire becoming entangled!

I asked Mr Lagos if the men felt any ill effects while working at such a depth? 'Very little,' he replied. 'Our main trouble was that our brains became a bit fuzzy. For example, should a lamp need some minor adjustment which would take us a few seconds on the surface, we had to think hard how to put it right'.

To my surprise I learnt that the wreck is singularly free from marine growth. Another point of interest is that it is lying slightly tilted to port. The tilt doubtless took place when the vessel struck the bottom, and I believe now that it saved my life.

I had been dragged down violently by the suction, suddenly to be shot up to the surface again. Obviously some trapped air must have been released when the tilt occurred. Maybe I came up in a bubble. I don't know.

I met some of the survivors who had been asked to take part in the TV picture at the studio. Leslie Morton, the slim lad now slim no longer, who, from his post on the lookout had yelled his warning that a torpedo was approaching.

Hughie Johnston, who had stood by the useless wheel watching the list indicator and ticking off the degrees to Captain Turner until told to 'go and save yourself'.

Parry Jones, one of the eight famous Welsh singers group, of whom four had been saved. He told us how he had stood on the stern gazing downwards at the four mighty propellers and huge 65-ton rudder, wondering if he would clear them if he jumped.

Then there was the charming lady, looking in her early forties, who shook hands with me and said: 'I was in the Lusitania too'.

Forgetting the intervention of time, I answered, 'I should remember you, but I'm afraid I don't'.

She smiled. 'I didn't expect you to. I was three months old then'.

We of the maturer years swept away the accumulated dust of 47 years and re-lived the dreadful tragedy. We told it again

A. A. BESTIC, a surviving officer of this once-famous ship, writes

SO I SHALL SEE THE LUSITANIA AGAIN

WRECK IS NOW ON FILM

THE first time I saw the Lusitania was when she was on her trials in the river Clyde. The next time, scats later, it was from the deck of a sailing ship in mid-Atlantic: she sped past us in a welter of foam.

The next time was when I joined her, and the last time was when she sank. Now I am going to see her again on television.

The mystery which so puzzled people in Kinsale and elsewhere, who refused to talk and, having chartered a small trawler, paid frequent visits to the famous wreck?

Doubtless interest would have waned considerably had it become known that they were only taking photographs, and not, as was romantically speculated, hunting for treasure.

Chief Diver

WHEN recently visiting the BBC studios in connection with a Lusitania film programme which they hope to transmit early this month, I met the chief diver, Mr Lagos, who had been in charge of the underwater photography off Kinsale.

He told me that the divers had actually swum down the 300 feet to the wreck, with nothing on but a breathing apparatus and thick underclothing. They were able not only to walk along the Lusitania's decks, but take photographs.

"We told it again on television, sitting in front of a huge 'drop-cloth' portraying a picture of the Lusitania about to slide beneath the surface..."

off the danger to Captain Turner until told to 'go and save yourself'.

Parry Jones, one of the eight famous Welsh singers group, of whom four had been saved, who told us how he had stood on the stern gazing downwards at the four mighty propellers and huge 65-ton rudder, wondering if he would clear them if he jumped.

Then there was the charming lady, looking in her early forties, who shook hands with me and said: "I was in the Lusitania too."

Forgetting the intervention of time, I answered, "I should remember you, but I'm afraid I don't."

She smiled. "I didn't expect you to. I was three months old then."

Survivors

I MET some of the survivors who had been asked to take part in the TV picture at the studio. Leslie Morton, the slim lad had had —

Stories Re-told

WE of the maturer years swept away the accumulated dust of 47 years and re-lived the dreadful tragedy. We told it again on television, sitting in front —

Blue R stood by one of the A.B.s, with New York for Liverpool on 1st May 1915. She carried 1,255 passengers, including 159 Americans, and 702 of a crew.

Fatal Blow

SHE was a queen of the ocean. Her launching was when the sunrise made modern liners like —

The Irish Independent, fifty years and one day after the sinking. Junior Third Officer Bestic remained friendly with Lusitania Captain William Turner, and was one of the last to visit him before the latter died in June 1933

on television sitting in front of a huge 'drop cloth' portraying a picture of the Lusitania about to slide beneath the surface. If it was meant to stir our memories, we didn't need it.

It is all so long ago now that this disaster often becomes confused today with that of the White Star liner Titanic which struck a submerged iceberg in the Atlantic when on her maiden voyage in 1912. The Lusitania, then the famous Blue Riband holder of the Atlantic, left New York for Liverpool on 1 May 1915. She carried 1,255 passengers, including 157 Americans, and 702 of a crew.

She was a queen of the ocean. Her luxurious salons and staterooms vied with the most modern hotel. Her 25 boilers, which ate up 7,000 tons of coal for the run, enabled her to streak along at over 27 knots.

Surely there could be little danger from the submarines, about which we had been warned both prior to leaving New York and by Admiralty wireless messages on the way home. We knew they could only travel at nine knots when below the surface.

On 7 May, when off the Old Head of Kinsale, Co. Cork, and but 24 hours from Liverpool, it happened. The torpedo struck her amidships.

Despite her 175 watertight compartments she sank in 20 minutes; and with her sinking, 1,198 people, including 134 Americans, were drowned. The sinister warnings about submarines had not been given in vain

[THE PROGRAMME WAS A BBC DOCUMENTARY *FIFTY FATHOMS DEEP*]

Bestic testified before the British Inquiry on 17 June 1915 and here is a précis of his evidence:

I heard an explosion. I was in the officers' smoke room at the time, and I went out on the

Bestic in Queenstown in the aftermath of the disaster, accompanied by an unknown man. A fellow crewman pulled Bestic into a raft, saving his life

bridge and I saw the track of the torpedo. It seemed to be fired in a line with the bridge, and it seemed to strike the ship between the second and third funnels, as far as I could see.

Then I heard the order given 'hard-a-starboard' and I heard Captain Turner saying 'lower the boats down level to the rail', and I went to my section of boats. My boat station was No. 10 on the port side.

I started to get No. 10 lowered down to the rail, but it landed on the deck. Captain Anderson was there beside me and he said: 'Go to the bridge and tell them they are to trim her with the port tanks'. I made my way to the bridge and sung out that order to Mr Hefford, the second officer. He repeated it, and I came back again and No. 10 boat was on the deck. We tried to push it out, but we could not do it. She had a big list to starboard on her.

I thought when we trimmed her with the port tanks she might right herself a little bit. She went on listing for about 10 minutes, I should say. Then she seemed to rectify the list a little bit. It gave us encouragement, and we thought she might come up altogether, or it might give us a better chance.

Captain Anderson was there, and I took most of my orders from him. Until the water came up and we could not do it any longer. I stepped over the side – two or three feet – into the water. A man named [Seaman Thomas] Quinn pulled me on one of the collapsible boats.

Patrick Browne (24) Lost
Trimmer
Kilboyne, Co. Mayo

Two Ballyheane men, Pat Browne, Kilboyne, and Pat Coyne, Buncomb, are also presumed to have been lost. They were engaged as trimmers on board.

(MAYO NEWS, 22 MAY 1915, P. 4)

Thomas Costello (30) Lost
Fireman
Killawalla, Co. Mayo

Costello was born at Westport, Co. Mayo. The *Connaught Telegraph*, 22 May 1915, reported that it was feared Costello had perished.

Patrick Coyne (24) Lost
Trimmer
Ballyheane, Co. Mayo

LUSITANIA VICTIMS

It is feared that two young men from Ballyheane named Coyne and Browne, who were on the ill-fated Lusitania, went down with her. There has been no account of them up to the present, and in the Church of Our Lady of the Holy Rosary, Castlebar, on Sunday, the Most Rev. Dr Higgins referred to their sad fate and asked prayers of the congregation for the repose of their souls.

(CONNAUGHT TELEGRAPH, 22 MAY 1915, P. 4)

Two Ballyheane men, Pat Browne, Kilboyne, and Pat Coyne, Buncomb, are also presumed to have been lost. They were engaged as trimmers on board.

(MAYO NEWS, 22 MAY 1915, P. 4)

This crewman is listed as Patrick Coyle on the *Lusitania* crew agreement, and under this name on Commonwealth War Grave Commission records and merchant navy memorial.

Daniel Daly (42) Lost
Fireman
Ranelagh, Dublin

GRIEF AND FURY IN LIVERPOOL

The scenes at Lime Street station were more poignant still. Shortly after 6 o'clock the train came in with over 600 of the crew …

I saw one elderly woman, with her shawl hanging from her shoulders and her grey hair in disarray, advancing slowly through the crowd, calling out, 'Is Dan Daly amongst you? Dan Daly the fireman?' She was a mother, seeking distractedly for her son. Clutching by the arm each member of the crew she encountered, she would moaningly ask whether he did not know Dan Daly the fireman, but none of them knew him.

At last she came upon a fireman who did know, and I heard the decisive answer which shattered her hopes. 'Dan is gone, Ma'am. He was down below at the time'. Throwing up her hands with a gesture of despair, the mother turned aside to lean over a packing case for support while she wailed and wailed in sorrow.

(THE TIMES, 10 MAY 1915, P. 10)

* Widow Mary A. Daly was Dan Daly's mother. She lived with her daughter-in-law, Dan Daly's wife Maud (*née* Hockey), at 405 Ashfield Street, Liverpool.

John Ferris Saved
Second-class steward
Fenit, Co. Kerry

Ex-Fenit Station Master Saved

Mr John Ferris, who was stationmaster at Fenit some years ago, was saved from the Lusitania *disaster. He was engaged as second cabin steward on the* Lusitania, *to which he transferred from the* ss Cameronia *about one hour before the* Lusitania *steamed out of New York. He attributes his life to his knowledge of swimming and floating. Mr Ferris was for three hours in the water.*

(Kerry Advocate, 22 May 1915, p. 8)

In a strange quirk of history, John Ferris is a distant relative of Sinn Féin TD Martin Ferris, also from Fenit, who was intercepted by the Irish Naval Service in 1984 while aboard the trawler *Marita Ann*, smuggling guns and munitions across the Atlantic for the Provisional IRA.

Joseph Garry (25) Lost
Ship's Surgeon
Kildysart, Co. Clare

Clare Doctor on the Lusitania
Ennis Saturday

One of the doctors on the ill-fated Lusitania *was Dr Joseph Garry, son of Mr Patrick Garry, JP, MCC, Shanabea, Kildysart, and a brother of Dr M. P. Garry, the well known Irish International rugby footballer, and at present Tuberculosis Sanatorium doctor, Clare.*

A telegram from Liverpool this evening states that Dr Garry's name does not appear in the list of saved so far ascertained, but other lists are expected.

(Cork Examiner, 10 May 1915, p. 5)

Kildysart Board of Guardians
The Late Dr Joseph Garry

… Continuing with deep emotion, the Chairman said we all learned with deep regret that one of the victims was Dr Joseph Garry, son of our popular and esteemed brother member, Mr Patrick Garry JP. Personally I know Dr Garry from childhood. He developed into a fine type of an Irishman, genial, unassuming and admired by all who knew him. It was sad to see such a brilliant Clareman cut off in the flower of manhood by German hate.

Mr Michael Griffin said it was with very sincere regret that he rose to second the resolution which was proposed and spoken to by their Chairman. He had the pleasure of knowing Dr Garry personally, and he thought a nicer or more unassuming young man never breathed the breath of life.

All the other members present asked to be associated with the resolution, which was declared in silence.

(Clare Journal, 20 May 1915, p. 2)

Richard Gaul – Lost
Greaser
Drinagh, Co. Wexford

WEXFORDMEN AMONG THE VICTIMS

Messrs M. O'Neill, a Wexford fireman, and Richard Gaul, Drinagh, Wexford, greaser, were amongst the victims of the Lusitania *disaster.*

(NEW ROSS STANDARD, 14 MAY 1915, P. 5)

Sadie Hale (24) Lost
Typist
Cranmore Gardens, Belfast, Co. Antrim

Originally from Ballymena, Sarah Rachel Orr Hale, or Sadie as she was known to her family and close friends, was a young unmarried woman who worked for Cunard as a typist in their office in Liverpool. In 1909 Sadie was placed on Cunard's Atlantic steamers on the New York run to provide typing services. She travelled frequently on the *Mauretania* and *Lusitania*. The usual arrangement for her employment was that she would work in Cunard's offices in Liverpool between voyages while remaining signed-on as crew for the next crossing.
On 14 January 1915 Sadie wrote a letter which was placed in an envelope marked – *Only to be opened after my death*

Mildmay
Blackburne Place
Liverpool

Dear Mother and Tillie,
I attach a paper showing how I desire my capital disposed of. My personal belongings I leave you to deal with as you wish.

I would like Mrs Larisch, of Mildmay, Blackburne Place, Liverpool, to get one of my trinkets as a remembrance, or, failing that, a piece of crystal or silver.

My books are at Plym, Manor Road, and I should like you to write to Miss Pilling, 20 Rufford Road, Liverpool, giving her a list of my library, and asking her to choose six volumes. The remainder you can keep.

Mrs Oxton, 52 Bebington Road, Higher Tranmere, Birkenhead, Cheshire should also get a trinket or a piece of crystal.

Amongst my belongings you will find a book containing addresses, and those marked with an 'X' I should like you to advise that I have died.

Drawing by Louis Raemakers. A surprising number of survivors claimed the submarine surfaced to survey its handiwork. 'The crew stood stolidly on deck,' said one. 'I could distinguish the German flag.' Nothing of the kind occurred

I have one large trunk at Mildmay, a green suitcase, a cardboard hat box, and a leather suit-case (the last-mentioned being in Miss Larisch's room). At sea I have one cabin trunk and a kit bag.

I hope this will be quite clear to you. I desire that my entire capital, which is invested in the Cunard S.S. Co. Ltd., Savings Fund, the Post Office Savings Bank and J. & E. Taylor, 3 Little Victoria Street, Belfast be equally divided between my nieces, Helen Margaret Taylor and Dorothy Hamill Taylor.

Sarah Rachel Orr Hale

In an unsigned letter written on the following day (15 January 1915) to her mother, the following passage was included:

I had to get up early and do my packing this morning, but now everything is finished, so tonight I shall only put my things in my trunk at Mildmay. By the way, you ought to know what I keep there when I am at sea. I have my large trunk, the green suitcase (the last is in Miss Larisch's room for safe-keeping). In my attaché case (which is in the large trunk) you will find a note which tells you what to do in case anything happens to me. Now, for heaven's sake, don't think that I am scared or imagine anything is going to happen to me this particular time. I merely give this information for all time so that there will be no difficulty in case of accident. I keep my bank book on the top tray of my large trunk. So that is all.

On St Patrick's Day 1915 Sarah wrote another letter:

Mildmay
Blackburne Place
Liverpool

Mother and Tillie Dear,
There is absolutely nothing being done in the office so I think it is well that I am going to sea, otherwise I might be out of a post ... I have effected my insurance by paying the first premium. I enclose the receipt, which I want you to hold until I return. In case anything happened, it is better for you to hold this. You would communicate with Mr E. Stephens, N. P. I. for Mutual Life Assurance, 1 Exchange Street West, Liverpool as he will hold my policy until I return. I shall try and get a card off the ship, but in case I don't, my deepest love to you all.
    Sadie
P. S. – My insurance, in case of death, I should like to be held for Helen and Joan [Dorothy?] when they attain their majority.

Helen and Joan were nieces mentioned in her previous letter.

Sadie's personal estate amounted to £443 12s 10d, according to documents uncovered after her death. But the question the courts had to establish was whether the series of letters she left amounted to a valid will. To be valid in English law a will must be signed by its maker in the presence of two witnesses who must see each other sign. Sadie Hale had simply written letters with no witnesses at all.

The father of the two nieces intended to benefit from the insurance sought an exemption under a provision of the Wills Act 1837 which stated that 'any soldier being in actual military service or any mariner or seaman, being at sea, may dispose of his personal estate in a manner as he might before the passing of this act, i.e. without these formalities'.

The two questions for the court, therefore were:

1. Was Sadie Hale a mariner or seaman?
2. Was she 'at sea' at the time she wrote her unwitnessed will in Blackburne Place, Liverpool?

In his summing up, Mr Justice Madden declared: 'That the deceased was among the victims of German barbarism who lost their lives in the sinking of the *Lusitania*, is clear beyond doubt, for her body was found and identified'. [Body number 127.] He concluded that as a typist who was in possession of a Certificate of Continuous Discharge (albeit lost in the sinking) under the Merchant Shipping Act 1894 she was indeed a 'mariner or seaman' and that as she was preparing for a voyage she was 'at sea' at the time she made the unwitnessed declaration.

Accordingly, her nieces benefited and were awarded the residue of her estate. As a result of Sadie's case it is accepted that civilian staff engaged on a merchant navy ship are indeed *seamen* and may make unwitnessed wills. A farsighted decision for 1915, but one which contrasts sharply with the similar case of Sir Hugh Lane (*qv*).

John Harman – Saved
AB Seaman
Cork and Liverpool

John Harman, of Cork, who resides at 4 Albert terrace, Rathbourne Street, Liverpool, said he was on deck, and he saw the torpedo coming through the water to the Lusitania. *He had hardly realised what it was when the explosion occurred. He went to the boats, and was one of those who helped to launch boat No. 15.*

(IRISH TIMES, 10 MAY 1915, P. 9)

Edward Heighway – Saved
AB Seaman
Strangford, Co. Down

SEAMAN'S HEROIC RESCUE WORK

The Belfast Evening Telegraph reports an interview with Edward J. Heighway, member of the Lusitania's *crew, who has arrived at his home at Strangford, Co. Down. He said that when the first torpedo struck, a 'mountain of water' rose to the boat deck. On the second torpedo striking, he rushed to the lifeboat of which he was in charge, lowered it, and called for passengers. But owing to the list the people had scrambled to the other side of the vessel, and would not return.*

Eventually the boat got 70 or 80 passengers, including a number of women and children, and it was lowered to the water, being with difficulty rowed away from the danger zone.

Heavy masses of chairs, boats and gear, mixed up with women and children, came tumbling about. Many people were killed as they fell. The great vessel 'took a straight dive and in a few seconds nothing was to be seen but a blinding mass of steam and wreckage', with dead bodies floating all about.

The most pathetic spectacle was that of mothers frantically clasping their babies to their breasts – some already drowned and others beyond human help. Heighway's boat picked up 20 living people. His party was rescued in an hour's time and conveyed to Kinsale.

Heighway, like his shipmates, lost all his belongings, all except the decoration received from the King for his gallant services at the Volturno *disaster, which he happened to have in his pocket.*

(IRISH INDEPENDENT, 12 MAY 1915, P. 6)

Photograph taken during Heighway's service on the Carmania

The *Volturno*, of the Canadian Northern Steamship Company, went on fire in the North Atlantic on 9 October 1913. Of the 654 aboard, 103 passengers and 30 officers and crew were lost. On that occasion Heighway, who was aboard the *Carmania*, plunged into the sea with a line in the darkness of night to rescue a man who fell overboard from the burning ship. Ironically the life he saved was German – third-class passenger Walter Trentepohl.

Heighway received his silver medal from King George V in May 1914, a year before he repeated his heroics in the *Lusitania* sinking.

James Hoey (25) Lost
Trimmer
Mary Street, Dundalk, Co. Louth

James Hoey, of 4 Mary Street (South), Dundalk, who was a trimmer on his first voyage on the Lusitania, *and has not been heard from since the torpedoing of that vessel. He is supposed to have been lost. The news has brought great grief to his aged grandmother and sister, with whom he resided in Dundalk. He was only 25 years old, and was a very promising young man.*

(LARNE TIMES, 22 MAY 1915, P. 9)

Hoey was born at Duleek, Co. Meath and his parents, John and Rose, were both dead.
The Commonwealth War Graves Commission records his age as 23.

Patrick Hopkins (25) Lost
Fireman
Castlebar, Co. Mayo

It is also feared that four other young men, named Costello from Killawalla, and Pat Cooney, Thomas Carney, and Pat Hopkins, from Crumlin, also perished on the occurrence.

(CONNAUGHT TELEGRAPH, 22 MAY 1915, P. 4)

Hopkins was born at Tawnyshowny, Castlebar and was the son of Patrick and Ellen Hopkins, of 15 Walmsley Street, Liverpool.

James Hume (19) Saved
AB Seaman
Belfast, Co. Antrim

THE SUNKEN LINER
YOUNG SEAMAN'S TERRIBLE STORY

James Hume, 19 years of age, who was a seaman on board the Lusitania, *has arrived at his home in Canmore Street, Belfast. He was in his bunk snatching a few hours' rest when he was awakened by the sound of the explosion, and going on deck, handed a lifejacket to a woman who was carrying a baby, assisting the woman to fix the jacket.*

In thankfulness she snatched a gold watch from her breast and pushed it into his hand, ignoring his protest. As a boat at which Hume was engaged was lowered, a sudden list of the liner caused the frail craft to upset. Hume ultimately climbed down to a rail and when the liner was half submerged he sprang into the sea, making a drop of 60 feet.

'All around the ship,' Hume continued, 'you could see nothing but heads bobbing up and down in the water, and when I looked back I saw the stern of the vessel in the air. People too terrified to jump were clinging desperately to the sides, and they went down when the ship sank'.

He gave a pathetic account of how about 40 people clinging to an upturned boat were swept away, one after the other, by the buffeting of the waves.

'I managed to swim over to a collapsible boat, which was floating bottom upwards, the canvas covering still being attached. There were about 40 of us clinging to it, including half a dozen girls whom the menfolk did their best to support.

'The boat was continually turning over on its side, however, and one by one the others lost their grip and disappeared. A child of about six years was washed up against me, and I endeavoured to support her, but lost consciousness and when I came to my senses I was aboard a fishing boat. I do not know what became of the child.

'I was over four hours in the water, and that with nothing on but an undershirt, so you may guess I was nearly frozen. My feet were so cut up that I could scarcely walk'.

In the course of his narrative, young Hume said that some passengers in the boats started singing to keep their spirits from failing. Rule Britannia and Tipperary were two of the airs he heard as he was clinging to the upturned boat. On a raft, on which several women were huddled, he saw a clergyman in an attitude of prayer.

(IRISH INDEPENDENT, 13 MAY 1915, P. 7)

A graphic description of the last scene aboard the Lusitania was given to a Telegraph representative by James Hume, a young seaman, who has just returned to his home, 98 Canmore Street, Belfast.

Hume, who is nineteen years of age, has only been at sea a couple of years, but in a few hours gained the experience of a lifetime.

The first news of the disaster was conveyed to his mother in a rather startling manner on Friday evening. Her husband, who is in the Ulster Division, had come home that day for Saturday's great parade, and with the hustle and bustle the Telegraph containing the dread news lay unopened on the table until about 8 p.m.

PARENTS' SUSPENSE

Mrs Hume was glancing casually through the pages when to her horror she saw the grim tidings of the Lusitania's fate. The hours of terrible suspense that followed may be well imagined, and it need scarcely be said that the wire which arrived on Saturday morning announcing her son's safety was received with joy by the anxious mother.

Hume spoke in great praise of the kindness of the people of Queenstown. He was provided with clothes – 'coat and trousers, about two sizes too large for me', he laughingly remarked – and a pair of tennis shoes, and was thus garbed when he reached Liverpool.

A sorrowful scene was presented at the Liverpool docks, he said, where crowds of people were gathered, anxiously scanning the faces of those who came ashore, all on the look-out for dear ones who had been aboard the ill-fated Cunarder.

One young woman rushed from the crowd and, clasping Hume around the neck, kissed him, only to drop back the next moment with the cry, 'Oh, I thought you were my brother'. She proved to be the sister of a fireman on the Lusitania.

(LARNE TIMES, 15 MAY 1915, P. 9)

Patrick Kearney (25) Lost
Trimmer
Crumlin, Co. Mayo

By the sinking of the Lusitania *many families around Castlebar are thrown into mourning.*

Three Crumlin men, Pat Kearney, Thomas Kearney, and Pat Hopkins, have lost their lives, as has also Thomas Sweeney, Parke, who was working on board the vessel.

(MAYO NEWS, 22 MAY 1915, P. 4)

Kearney was a son of Patrick and Bridget Kearney, who were then living at 15 Walmsley Street, Liverpool. He is believed to be no relation of his namesake, Thomas Kearney.

Trimmers and firemen labouring in the bowels of the vessel had little chance of escape. Those not killed immediately by the force of the blast were nonetheless stunned, then bowled off their feet by the inrush of water. The lights went out, plunging the workspaces and tunnels into pitch darkness. At the same time the impact pushed thick clouds of soot into the air from the shocked bunkers. Broken steam pipes and gashed boilers next poured scalding vapours into any remaining pocket of space, turning the place into Dante's Hell. The chances of salvation for any man below were remote.

Thomas Kearney (25) Lost
Fireman
Castlebar, Co. Mayo

It is also feared that four other young men, named Costello from Killawalla, and Pat Cooney, Thomas Carney, and Pat Hopkins, from Crumlin, also perished on the occurrence.

(CONNAUGHT TELEGRAPH, 22 MAY 1915, P. 4)

Kearney was the son of Peter and Mary Kearney of Spink, Tonneyshawn, Castlebar.

James McDermott (38) Lost
Ship's Surgeon
From Cork City
Lived in Wallasey, Liverpool

Dr James McDermott, the doctor on the Lusitania, *who it is feared is amongst the drowned. Dr McDermott, who was a native of Cork (he resided in his boyhood and student days at Eldred Terrace, Douglas Road), was well known and esteemed here.*

He was a man of fine appearance and great charm of manner, and was very well liked by the officers and crew of the Lusitania *and other ships of the Cunard line on which he had been the doctor. He had been for seven years in the service of the Cunard Company. Dr McDermott was the eldest son of Captain McDermott, formerly Board of Trade Superintendent in Cork, and now residing in England. His friends in this city deeply mourn the sad fate of Dr McDermott.*

(CORK EXAMINER, 12 MAY 1915)

A large crowd awaited the arrival of the train due in Cork at 9.25 from the West as it was surmised that some of the survivors would arrive in Cork by the train. Amongst those in waiting was a sister of Dr McDermott, who was Medical Officer aboard the Lusitania, *and was well known as wing three-quarter in the University rugby team when a student. The paucity of news regarding survivors caused the gravest anxiety. On arrival of the train it was ascertained that none of the survivors were on board.*

(CORK FREE PRESS, 8 MAY 1915)

Dr McDermott's body was recovered and interred in the Old Church Cemetery, Cobh, in private plot number 474. It has later been marked by a stone erected by the Commonwealth War Graves Commission.

James Moran – Saved
Greaser
Erren, Co. Mayo

They were engaged as trimmers on board; and another Ballyhaunis man named Moran, of Erren, who occupied a similar position, has, we are pleased to learn, been saved.

(MAYO NEWS, 22 MAY 1915, P. 4)

James Murphy – Saved
Fireman
Swords, Co. Dublin

James Murphy, who was a fireman on the Lusitania, is a native of Swords, Co. Dublin. He was jammed between two lifeboats when in the water, but was rescued.

(IRISH INDEPENDENT, 15 MAY 1915, P. 3)

Murphy was treated in the Queenstown Infirmary for a variety of injuries.

Michael O'Neill (44) Lost
Fireman
Wexford

ONE OF THE LUSITANIA'S VICTIMS

One of the victims of the stupendous German crime which caused the destruction of the Lusitania and the murder of 1,500 men, women and children, was Michael O'Neill, brother of Mr John O'Neill, William Street, New Ross, a baker in the employment of Mr Murphy, UC, John Street.

Michael was one of the Lusitania's stokers, and the anxious enquiries of his brother elicited the sad tidings that he was not one of the survivors. Prayers were offered up at all the Masses in both churches on Sunday last for the repose of the soul of the deceased. He was a man of about 42 years of age, and a native of Wexford, where another brother of his resides.

(NEW ROSS STANDARD, MAY 21, 1915, P. 5)

Stephen Rice – Saved
Fireman
Co. Armagh

Stephen Rice, a Co. Armagh fireman, was picked up after hours in the water. He is suffering from bruises.

(IRISH INDEPENDENT, 15 MAY 1915, P. 3)

Rice was treated in Queenstown Infirmary.

Laurence Rossiter – Saved
Fireman
Main Street, Wexford

WEXFORD FIREMAN ON THE LUSITANIA
'I OWE MY LIFE TO BEING ABLE TO SWIM'

Mr Joseph Rossiter, linotype operator in the News office, Waterford, has received a letter from his brother, Mr Laurence Rossiter, who was a fireman on board the Lusitania, and is one of the fortunate survivors. In the course of his letter he says:

'I need not tell you that we had a terrible time while it lasted, and I hope never to see the same sight again … I owe my life to being able to swim. I never troubled about a lifebelt. I am broken up, and when I will be able to go to work again, I do not know. However I am thankful that I was saved. I was in the military hospital in Queenstown for three days. The scenes there are beyond describing'.

Mr Rossiter, who is a Wexford man, is now in Liverpool. He is a son of the late Mr Nicholas Rossiter, Main Street, Wexford.

(NEW ROSS STANDARD, 21 MAY 1915, P. 5)

Charles Scannell (25) Saved
Fireman
Robert's Cove, Minane Bridge, Co. Cork

CORKMAN'S THRILLING STORY
FOREBODING OF DISASTER
DROWNING VICTIMS' CRIES

Charles Scannell, 25, a native of Roberts Cove, Minane Bridge, near Tracton, County Cork, a fireman on board the Lusitania, tells a thrilling story of what he saw after the ship was torpedoed. Some three or four years ago he was seen on several athletic fields in the county, and many of his confrères in those early strenuous days of his will readily remember him.

'This was my second trip on the Lusitania,' said Mr Scannell, 'and we did our ordinary round of duty until we were torpedoed. I was in the stokehold on the 8 a.m. to 12 noon watch that day, and on being relieved at the latter hour, washed, had a meal, and retired to my bunk in a room occupied by 16 others and myself.

'I don't know exactly how to put it, but I had before that a strange foreboding of the disaster, so much so that when I retired from my previous watch I could not sleep – I had a feeling that something was going to happen and was unable to rest.

'Anyway I got into my bunk about 12.30, and I must have been nearly a couple of hours there sleeping lightly when I heard a terrific noise, which brought me to my feet in an instant. The others in the room were all awake, and as I opened my eyes I saw them making for the door.

'"What's up?" I asked one of my mates, and his answer was, "She's torpedoed". I seized my trousers, and was drawing it on when a man rushed in shouting "Stanley, Stanley" – he was one of my mates [Hugh Stanley] – "we're torpedoed". At this time I had only a shirt and underpants on, and it was in this attire, I may say here now, that I eventually came ashore at Queenstown.

'But to resume: I ran from the room, and as I did so the vessel listed heavily and I was flung against the side. I had hardly recovered myself when there was an inrush of water from both sides which nearly swept me off my feet. With difficulty I made my way to the top deck, and there I saw the people crowding to the boats. It was all confusion.

'I managed however to get into one boat, but it was too crowded and I got out again. Then I got into another boat, but that was also full up and I left it. It struck me then that I had better hunt around for a lifebelt, and I did so, but almost immediately met a man with two cork jackets in his hands. I asked him for one, but he said, "One is for my poor wife, but I can't find her". After a bit I succeeded in getting a lifebelt from a passenger who had two. He tried to fasten it on me, but the tapes gave way – it was apparently an old one – but between us we fixed it somehow.

'Seeing the way the ship had now listed and difficulty of getting at the boats, I made for the stern and slid down the log line, tearing the flesh badly off my hands, as you can see'. Mr Scannell here held up his hands – one entirely bandaged, the other partly. 'Just as I was tipping the water,' he continued, 'a man coming down the line after me bounced into me, and my lifebelt came off. It fell into the sea.

'I went after it, got it, and placed it round me as well as I could, and in that way it proved useful. I saw a boat some distance from me, I made for it, but I suppose those in it didn't see me, for it pulled away from me, and I was unable to overtake it. I saw another a little later, but failed to reach that also.

'Swimming near me was the chap who knocked off my lifebelt coming down the rope, and he said, 'Never mind, we'll get into the track of some of them'. Then, hearing a tremendous noise, I turned and saw fire and smoke bursting out, and with that burst the ship went down. Around me there were scores of people shouting and screaming, and all struggling. It was simply fearful.

'I still swam on, and suddenly found myself in a current that was dragging me back in the direction of where the vessel disappeared. After an effort I got out of this, and soon after saw an upturned boat with about 20 people on it, amongst them being the Second Engineer [Alex] Duncan and a fireman. I reached it all right, and they pulled me up, and there with all the others I saw my friend again who slid down the rope behind me. He had got onto the boat only a few minutes before I did.

'To the best of my belief I was about an hour in the water before I found this place of safety, and while drifting about on it I saw any number of people being carried past, some actually drowning – no sound from them; others still crying feebly, while more were yelling. I heard several invoking curses on Germany, and that sort of thing. It was a dreadful sight. We were four hours on the boat, and the scenes that I saw during the greater part of the time I shall never forget.

'Eventually a trawler came along, took us on board, and brought us into Queenstown, where I was provided with a suit of clothes. As far as I can learn since, only two of the seventeen room-mates of mine were saved in addition to myself, namely Hugh Stanley and Patrick McMahon. There were in all about 200 firemen and trimmers in the ship – the "Black Gang", as they are called, and the majority of these were drowned, and I have no doubt that all the men in the stoke holds on the 12 to 4 watch went down too'.

Asked if he had any idea as to the rate of speed the Lusitania was travelling at the time she was struck, he said he could not say what it was at that particular moment. All he could say with any degree of certainty was that when he left the stokehold at 12 and went to his bunk she was doing about 15 knots, or a little more than half her normal speed.

Mr Scannell, who was sent on to Liverpool on Saturday, and returned yesterday, left for his home of Robert's Cove last evening.

(CORK EXAMINER, 13 MAY 1915)

Owen Slavin – Saved
Trimmer
Dundalk, Co. Louth

INJURED SURVIVORS
IRISHMAN LOSES HIS ARM

At the South Infirmary there are two more survivors, Patrick Reynolds, Liverpool, and Owen Slavin, Dundalk. They are both doing well.

Mr Slavin was the victim of a most unfortunate accident. Shortly after the first torpedo hit the liner he was hit by some falling object on the arm and knocked down.

After this he found himself in the water and was picked up by one of the boats. He was removed to Queenstown in a very exhausted condition. There it was found that the fracture was so serious that the arm had to be amputated.

(CORK EXAMINER, 12 MAY 1915, P. 6)

One man told a strange story. He was a member of the ship's crew and was at his station when she was going down. He endeavoured to get his boat lowered, it being full of passengers. They worked at her for twenty-five minutes to no avail, and they all went down with the Lusitania. He knew no more, but believed that there was no explosion on the ship as she went down.

THE LUSITANIA TRAGEDY.

When he became conscious, he was on the surface and seeing an upturned boat he seized its keel with his right hand. He prepared to make himself secure and made an effort to catch the keel with his left hand only to make the horrifying discovery that his arm was gone – blown clean away. He felt no pain, and was not aware of anything untoward having happened to him. He was taken on board a boat and his arm was then bound up and fastened with a rope to prevent his bleeding to death.

(CORK FREE PRESS, 10 MAY 1915, P. 7)

ARM AMPUTATED WITH A PENKNIFE

Owen Slavin, left, a coal trimmer from Dundalk, with Patrick Reynolds, Liverpool, sitting. Slavin's left arm was amputated in order to save his life

Dr S. B. D. Vescovi, an Italian, returning home from Chile, said he was on deck near the cafe when he felt a shock, and water and debris were thrown upwards. Then the people rushed about. Then suddenly the ship sank and he went down with her. He was in the water some hours, but at length reached an upturned boat on which there were several ladies.

A Greek steamer had picked them up. On the steamer he found one man's arm was so badly injured that he had to amputate it with his penknife. He also dressed the injuries of another man, who had three fingers crushed. Lady Allan was also aboard the boat suffering injuries, and to her and other ladies he gave restoratives.

(IRISH TIMES, 10 MAY 1915, P. 8)

Jeremiah Sweeney – Lost
Fireman
Castlebar, Co. Mayo

Jeremiah, named in a newspaper list as 'Thomas' Sweeney, was the son of widow Ellen Sweeney, of Turlough, Castlebar, Co. Mayo. His father was called Patrick.

By the sinking of the Lusitania many families around Castlebar are thrown into mourning. Three Crumlin men … have lost their lives, as has also Thomas Sweeney, Parke, who was working on board the vessel.

(MAYO NEWS, 22 MAY 1915, P. 4)

Francis Toner – Saved
Fireman
Co. Dublin

HIS THIRD ESCAPE
A FIREMAN'S THRILLING EXPERIENCE
WAS IN TITANIC DISASTER

Frank Tower, fireman on board the Lusitania, *who was amongst those rescued and brought to Kinsale, tells a thrilling tale. He is a Liverpool man whose home is at 23 Craton Street. 'This is the third big shipping disaster I have been in,' he said to our special representative, 'and if I am in another I think it will be my last', he added good-humouredly.*

Tower is middle-aged, strongly built, cool and courageous. He was a fireman on the Titanic *when that great vessel went down in 1912. His next experience was with the* Empress of Ireland, *which went down last year in the St Lawrence river and over 1,000 passengers and crew were drowned.*

'I was down below at my work when the Lusitania *was struck,' said Tower. 'The torpedo created a great shock and I immediately went on deck. I didn't hear a second torpedo strike the vessel, but there must have been a second, for there was a terrible explosion. As a result of that many firemen were killed'.*

(IRISH INDEPENDENT, MONDAY 10 MAY 1915)

Frank Toner appears to have been the source of the legend of 'Lucky Tower' – a story about a fortunate stoker who was said to have survived three great sea disasters in turn. Tower appears to be a corruption of Toner.

The first mention came in the *Cork Examiner*, above, in its second edition since the sinking. In the middle of a page is a picture headed 'Firemen Survivors'. The caption reads: 'The man with the grey moustache in the centre of the picture is Toner, a fireman. He had been a hand on the *Titanic*, was in the wreck of the *Empress of Ireland*, and lastly the *Lusitania*'.

On page nine of the same edition is a short piece entitled 'Fireman's Version' giving this interview:

Frank Toner, a fireman on board the *Lusitania*, was amongst those saved and landed at Kinsale. In an interview with our representative on Saturday he said he was below at the time of the explosion. The torpedo hit the vessel at the bow end of the bridge and tore a great hole in her side. Immediately he called out to one of his mates. 'Come on, get up to the top. This torpedo has done us in all right!'

They climbed on top and found that the vessel was already sinking fast. 'We made a jump for it,' he said, 'and I was pulled on to an upturned lifeboat and remained there with nine others'. He further explained that six of those were women, but before they were met by any other boat, two of those had died.

Questioned as to the speed, etc., of the *Lusitania* at the time, he said she was going about 15 knots. The weather was beautifully fine and clear, the sea was calm, and under the instructions of the captain everything had been got ready for an attack, but he could not say why she was going so slowly at the time.

The saloon passengers at the time he jumped were, he said, on the saloon deck and nearly all of them must have been drowned because they did not seem to make any attempt to escape, perhaps with the idea that the *Lusitania* would not sink so quickly, or perhaps with the idea that the rescue was close at hand.

He was perfectly satisfied that the ship sank within twenty minutes, as from the first moment she was struck she began to go down – just like a flat stone thrown into a pond, the fore-part being immediately submerged.

The photograph originally printed by the *Cork Examiner* was subsequently corrected after the captain of the *Wayfarer*, then in port, pointed out that the man identified as Toner was one of his crew members – a fireman named Ralph.

Elsewhere the *Cork Examiner* reported that

one of the survivors, Frank Toner, who was employed on board the *Lusitania* as a fireman, attracted a considerable amount of attention, and though he could not be induced to refer at any length to the prominent and plucky part he played in the disaster, some of his companions in the military hospital gave accounts of the great bravery he displayed.

He has a unique record, having gone down on three liners within a couple of years, but on each occasion his life was spared. He was one of the crew of the *Titanic* which sank on her maiden voyage with such disastrous results, but he was rescued. He was also employed on the Canadian Pacific liner *Empress of Ireland*, which sank in the St Lawrence with a heavy loss of life, but Toner was again fortunate enough to be saved. On Friday afternoon he was rescued for the third time.

He was a fireman on board the *Lusitania*, and when the liner began to settle down, he came on deck and worked untiringly in helping women and children into the boats, but he never gave any consideration to his own interests. As the *Lusitania* listed to starboard and her masts were lowered towards the water, he climbed one of the masts but soon got into difficulties.

He became entangled in the wireless apparatus, but succeeded in setting himself free as the ship disappeared. He was precipitated into the water, but was quickly pulled onto an upturned boat where he remained until rescued by the patrol boat *Heron*. During the time that he was on the upturned boat he rendered valuable aid in helping parties struggling in the water to the boat, and his actions throughout were certainly most heroic.

In the proceedings of the Kinsale inquest into five bodies landed there, District Inspector Alfred Wansborough named survivors he found on the naval patrol ship *Heron*, among them 'Francis Toner, 23 Crichton Street, off Wareham Street, Liverpool'.

The *New York Times* next carried the picture shown here, saying it depicted a triple tragedy survivor named 'Turner'.

The same picture was carried in a book on the disaster which was published within a month of the sinking. *Horrors and Atrocities of the Great War* referred to the serial escapee as 'Tonner, a County Dublin man, and a stoker on the *Lusitania*, who was one of the survivors landed at Kinsale'.

Toner and Turner certainly sound similar. There was unquestionably a Toner on the *Lusitania*, while on the *Titanic* there is a perplexing entry for a fireman up to now identified as 'Tozer'. No one served under that name on the *Empress of Ireland* however, although there was a cook named Turner.

Sailors are known for their tall stories. Another man later claimed to be a survivor of the three famous shipwrecks:

'JONAH' OF A TRANSPORT
A SEAMAN'S STORY OF MISFORTUNES

Charles Dunn, a seaman, pleaded guilty at Liverpool yesterday to a charge of failing to join an Admiralty transport.

He had served on the Titanic *and* Empress of Ireland, *both of which foundered at sea, and also on the* Lusitania *and the* Florazan, *both of which were torpedoed by German submarines.*

In consequence of these experiences, he was known to seamen generally as 'Jonah' and it was stated that the sailors on the transport intended to throw him overboard if he dared to make the trip. He therefore left the ship and joined the Royal Navy Reserve, but was discharged as being unfit for further service.

The Admiralty solicitor said the man was well known, and his portrait with the story of his adventures had appeared on the cinematograph screens of various music halls.

The Magistrate, addressing the accused, said: 'I think a man who has been through so much deserves some consideration. I shall, therefore, bind you over to be of good behaviour, but if you get into any further trouble you will not be let off again'.

(THE TIMES, 3 FEBRUARY 1916, P. 5)

Charles A. Dunn was the intermediate sixth engineer on the *Lusitania*. There was a trimmer identified as 'John' Dunn saved from the *Empress*. No one served under the name 'Dunn' on the *Titanic*.

James Toole (38) Lost
Fireman
Co. Louth

MORE BODIES PICKED UP
FROM OUR CORRESPONDENT BEREHAVEN, WEDNESDAY NIGHT

Two more bodies were today recovered at Firkall, 12 miles to the west of here. One was that of a ship's officer, dressed in black uniform with three gold braid bands on each sleeve; on the inside of the shirt collar the name 'Piper' was written, and he wore a gold ring inscribed 'S. P. E'. He was a fine type of manhood, about 6ft 1in. in height. He had a set of false teeth in both jaws. No papers which would establish identity further were found on him. [John Piper, Chief Officer.]

The other body was that of a fireman, and from insurance cards and other papers found on him, he is believed to be James Toole, 12, Blackstone Street, Liverpool. A man of sturdy build, swarthy complexion, strong face, and about 5ft 8in. in height.

He was when recovered in a good state of preservation, as was the body of the officer. It was late in the afternoon when the second body, that of the fireman, was picked up. Both were conveyed to Garnish [island], where they now lie with the three found yesterday, awaiting the arrival of the Cunard searching boat for removal.

(CORK EXAMINER, 20 MAY 1915, P. 6)

Toole was a husband of Bridget Toole (*née* Geeney), and lived in Liverpool. He was from Louth, where his late parents, Patrick and Anne Toole, had raised him, and where he first gained experience as a seafarer.

Tagged as body number 232, Mr Toole was interred in Common A mass grave in Cobh's Old Church Cemetery.

Chief Officer Piper (body 231) was buried three days later in Kirkdale cemetery, Liverpool.

Phillip Henry Traynor (28) Lost
Trimmer
Derry City

DISPUTE OVER COMPENSATION

The Lusitania disaster was mentioned in cases before the Derry magistrates on Thursday when a series of summonses for assault and threatening language were heard. Mary Ann Traynor summoned her mother-in-law, Mary Traynor, Nelson Street, for abusive language, and her sister-in-law Mary McCay, for assault. The latter had a cross-case for threatening language, and there were minor summonses.

Mr Andrew Robb, for Mary Ann Traynor, stated that his client's husband had been lost on the *Lusitania*. The Cunard company paid £250 into court, and deceased's wife was now in receipt of a pension of £222 a year. After the disaster Mary Traynor took her daughter-in-law into the house, and they lived in a friendly manner, but when it was known that the money was all likely to go to deceased's wife, the mother started to give her daughter-in-law a bad time, the result being that she had to leave her, and since was unable to pass up and down the street without being subjected to abusive language by the defendants.

On Monday last Mrs McCay caught her by the hair, trailed her to the middle of the street, and struck her on the face several blows.

Mrs McCay – 'She was too drunk to know what I was doing'.

After a protracted hearing, the magistrates fined Mrs McCay 10s 6d and bound her to the peace. The other cases were dismissed.

(Belfast Weekly Telegraph, 6 November 1915. p. 3)

Other Irish crewmen, all lost in the sinking of the Lusitania:

Daniel Barrett
Fireman – Age 18
Son of Cornelius and Norah Barrett, of 2, Middle Street, Liverpool. Born in Cork.

W. Barry
Fireman – Age 26
Born in Dublin.

Patrick Brennan
Greaser – Age 47
Son of Michael and the late Catherine Brennan; husband of Annie Brennan (née Lacey), of 55, Langtry Road, Kirkdale, Liverpool. Born in Dublin.

Patrick Campbell
Fireman –Age 35
Son of Julia and the late Thomas Campbell; husband of Elizabeth Campbell (née Rice), of Cloutigoura Post Office, Newry, Co. Down. Born in Fisherhill, Co. Mayo.

Bernard Cassidy
Fireman – Age 59
Son of Thomas and the late Catherine Cassidy; husband of Elizabeth Cassidy (née Handley), of 26, Exeter Street, Liverpool. Born in Newry, Co. Down.

James Coady
Fireman – Age 53
Born in Wexford.

Patrick Collins
Fireman – Age 35
Son of the late Michael and Mary Collins.

Born in Dunmanway, Co. Cork.

Michael Corboy
Fireman – Age 49
Son of the late Daniel and Mary Corboy. Born in Newry, Co. Down.

Patrick Curran
Fireman – Age 44
Son of the late Patrick and Julia Curran; husband of Margaret Curran (née Dixon), of 9, Saltney Street, Liverpool. Born in Dundalk, Co. Louth.

John Donnelly
Fireman – Age 23
Son of Judith Donnelly, of 272, Derby Road, Liverpool, and the late Peter Donnelly. Born in Co. Armagh.

John Doyle
Fireman – Age 35
Son of Lawrence Doyle, of 368, Vauxhall Road, Liverpool, and the late Ann Doyle. Born in Glynn, Co. Wexford. Brother to Peter Doyle, below.

Peter Doyle
Leading Fireman – Age 32
Son of Lawrence and the late Ann Doyle; husband of Bridget Doyle (née Kelly), of 70, Dryden Street, Liverpool. Born in Wexford. Brother to John Doyle, above.

John Duggan
Trimmer – Age 31
Son of Margaret Duggan, of 38, Craddock

Street, Kirkdale, Lancs., and the late John Duggan. Born in Co. Kerry.

James Dwyer
Trimmer – Age 20
Born in Wexford.

Edward Finnegan
Trimmer – Age 22
Son of Mrs Mary Finnegan, of Drimahill, Castleblaney, Co. Monaghan. Born in Carrickmacross, Co. Monaghan.

Peter Gavan
Trimmer – Age 38
Born in Mayo.

M. Geraghty
Waiter/Assistant Butcher – Age 38
Born in Dublin.

Michael Grant
Fireman – Age 36
Born at Dundalk.

Philip Keating
Fireman – Age 31
Brother of Miss Annie Keating, of Crossreagh, Mullagh, Co. Cavan. Born in Cavan.

Thomas Ledene
Able Seaman – Age 50
Son of the late Mr and Mrs Ledene; husband of the late Margaret Ledene. Born in Limerick.

Daniel Lee
Fireman – Age 50
Son of the late Mr and Mrs Lee; husband of Bridget Lee (*née* Bracken), of 101 Gildorts Gardens, Liverpool. Born in Co. Westmeath.

Isaac Linton
Fireman – Age 48
Son of the late Isaac and Sarah Linton; husband of the late Annie Linton (*née* Garrett). Born in Co. Down.

Patrick Loughran
Trimmer – Age 19
Son of Michael and Mary Loughran, of 40, Queen Street, Newry, Co. Down.

Patrick Markey
Trimmer – Age 30
Son of the late Thomas and Elizabeth Markey. Born in Dundalk, Co. Louth.

Peter McBride
Trimmer – Age 52
Ravensdale, Co. Louth.

Owen McCann
Trimmer – Age 28
Born in Dundalk, Co. Louth. Lived in Carlingford, Co Louth.

Thomas McCann
Fireman – Age 22
Born in Armagh.

Bartholomew McCarthy
Fireman – Age unknown
From Wexford.

Daniel McConkey
Waiter – Age 42
From Hillsborough, Co. Down. Lived in St Ambrose Grove, Liverpool.

James McCormick
Fireman – Age 44
From Cork.

Thomas McCutcheon
Fireman – Age unknown
From Cootehill, Co. Cavan.

Michael McGeough
Fireman – Age 30
From Skyhill, Co. Louth. Lived in Dundalk.

Michael McGuigan
Trimmer –Age 43
From Newry, Co. Down.

Bernard McKenna
Trimmer – Age 29
From Castlebellingham, Co. Louth.

Kenneth McKenzie
Waiter – Age 22
From Belfast.

Patrick McMahon
Fireman – Age 37
From Monaghan.

Peter McNulty
Trimmer – Age 30
From Newry, Co. Down. Lived in Litherland, Liverpool.

Terence McParland
Fireman – Age 26.
From Forkhill, Co. Armagh. Lived in Bootle.

Matthew Murphy
Fireman – Age 58
Son of the late James and Ellen Murphy; husband of Margaret Murphy (*née* Donnelly), of 19, Southey Street, Marsh Lane, Bootle, Lancs. Born in Wexford.

Bernard Patrick Norton
Fireman – Age 44
Son of the late James and Elizabeth Norton. Born in Athlone, Co. Westmeath.

Michael O'Hare
Greaser – Age 35
From Newry, Co. Down.

John Orange
Fireman – Age 24
Son of Joseph Orange, of Chapel Street, Balbriggan, Dublin, and the late Mary Anne Orange.

Robert Pinkerton
Chief Baker – Age 50
Son of the late Robert and Margaret Jane Pinkerton; husband of Eliza Jane Pinkerton (*née* Clokey), of 40, Linacre Road, Liverpool. Born in Belfast.

Joseph Rafferty
Fireman – Age 23
Son of Patrick and Rose Rafferty, of Lower Willville, Carlingford, Co. Louth.

Michael Rice
Fireman – Age 60
Son of the late Patrick and Mary Rice. Born in Co. Armagh.

Edward Ryan
Fireman – Age 44
(Served as Rice) Son of Ann Ryan, of Corrags, Newry, Co. Down and the late Patrick Ryan; husband of Margaret Ryan (*née* Irving), of 94, Gildarts Gardens, Limekiln Lane, Liverpool. Born in Newry.

Geoffrey Sheridan
Fireman – Age 50
Son of the late Anthony and Mrs Sheridan; husband of Clara Sheridan (*née* Blundell), of 67, Strand Rodd, Bootle, Liverpool. Born in Ireland.

Patrick Sheridan
Fireman – Age 56
Son of the late John and Mary Sheridan; husband of Charlotte Sheridan (*née* Smyth), of 6, Boreland Street, Bootle, Lancs. Born in Co. Westmeath.

Michael Ward
Fireman – Age 28
Born in Galway.

Martin Welsh
Trimmer – Age 28
Born in Mayo.

Sure, Lady, I Won't Drop Her
One mother had the glad experience of being rescued with her little daughter and her husband. She passed the child to the willing hands of the Irish boatmen, and the first passenger whom she noticed on the little fishing vessel was her own husband, who had been picked up a few minutes previously
(Drawn by Christopher Clark for *The Sphere*, 15 May 1915)

The Rescue

We saw the ghastly procession of those rescue ships as they landed the living and the dead that night under the flaring gas torches along the Queenstown waterfront.

The arrivals began soon after 8 o'clock and continued at close intervals until about 11 o'clock. Ship after ship would come out of the darkness, and sometimes two or three could be just described awaiting their turn in the cloudy night to discharge bruised and shuddering women, crippled and half-clothed men and a few wide-eyed little children …

Women caught at our sleeves and begged desperately for word of their husbands; and men with choking efforts at matter-of-factness moved ceaselessly from group to group, seeking a lost daughter or sister or even bride.

Piles of corpses like cordwood began to appear among the paint-kegs and coils of rope on the shadowy old wharves …

US CONSUL WESLEY FROST

The news, when it reached Queenstown, left its hearers dumbfounded. The world's fastest passenger liner had been destroyed outside the harbour. Gradually seized by the need to do something about the massive loss of life unfolding a few miles away, a variety of craft began readying to put to sea. They included lifeboats, trawlers, tenders, steamers and royal navy sloops, although the ageing cruiser *Juno* was recalled in case she too fell victim to the 'pirates'. The press, left behind on a gigantic story, struggled to gather what facts they could. Only when the rag-tag flotilla began to make its way back to Queenstown that night did the appalling scale of the disaster become apparent.

Stormcock

LANDING SURVIVORS
PATHETIC INCIDENTS

The scene at Queenstown as the first of the rescue ships drew near was a thrilling one. It was the tug Stormcock, *and she came into the harbour towing a long line of boats, the last rays of the sun that had made a glorious day lighting her way on her sad homecoming.*

Every minute drew sightseers filled with pity to the wharves and quaysides, and by the time she neared the Cunard wharf, where she was to disembark the survivors, a great crowd had collected. The police under District Inspector Armstrong had closed the Cunard quay against the public.

Bluejackets and soldiers were quickly on the scene, but there appeared to be a lack of organisation for quite a time. In fact it may be said that the bustle was of quite an unexpected character. Dusk had fallen when the ship drew alongside.

As quickly as possible gangways were run aboard, and those survivors who were able to do so rapidly left the ship and collected on the quay. Here it could be clearly seen the rapidity of the effect of the terrible power of the torpedoing. Passengers lightly clothed, in some cases in shirt and trousers; firemen wearing but dungaree trousers and 'sweat rag', ship's butchers still having their blue overalls on them, and stewards in the bedraggled remains of the smart uniform that denoted their calling.

(CORK EXAMINER, 11 MAY 1915, P. 5)

Flying Fish

The *Flying Fish* operated as both a tug and tender, ferrying the passengers and mails to the liners making the Queenstown stop. She was owned and operated by the Clyde Shipping

Company. Her Captain, Tomas Brierley, a father of 13, was 54 years old at the time of the sinking. His vessel was tied up when he noticed a large amount of naval tonnage getting steam up to rush for the harbour mouth. He guessed there was an emergency and joined in.

As soon as the *Lusitania's* distress signal was relayed to the admiralty, the naval commander at Queenstown, Vice Admiral Sir Charles Coke, sent all serviceable craft to the rescue. These included the ageing and vulnerable cruiser *Juno* (which was recalled to Queenstown at the harbour mouth because of her perceived vulnerability) along with the sloop *Bluebell* and tugs *Warrior*, *Stormcock* and *Julia*.

The *Flying Fish* encountered the Manx lugger *Wanderer* about two miles off the Old Head, and took on its tempest-tossed complement of survivors. Having returned them to Queenstown, it made a further sortie and stayed out until long into the hours of darkness. It also made several trips to the vicinity in the following days.

Captain Brierley died in 1920 and is buried in the Old Church Cemetery, not far from the many victims of the *Lusitania*, among them some who had been taken from the sea by his vessel.

'FLYING FISH' LANDS 17

This morning, at 6.30, the tug Flying Fish *berthed at the Cunard wharf with the bodies of 8 women and 9 men. The work of removing these bodies to the morgue was the same distressing spectacle such as Queenstown has had to suffer since last Friday night. It was a dismal sight to watch the stretcher bearers taking the victims in.*

The corpses showed no great disfiguration, but some of them bore severe injuries, and in more than one case the faces were covered over … the Flying Fish *put out to sea again, to pursue with other tugs and varied crafts the gruesome task of recovering bodies.*

… She hopes to reach Schull early tomorrow morning, where she will pick up the bodies of 2 boys and 3 women, and at Myross (Glandore Bay), 1 body awaits her.

(CORK EXAMINER, 13 MAY 1915, P. 5)

Bluebell

The *Bluebell* was a flower-class naval sloop, and not a tug or a trawler as commonly cited. She was one of the few serviceable vessels available to Vice-Admiral Sir Charles Coke, head of the Queenstown Command. Coke had been pressing urgently for destroyers, but was told they were all needed for the more important mainland defences.

A flower-class sloop, probably the Bluebell, *putting out from Queenstown, c. 1916*

CAPTAIN SAVED

Later it was ascertained that Capt. Turner was not drowned, but had been picked up by HMS Bluebell *and subsequently taken to Queenstown on a Government launch.*

(CORK EXAMINER, 8 MAY 1915, P. 8)

The *Bluebell* found William Thomas Turner clinging to a floating spar with the aid of seaman Jack Roper. Having been rescued, the captain of the *Lusitania* was taken below to the mess, where he sat beside a stove, his head bowed or buried in his arms. During the journey, a woman passenger suddenly began berating him for the loss of her child, who had been placed in a raft which promptly capsized.

The *Bluebell* also rescued *Lusitania*'s Junior Third Officer Albert Bestic. To cheer up his captain, he told him: 'I'm glad to see you made it, Sir'.

Evidently feeling sorry for himself, Turner replied: 'Why should you be? You're not that fond of me'.

Turner was described as 'a very pathetic figure' as he walked through Queenstown the next day. To a reporter who approached him, he said: 'All I can tell you is that I stuck to my ship until she went from under me'.

A year later, this same royal navy vessel achieved fame in detaining the German gun-runner *Aud* (actually the *Libau*, posing as a neutral Norwegian) crammed with armaments to support the 1916 Easter Rising. The *Aud* had been due to *rendezvous* with Republicans in the same area as the *U-19* was putting Roger Casement ashore, but the British had increased surveillance in the Tralee area and along the coast because of code-break intercepts that such a shipment was under way.

The *Aud* eventually tried to flee, but was intercepted by the *Bluebell* and ordered to Queenstown. Trapped, the *Aud* scuttled herself with explosive charges on arrival in the mouth of Cork Harbour … and the *Bluebell* had the job this time of picking up German lifeboats.

Despite recognising the paucity of his resources at Queenstown and cam-paigning for more, the career of Vice-Admiral Coke did not survive long after the *Lusitania* sinking. He had already been replaced as senior naval officer at Haulbowline, the British base, by 1914 – only for his successor, Admiral Robert Stokes, to die of pneumonia within four days of arrival. Stokes is buried in the Old Church graveyard.

Vice-Admiral Coke

Coke was then restored 'temporarily' to the overall command of Irish waters, and was in charge, at the age of 60, when the sinking occurred.

The vice-admiral had hosted Winston Churchill, the First Lord of the Admiralty, when the latter visited the royal navy base at Queenstown in July 1912. Churchill promised Coke a cruiser squadron – but never delivered.

When the *Lusitania* was sunk, Churchill considered that her captain must have been a 'knave', possibly in the pay of the Germans – despite the Cunard vessel's lack of a naval escort in an obvious war zone!

In autumn 1915, Coke was recalled from Queenstown. He was retired at his own re-quest in April 1917, 'in order to facilitate the promotion of junior officers'.

He lived into his ninety-first year, dying at home in Exmouth in February 1945 – the same month that Churchill met Roosevelt and Stalin at Yalta to plan the post-war world.

Colleen

WEXFORD MAN IN THE RESCUE PARTY
'MOST TERRIBLE SIGHT'
PRIESTS GIVING ABSOLUTION DROWN IN THE LUSITANIA

Mr James Carr, Distillery Road, Wexford, is a stoker in the transport steamer Colleen, *which put out from Queenstown to the rescue. He is an ex-naval man, and was recalled for service at the be-ginning of the war. In a letter from Queenstown to his wife, which she received on Monday morn-ing, he states:*

'We were coaling one of the vessels when word came that the *Lusitania was sunk about fifteen miles from here, and we were ordered out at once. During the whole night we were bringing dead and alive to the port, and at present there are nearly 200 people dead here.*

'Men and women amongst the survivors were practically naked when landed. It was the most terrible sight I ever saw. I carried one woman up to the hospital in a dying state, and she was dead by the time I got there. She had some thousands of pounds stuffed in her stockings.*

'I also helped in the removal of another woman with a baby to her breast, and both were dead. People are arriving here from all parts to claim the bodies. Many of the survivors are in a very bad state, and are being treated in the hospitals. We all got great praise for the way we worked'.

Describing the conditions of the survivors on being landed, he says: 'One young woman came ashore smiling. She was covered with flannel and in her bare feet. Her husband was with her, and one of his legs was broken. She maintained a good-humoured appearance and told him not to give up heart. This woman was one of the best I ever saw, because she had suffered for four hours in the water before she was picked up.'

Mr Carr states that two priests on the Lusitania went down with the ship. 'They were', he said, 'craved to get into the boats, but they would not do so as they continued at the work of giving Absolution to the people, and when the vessel went down they also disappeared'.

(NEW ROSS STANDARD, 14 MAY 1915, P. 12)

Courtmacsherry Lifeboat

The Courtmacsherry lifeboat crew were early summoned to the scene of the disaster. They were accompanied by Mr Longfield and Rev. Mr Forde.

By the time the boat reached the scene a large number of vessels were hurrying up to the rescue. These vessels included a number of destroyers, which were making a large circle about the place where the liner was known to have gone down.

The Courtmacsherry lifeboat was still on the scene at ten o'clock.

(CORK EXAMINER, 8 MAY 1915.)

The Rev. J. W. Forde blamed the fact that the lifeboat was dependent solely on muscle-power for its failure to save life. He wrote a report the next day to the Royal National Lifeboat Institution (RNLI):

At about 2.30 yesterday, 7th inst., intelligence reached me by messenger that a large steamer was sinking some miles off. I at once proceeded to the boathouse where I found coxswain and crew launching the boat immediately. We had no wind, so had to pull the whole distance.

On the way to the wreck we met a ship's boat crowded with people who informed us the Lusitania had gone down. We did everything in our power to reach the place, but it took us at least three and a half hours of hard pulling to get there and then only in time to pick up dead bodies.

The Queenstown boat reached the wreck towed by steam trawler, almost together with us, and we all with other boats there then remained until about 8.40 engaged in that work. We were towed back a portion of the way by a steam drifter and reached the boathouse about 1.00 a.m.

Everything that was possible to do was done by the crew to reach the wreck in time to save life but as we had no wind it took us a long time to pull the ten or twelve miles out from the boathouse which we had to go. If we had wind or any motor power our boat would have been amongst the first on the scene.

It was a harrowing sight to behold. The sea was strewn with dead bodies floating about, some with lifebelts on, others holding onto pieces of rafts, all dead. I deeply regret it was not in our power to have been in time to save some. Went with the boat to the wreck and did what we could. Lifeboat was ten hours on service.

Crew of the Courtmacsherry lifeboat Tim Keohane, Cox; Mike Keating, John Murphy, his son Jerry Murphy, John Moloney, Con Whelton, his son Con Jr, Paddy Crowley, Mike Flynn, David Moloney, Pat Flynn, John Keohane, Pat Madden, Lar Moloney.

Left, an identical boat to Courtmacsherry's lifeboat, the Kezia Gwilt

Antoinette

This rescue boat incredibly was sunk by the *Lusitania* six days after that liner had sunk!

BALTIMORE FISHING BOAT SUNK
THRILLING EXPERIENCE OF THE CREW
(FROM OUR CORRESPONDENT) BALTIMORE, THURSDAY

A terrible disaster was providentially averted about midway between Sherkin Island and the Fastnet Lighthouse last night.

The crew of the Antoinette, *a fishing boat belonging to Mr Cadogan of Sherkin, put out to sea last night, and as the weather was rather stormy, decided to carry with them a yawl. A few hours later this yawl saved them – they numbered eight, all told – from a watery grave.*

It appears that they came in contact with a quantity of wreckage from the ill-fated Lusitania, *and the fishing boat, having her sails set, was going at a high speed when she struck what appeared to be a huge raft, which cut her in two, sinking her almost immediately.*

The crew had barely time to get the yawl out of the boat and enter it when the former went down, this making the second boat which Mr Cadogan has lost within a comparatively short period. The crew were in an exhausted condition in their frail craft, and being tossed about in the heavy seas and in imminent danger of their lives, when they were picked up by the Eileen Bawn, *owned by Mr Denis O'Donovan, which had them safely landed at Baltimore.*

(CORK FREE PRESS, 14 MAY 1915, P. 3)

Two further bodies were [each] brought in by the boats Antoinette *and* Reliance, *also wreckage and a lifeboat. Two addresses were found on the bodies, viz., Harrison, Main Street, Bridgeport, Connecticut, and P. Seccombe, West Hill, Peterborough.*

One appeared to be a bandmaster named Cameron [Charles W., 38, buried in Old Church cemetery] from music papers and a uniform coat found.

[The band was reportedly playing It's a Long Way to Tipperary *at the time the torpedo struck. They 'suddenly stopped playing and rushed up on deck', according to survivor George Slingsby.]*

A gold watch, stopped at 4 p.m., and a gold medal and sovereign purse, was found on the body of a man about 45 years, with a coupon and sample for a toothbrush factory, Florence and Company, Connecticut.

(CORK EXAMINER, 11 MAY 1915, P. 5)

Dan O'Connell

About 4 o'clock, the steam trawler Daniel O'Connell, *that had been fishing eight miles south-west of the Old Head, came on the scene, and picked up two of the ship's boats which were on the spot. These contained 65 passengers, mostly women and children, all of whom were in a deplorable condition.*

The trawler was taking these survivors to Kinsale, but was intercepted by a Government tug, which took them to Queenstown.

The steam trawler, Daniel O'Connell, *it will be remembered, rescued the crew of the three-masted schooner, the* Earl of Latham, *on Wednesday last, after that boat had been torpedoed eight miles south-south-west of Kinsale.*

(CORK EXAMINER, 8 MAY 1915, P. 8)

LUSITANIA TRAGEDY.
LIFE-SAVING WORK.

> *Poor quality picture of the Dan O'Connell, with the crew below. They witnessed the sinking of the schooner Earl of Latham by the U-20 off the Old Head on 5 May, and two days later they were on hand to rescue survivors from the Lusitania, sunk by the same submarine in the same vicinity. They also picked up 50 bodies*

Upwards of sixty-six women and children were rescued by the Dan O'Connell, which proceeded in all haste to Kinsale, but on the way she was intercepted by the Admiralty tug Stormcock, and these survivors were transferred to her and taken to Queenstown.

(CORK EXAMINER, 10 MAY 1915, P. 9)

THE DAN O'CONNELL

Throughout the town and district of Kinsale the conduct of the steam drifter Dan O'Connell as well as the Elizabeth and the Wanderer, meets with general commendation. It was the Dan O'Connell that rescued the crew of the schooner sunk by a German torpedo last week, and her captain informed our representative yesterday afternoon that the Lusitania went down in the same spot as the schooner.

The captain of the Dan O'Connell was the first to announce the presence of the submarine off the coast to the Admiralty, and this intimation was given immediately after the sinking of the schooner.

(CORK EXAMINER, 11 MAY 1915, P. 6)

Elizabeth

Edward White of Arklow, skipper of the trawler Elizabeth. He disputed with a royal navy officer about bringing the survivors to Kinsale. White is standing in front of his own vessel in the Manx fishing boat Wanderer. Notice the abandoned shoe to lower left.

Edward White, Arklow, skipper of the motor drifter Elizabeth stated he went out fishing from Kinsale and met a small fishing boat four miles off the Old Head. Those in that boat told him there was a liner after being wrecked, and indicated the direction.

Witness directed his boat to the spot and reached there about half-past four. They saw some small lifeboats on the water. They took in a number of persons from one boat, and took it in tow. There were 63 persons in the lifeboat.

Some of the women were very much excited, and asked to be taken to the nearest place. As they had got inside the Old Head of Kinsale the [admiralty tug] Stormcock overhauled them and asked to have the passengers transferred over to them. Witness pointed out that they would be into Kinsale in twenty minutes, while it would take at least an hour and a half to get to Queenstown.

The people in the lifeboat began to talk together. Some wanted to get to Queenstown, and some to the nearest place. They would have been into Kinsale while they were delayed by the Stormcock.

He had lost the night's fishing owing to having gone to the scene of the wreck to pick up survivors.

John Forde, of the steam drifter Dan O'Connell, of Arklow, was the next witness. He said the drifter picked up sixty of the passengers. He was told by his captain to go as pilot into one of the lifeboats which was towed into Kinsale by the Elizabeth.

When they got inside the Old Head the Stormcock overhauled them and demanded the passengers. Witness went aboard the Stormcock, and said he wanted to get back to Kinsale himself, and the Captain of that vessel [Commander Shee] said he could not do anything with him, and added: 'I suppose what you want is to make money'.

He also said the fishermen were causing a lot of trouble, and he would run down the Elizabeth only she had passengers on board, and that he would acquaint the Admiralty of their conduct.

A juror – 'I suppose the way you are causing trouble is saving lives'.

(CORK EXAMINER, 11 MAY 1915, P. 6)

Heron

It was late in the evening – about eight o'clock – when the rescued were brought to the [Kinsale] inner harbour on board the Heron, *a naval patrol boat. She was flying a signal for help, and her ensign was at half-mast. Large crowds immediately gathered along the quayside, and there were many touching and pathetic scenes as the victims of one of the most inhuman crimes ever committed were landed.*

It was soon learned that the Heron *had sixteen rescued people on board – thirteen men and three women – but it soon became known that three of the men and two of the women were dead, while another woman was in a state of collapse.*

The dead bodies were immediately removed to the Morgue attached to the Barracks, while the survivors were promptly attended to.

(CORK EXAMINER, 10 MAY 1915, P. 9)

Osprey

Our Baltimore correspondent writes – The commendable bravery and pluck displayed by Captain Elliott and his crew in proceeding to the scene of the disaster without a moment's hesitation or delay on Friday evening has met with the warmest admiration here.

Also the plucky men who volunteered to accompany him: Messrs D. McCarthy Morrogh, solr; Denis O'Donovan, Mr Ward, Mr Cornelius Hegarty. It was a great risk.

The Osprey *on her outward journey first encountered a patrol boat between the Galley Head and Seven Heads, when they were informed that little good was to be done, and that they were beyond all aid. However, they went to the scene, and kept moving around all night till daybreak, when they observed several upturned and battered boats, and having examined all carefully, there were no human beings, dead or alive, found in any. There were fourteen boats in all – some in perfect order.*

Moving about in the calm waters they observed all kinds of clothing of men, women and children. They returned to Baltimore this morning, bringing with them a big stock of miscellaneous articles which they found floating and picked up, including tobacco pipes, pouches, deck chairs, and all sorts of household utensils – all marked Lusitania.

Captain Elliott picked up a notebook in the wreckage belonging to Samuel Max Kubelick, estate agent, Quebec [see appendix: Property handed in at Queenstown]. From the different papers, at present in the hands of the customs officer, it would appear this gentleman, who is presumably among the drowned, was an Austrian, but became a naturalised Englishman.

He had letters of introduction to several English firms from Messrs Hitchmon & Co., fish merchants, Quebec, his father-in-law apparently being a member of the latter firm. Some photos were also found.

(CORK EXAMINER, 10, 11 MAY 1915)

The Queenstown Lifeboat

TO THE EDITOR, FREE PRESS

Dear Sir,

As some subscribers to the Lifeboat Institution have asked me what services were provided by the Queenstown lifeboat on the occasion of the sinking of the *Lusitania*, I have pleasure in stating that on receipt of a telegram at 2 p.m. from the Old Head of Kinsale to the effect that the *Lusitania* appeared in difficulties, the lifeboat was at once launched and sent to the scene.

The trawler *Bradford* was good enough to take her in tow, and she arrived at the scene at 4.40 p.m. By that time most, if not all the living survivors had been taken on board the various steamers in the vicinity, and the lifeboat was directed to pick up all floating bodies. This was done and 29 people, all dead, were found and conveyed to the trawler. By 9 p.m. it had become too dark to distinguish anything, and the boat returned to Queenstown where she arrived at 1 a.m.

The coxswain of the lifeboat reports that several people appeared to be drowned or suffocated from the lifebelt jackets being improperly put on. One girl, about 19 years old, had her belt round her hips and floated feet up. It must have dropped before she became immersed.

Many others had the jackets across their mouth and were apparently suffocated and not drowned. In their cases the jackets must have been displaced in the water. I think the proper way of using lifejackets might with advantage be taught at all First Aid lectures, and I shall have pleasure in sending a jacket with a man to explain its use to anyone wishing it.

There is little doubt that ignorance in this matter was the cause of many deaths.

I am, dear sir, your obedient servant,

George Usborne,

Hon. Sec.

Queenstown Branch, R.N.L. Inst.

(CORK FREE PRESS, 11 MAY 1915, P. 8)

Usborne in 1915 was also a captain in the royal navy, and harbourmaster at Queenstown.

Village Maid

BALTIMORE, MONDAY NIGHT

Seven bodies were brought here at 8.30 tonight, picked up eight miles off Galley Head – five men and two women, the latter wearing rings, apparently married. One seemed a wealthy lady, having massive gold rings. Many willing hands removed the bodies to the boathouse. They were brought by the boat Village Maid *of Sherkin, owner L. [Louis] Nolan.*

Another Baltimore message says – The steam trawler Bradford *arrived in the harbour here this afternoon. They were at the scene of the wreck, and picked up 38 dead bodies, besides several boats belonging to the* Lusitania. *One of her boats, also drifting westward, was picked up by a Cape Clear crew today.*

(CORK EXAMINER, 11 MAY 1915, P. 5)

VICTIMS AT BALTIMORE PENNED UNDER A RAFT
BALTIMORE, WEDNESDAY

An Arklow boat, the Lucy Mary, *arrived here this afternoon after passing a raft off the harbour with two bodies pinned underneath – a man and a young little girl. They were unable to extricate the bodies, the raft being upturned, and it was too heavy to tow it ashore.*

Mr Nolan's boat [Village Maid] *proceeded in the direction of the floating raft, and it is expected he will succeed in bringing it ashore. A lifeboat in perfect condition was brought in here last night by Mr Nolan, and a purse containing some dollar notes was also picked up.*

(CORK EXAMINER, 13 MAY 1915, P. 5)

Wanderer

The Manx fishing boat *Wanderer* was first on the scene of the sinking. She was a lugger of about 20 tons, out of the tiny port of Peel, and had been fishing a few miles away.

The photograph (p.106) shows the crew of seven who went to assist the stricken liner. Captain William Ball appears third from left, with his son Stanley alongside, centre. The men are wearing a special medal conferred on them in the Isle of Man and are standing on Tynwald hill.

Crewman Thomas Woods was alone on deck, having sent 'little Johnny Macdonald' below to make tea, when he saw the *Lusitania* list. He gave the alarm, and the crew quickly tumbled up on deck. The skipper's first words, according to a Manx journal of November 1915, were: 'Go for her, be British' – an echo of the reported words of the *Titanic* captain three years earlier.

In a later letter to the vessel's owner, Captain Ball wrote:

We had rather an exciting experience on Friday afternoon, about 2.30 p.m. We were coming in with about 800 mackerel ... when we saw the *Lusitania* sink, after being torpedoed by a submarine, about three miles SSW of us. We made straight for the scene of the disaster.

We picked up the first [life]boats a quarter of a mile inside of where she sunk, and there we got four boat loads put aboard us. We couldn't take any more, as we had 160 men, women, and children. In addition, we had two boats in tow, full of passengers. We were the only boat there for two hours Then the patrol boats came out from Queenstown.

We had a busy time making tea for them – and all our milk and tea is gone and a lot of clothes as well, and the bottle of whiskey we had leaving home. The people were in a sorry plight, most of them having been in the water. We took them to within two miles of

A postcard issued by the Manx Postal Museum shows the Wanderer *and the* Lusitania, *artistic licence telescoping the distance between the two. This painting, by John Nicholson, was also produced as a stamp to mark an anniversary of the sinking. PL11, the lugger's designation, shows she was from Peel.*

the Old Head, when it fell calm, and there was a little air ahead. The tug boat *Flying Fish* from Queenstown then came up and took them from us … It was an awful sight to see her sinking, and to see the plight of these people. I cannot describe it to you in writing.

Captain Ball told the *Cork Examiner* that the *Wanderer* was the only vessel on the scene for about two hours. He transferred his passengers, and then 'went fishing, as there were lots of boats at the scene'. Ball praised the actions of a stewardess who was amongst the rescued: 'She was a very brave woman. She was a doctor and everything. She, in my belief, saved many lives on board'.

Stanley Ball added that the *Wanderer* had seen the *Lusitania* going east:

We knew it was one of the big liners by her four funnels, so we put the watch on. We were lying in bed when the man on watch shouted that the four-funnelled boat was sinking. I got up out of bed and on deck, and I saw her go down. She went down bow first.

We picked up four yawls. We took 110 people out of the first two yawls, and about fifty or sixty out of the next two; and we took two yawls in tow. We were at her a good while before any other boat. The first person we took on board was a child of two months. We had four or five children on board and a lot of women. I gave a pair of trousers, a waistcoat, and an oil-coat to some of them. Some of us gave a lot in that way. One of the women had her arm broke, and one had her leg broke, and many of them were very exhausted.

Another crewman, Harry Costain, said: 'I never want to see the like again. There were four babies about three months old, and some of the people were almost naked – just as if they had come out of bed. Several had legs and arms broken, and we had one dead man, but we saw hundreds in the water. I gave one of my changes of clothes to a naked man, and Johnny Macdonald gave three shirts and all his drawers'.

Lookout Thomas Woods said it was 'the saddest sight I ever saw in all my life. I cannot tell you in words, but it was a great joy to me to help the poor mothers and babes in the best way we could'.

Those saved by the *Wanderer* included David A. Thomas, the coalmine owner and millionaire, and his secretary, A. L. Rhys Evans. Mr James Brooks, of Bridgeport, Connecticut, wrote: 'I even had to sit with my leg hanging over the side because there was no room to put it on the inside'.

The Manchester Manx Society invited the skipper and each crewman to accept a

medal, designed by Mr F. S. Graves, to mark their gallantry and the *Mannin* journal reported that the society was voicing the sentiments of all Manxmen. Lord Raglan made the presentation on 5 July 1915:

> I am quite sure that we shall always feel gratitude to you and to those with you … The consciousness of having saved so many lives must in itself be a great reward … but there would indeed be a lack of generous feeling in the world if this admiration did not find some tangible expression.

It is notable that while the British government famously struck at least 25,000 copies of a German medal commemorating the disaster for their own propaganda purposes, there were few official rewards for any of the rescue crews that put to sea that day.

The crew of the Wanderer, *skipper William Ball third from left, stand with their medals on Tynwald Hill, Isle of Man, July 1915.*

Second class survivor Nora Bretherton inserted the advertisement below in the *Cork Examiner* of Monday, 10 May 1915:

Missing
A baby girl, 15 months old, very fair hair, curled, rosy complexion, in a white woollen jersey and leggings. Tries to walk and talk. Name Betty Bretherton. Please send any information to Miss Browne, Bishop's House, Queenstown.

Betty's body was recovered the following day (number 156, pictured left), but Norah had gone home to Dover with her surviving son, Paul, 3. Betty was buried in the Ursuline convent, Blackrock, Cork.

Reporting

Kultur's Rich Haul

In the following letter, telegraphist Albert J. Ashdown RNVR gives a most moving picture of a rescuer's work with the survivors of the *Lusitania*.

We have been digging a grave this morning – a giant's grave, 25ft x 12ft x 8ft, in which will be laid British and American women and babes whose names fill the latest 'Roll of Honour'. The 'Great German Naval Victory' has come and gone.

What a sight! I have been expecting to wake up ever since, it seems so unreal, so inconceivable that this diabolical crime can have disgraced the fair earth.

A tough and rugged member of the British Navy said to me: 'Well chum, I have always considered myself to be about the limit in hard-heartedness, but the waterworks had the upper hand tonight'. His cheeks bore witness to his truthfulness. I think we all felt decidedly 'throaty'. Anyhow, we refrained from looking into each other's eyes as the throng of injured men, overwrought and sobbing women, and poor little children were handed up the gangways in silence to the warmth and light of the Cunard Company's offices.

The average raiment of each child and woman was about three-quarters of a domestic blanket, while many of the men were not even as well off as that. Our sailors did what they could, but the present regulation uniform does not go far.

As boat after boat put alongside, a volunteer band of bluejackets went aboard and got the poor creatures on land as quickly as possible. There was a man whose head and face were covered with rough bandages and dried blood, and another making a brave show on his improvised crutches – broom and walking stick. And the ladies, some young, many old and infirmed, a few sobbing bitterly, the majority (some in great pain) hiding their sufferings with their smiles, and one poor girl who had received a mental blow (the effects of which may never leave in this life) was babbling nonsense and laughing wildly.

Many clamoured for a solace which we know can never be granted in this world of seeing husbands and children gone to the 'Far Beyond'. Many were vainly hunting for dear ones lying 60 fathoms beneath the calm sea.

And then the children! Massacred innocents! it was hard to look and still believe in God's goodness. With a hasty 'Here you are', the naked little body of a boy about eight years of age was thrust into my arms. Some mother's little laddie, poor little man, he will never again give anyone any more trouble – or joy. It is feared his parents will never know of their loss on this side of the grave. Then the body of a woman with a child tightly hugged to her breast, one little arm encircling her neck and the other tucked away in her blouse. Tenderly they were handed out and will be buried as one.

As boat after boat put in the proportion of dead to living became greater until at last they were freighted only with dead. There they lay in the hold of the fishing trawlers, a rich haul for Kultur. That picture has been a tonic, if one were indeed needed. There was not a man among us who could not that night confidently have tackled any ten of the German vermin single-handed.

Any man who could go and not go after learning of these choicest brands of German infamy has not the spirit of even a decent beast, leave alone that of a Briton whose kith and kin have been foully murdered by the venomous race that has run amuck. I wondered as I looked as to what could so far forget its own mother, mate and young, as deliberately and coldly to perpetrate such a horror on innocent babes and women. These sneaking pirates are apparently a band of natural cut-throats, of which there will be an inexhaustible supply while Germany exists. Surely we are now all of one mind that it is time to cut out the talking and do something.

We bury them tomorrow. A soldier's grave for women and children. Not the first. Is it to be the last? The men of the nation will supply the answer.

Bodies lying in the Cunard shed at Queenstown, Cotton has been placed in the mouths to prevent fluid leakage from the lungs, a standard mortuary practice. The bodies are laid out sequentially. Nearest the camera is No. 119, Charles Lapphane, a third-class waiter. Then comes second-class passenger John Mainman, followed by first-class passenger William Henry Helm Brown. Next are Mary Jane Press and 40-year-old Catherine Barr, both second-class passengers.

All were buried in Queenstown's Old Church Cemetery, with the exception of body 117. These remains, belonging to British subject Brown, were forwarded to the American Express Co., Liverpool, for interment locally. His widow, Winifred, remained in Buffalo, New York.

Pathetic sights were witnessed as persons passed in and out of the temporary morgues. Women had to be helped in by friends. They went through the rows of dead, expecting to see some dear one, but in the great majority of instances they were unable to identify anyone belonging to them amongst the dead. This was only natural, considering that only 139 bodies or about one-eleventh of the total missing, were up to then landed at Queenstown.

The bodies were placed in three temporary morgues – one at the Town Hall where some forty bodies were placed; another in the Cunard Company's premises, and the third a shed on one of the quays. Descriptions were taken by the police, and numbers placed on them. Whatever valuables were found on them were taken charge of, and it is expected that these may lead to the identification of some more of the dead.

Many of the bodies bore marks of injury, nearly in all cases about the head, probably caused by either striking against the side of the steamer in jumping off, or by being struck by pieces of wreckage. Some of them very clearly made a hard struggle for life, judging by the expressions they wear in death. Others wear a most calm, happy expression.

One lady, who looks to have been in opulent circumstances, looked as if she were at any moment about to wake from a peaceful sleep. In one corner of the Town Hall morgue there was a child of about a year old, crouched up in a sitting attitude, looking quite happy. In another of the morgues there are two children, six or seven years old, locked in one another's arms.

(*Cork Examiner*, 10 May 1915, p. 7)

In this heap of slain is a couple of children, apparently twins, of about two years of age, whose little cheeks glow rosy-red with the bloom of young, vigorous health, though cold in death.

It is a sight which would make the Kaiser and his merry men rock with laughter and drunken celebration while earth, heaven and hell join in weeping.

(Westmeath Examiner, 22 May 1915, p. 8)

Images of victims published in the Daily Sketch and Cork Examiner respectively. A total of 223 bodies were initially recovered

Twenty years ago today – A Reporter's Recollections of the Sinking of the
Lusitania
Special to the Examiner

Around the opening of May 1915, reporters employed by the three newspaper offices which then existed in Cork were not unduly pressed with the usual routine work. The war was on nine months, and war news filled all the papers. There were the agency accounts, the official communiqués, the reports from special correspondents, and last, but not least, the casualty lists.

Trade was good and advertisers were everywhere demanding more space than many papers could afford to give them. Supplies of printing paper were getting curtailed. Hence meetings of Corporations, County Councils, Rural Councils, Boards of Guardians, Petty Session Courts, etc., etc., were rationed as to space. Discussions which a short time before might be allowed to run to columns were reduced to a few lines.

We had some occasional war excitements: A few contingents of wounded were landed at Cork or Queenstown (now Cove). Soldiers were interviewed, but the military mind became doubtful of the utility of such publicity in winning the war. A military information and censorship office was established at Queenstown. (For the sake of clearness I shall stick to the old name throughout, as all I have to say refers to the place as it was thus known). A most obliging gentleman was placed in charge, a barrister by profession before he became a war-time officer, but he rarely had much information to give away. In fact his job was to see that the papers did not publish too much.

We had a few 'scares'. One night the forts at the entrance to the harbour started to blaze away at some object out at sea. The shooting seems to have been rather wild, because one or two shells dropped in the neighbourhood of Crosshaven. Next morning the story ran that a German submarine was seen making for the harbour. There was even a suggestion that the Crosshaven shells must have come from seawards; therefore the submarine or whatever it was must have returned the fire. It took the greater part of a day to track down that story, between Crosshaven and the Military Information Bureau at Queenstown. In the evening the latter issued an anaemic communiqué to the effect that some object was sighted out at sea, and the forts opened fire. It left a lot of questions unanswered.

A Spy Scare

There had been a comic spy scare at Crosshaven earlier in the war. An English engineer, who had some connections in Cork, was over for a holiday and like many others had a camera and went with friends to Crosshaven for an afternoon. He was seen taking a photograph, and there happened to be a concealed gun emplacement half a mile or more away. He was arrested, and a State trial was staged at Carrigaline Courthouse. I saw the offending 'snap', and a microscope would not reveal the slightest bit of information of use to the enemy if he could get hold of the print. But the unfortunate defendant, like hundreds of others, had been in Germany the previous year and there were some notes in his pocket-book regarding train times and connections. That was enough. He was solemnly returned for trial at the next Assizes in Cork. But he was never put on trial. Someone had a brain wave and made enquiries in England as to his bona fides, and the case was dropped.

We may have had a few other 'thrills', but there were few and faint opportunities to any of us to cover ourselves with glory as war correspondents, even at a distance from the war.

'An Easy Weekend'

If I remember correctly, most of the Cork Pressmen were anticipating a quiet weekend on May 7, 1915. It was a Friday, and after a more or less satisfactory interview with the gentleman who paid our salaries, I for one went home for an early dinner [lunch], with the intention of attending a funeral afterwards. When Pressmen go unofficially to funerals work is slack. Shortly after 2 o'clock I left home and met a member of another department cycling to his home for dinner. He told me that word had just reached the office that the Lusitania had been torpedoed off the Old Head of Kinsale. Where the first information came from, I do not know even now, but I fancy it was from the Cork

A few of the Lusitania survivors. The youth in the foreground is William Burrows, who was a bellboy on the Lusitania. He took control of one of the boats and steered the passengers to safety.

(IRISH INDEPENDENT, 10 May 1915, p. 3)

Burrows was 15 years old, one of 10 stewards' boys, half of whom drowned. Coming back to the ship on the night before leaving for Liverpool, a New York policeman on the gate told him: 'You're not going to get back this time, sonny. They're going to get you this time'. Burrows laughed at him.

'I was about three decks down in the bathroom when all of a sudden there was a terrific bang,' he recalled decades later. 'All the lights were out. I made my way up to the top deck as fast as I could, and when I finally arrived she was listing over to the starboard side, pretty steep.

'I managed to get bundled into number 13 lifeboat, and I was lowered away down to the water's edge. The thing I noticed was all the water rushing in through the portholes – it was such a lovely day, you know – all the water rushing in, every porthole open. Of course that made her sink much quicker than she would have done, I think.

'When we were a little distance away from the ship there must have been a terrific explosion down below, because you could see all the cinders and everything and debris getting blown out of the funnels. And of course her stern end came right up out of the water and then she went straight down, clean as a whistle.

'We picked several people up out of the water, and then the Stormcock, a patrol boat, came and picked us up. I managed to get ashore in me shirt sleeves – I'd left me little bellboy's jacket hanging in the bathroom.

'The water was just flat as a billiard table. It was a lovely day, a lovely sunshiny afternoon. Only when we got in the lifeboat we saw these people struggling, you know, a lot of them had lifejackets on. But the main thing I noticed was all the water rushing in through the portholes. I know I made quite a few trips after that, and as soon as you were in the danger zone all portholes were battened down'.

Escaped from the Pirates.

Little Robert Kay, seven years old, was one of the intended victims. He had a narrow escape. His mother and sister were drowned. The sister was a beautiful child of 9 years of age. They were on their way to England to the grandfather, a Mr. Belcher, who resides at St. Helens. The poor little fellow had a most trying experience, and was so very fatigued that he rested in bed at the Imperial Hotel, Queenstown, until Monday His grandfather arrived at Queenstown yesterday, and there was a most affecting scene when he met his poor little grandchild.

Post Office. Some there read a message going through and passed along the tip. Needless to say, the navy or army did not go out of their way to give prompt information to newspapers.

A few minutes later, when I got to the office, I found an impatient Chief Reporter lying in wait for the first member of his staff who came within hailing distance. It happened that there was a convenient train to Queenstown, and that is how I happened to be the first Pressman to reach Queenstown on that momentous afternoon. I was accompanied by our staff photographer, Mr Tom Barker, a pioneer at press photography, and an adept at all the niceties of the game. When he could not secure news pictures it was as well for others to give up hope. He was also a good news gatherer.

ARMY AND NAVY

Arriving at Queenstown, our first objective was the Information Officer or Censor. The office was in a terrace overlooking the railway station and portion of the harbour. He received us with his usual courtesy, but had no information to give. All he knew – or professed to know – was that the Lusitania had been torpedoed a few minutes after two o'clock, and that destroyers had gone out to her rescue. It was a naval business, and Admiralty House was in control.

He rang up Admiralty House, but they 'had no information' there. The information part was my share of the business. Tom Barker was concerned with pictures. Cameras were not popular with the naval authorities at Queenstown just then, and one could easily get arrested for taking photographs. Barker wanted to know whether the authorities would allow him to take photographs. Our military friend saw no objection; in fact photographs of shivering survivors and rescued corpses would be good war propaganda, especially if they happened to be American citizens. He did not put it as crudely as that, but the suggestion was present. He rang up Admiralty House again. Whoever was there quoted regulations and prohibitions. Photography in a military area or a naval base was not permissible.

As far as we could make out, the Admiralty did not love reporters or Press photographers, and it was clear they were not going out of their way to facilitate us.

Barker, who was equal to all occasions, had an inspiration. In a casual way, he said an army of London special correspondents and photographers would be over in the morning, and they would write up and photograph as they pleased, and would have the backing of the Government itself. One brain wave gave rise to another. The military gentleman had his. He rang up Admiralty House once more, and put that aspect of the case before them. They promised to consider the matter and let us know later on.

VERSATILE TOWN CLERK

Our next objective was the Office of the Town Clerk, Mr Jas Campbell. This was always a sort of exchange bureau for Pressmen, for what Mr Campbell did not know about Queenstown and its doings was not worth knowing. He was a man of many parts. With his municipal or civic duties he combined those of correspondent for some foreign news interests, and was Spanish Consul. We found he had been on to Admiralty House in his varied capacities. As Town Clerk he was in charge of sanitary arrangements, and had something to do with the reception of corpses. The morgue was right under his offices. As Spanish Consul, he was interested in any Spanish nationals on board the Lusitania, and would have to look after them, dead or alive. But Admiralty House gave little away. I had a shot at them, but when they would not tell a Town Clerk and a Consul anything worthwhile, it was not to be expected they would expand to a common garden reporter.

MANY RUMOURS

Rumours of all sorts ran like wildlife through the town. One of those was that the Lusitania had sunk with all hands, another that she was still floating. All these had to be explored, if I might put it that way. The only place where definite information could be got was Admiralty House, which we knew right well must be in communication with the rescue ships sent out by themselves. But the results of inquiries there were invariably negative.

Then a destroyer which had gone out in a great hurry was seen returning. This gave rise to two or three further rumours. One was that she had been recalled by the Admiral, who by some means had discovered that German submarines were lying in wait outside the harbour. Another rumour was that the other rescue ships had taken on board the Lusitania people; a third that she was being towed in. I met a Town Councillor somewhere in the street and he told me that the Lusitania was coming into Queenstown under her own steam. He heard it from someone who had it from somebody, who was told so by a sailor, a signal man, a radio operator, or some equally important personage in the know. There was no doubt about it. Back I hied to the Town Hall, and discovered the good news was there before me.

Tom Barker

All the local Press correspondents of Queenstown were gathered in the office, as well as Tom Barker and one or two reporters who had been sent on from Cork. There were a few town councillors present also, if I remember rightly. The Queenstown men were all jubilant.

Here is the reason. During the controversy over the landing of mails at Queenstown and the calling of the bigger liners at Queenstown instead, Captain Turner of the Lusitania had made some disparaging statements about the safety of the harbour and the facilities for entering it. He said one of the big ships, the Mauretania, I think, scraped mud on one occasion when entering. The Queenstown men resented this imputation on their harbour, and now it would be poetic justice if Captain Turner had to bring the Lusitania in for safety. Mr Campbell, a Queenstown man before everything else, put the position that way very frankly. Tom Barker had got permission to take photographs so long as they did not include any part of the harbour, and his immediate concern was that survivors or the whole ship's complement would be landed while the light lasted.

ADMIRALTY HOUSE AND PRESS

Of course, we had to get official confirmation or denial of the story, and for once Admiralty House was definite; the Lusitania was not coming into the harbour under her own steam or any other steam. Their information was that she had sunk, and the rescue vessels were picking up survivors. They could not say when the latter would arrive.

Strolling about with a colleague, we met District Inspector Armstrong, of the RIC, an old friend, who never let a Pressman down if he could help him. He did not know when any of the rescue ships might be expected, but he knew that ambulance services were being got ready, and said something about 9 or 9.30, and I knew Armstrong well enough to know that when he passed a tip you could rely on it. He also said he thought the first destroyer in would tie up at the Blackrock Railway Company's 'Blue' boat wharf.

By this time most of the Pressmen of Cork's three morning newspapers were in Queenstown; a few had been sent to Kinsale or Clonakilty as a result of a message that local fishing boats had landed a number of survivors there, but the main force of the Press was concentrated on Queenstown.

The evening trains also brought down a number of Cork doctors, nurses, and medical students, as well as curiosity seekers.

SURVIVORS AND BODIES ARRIVE

At last one of the rescue ships was seen coming into the harbour and making for the Blackrock Railway's landing place. Bluejackets under petty officers formed cordons and lines. The Press were at the gates awaiting admission, under the leadership of the late Mr Ernest Tuohy, one of the keenest news journalists Ireland ever produced. We tried to impress the British Navy with the dignity of the Press, but it remained heartless. Its orders from Admiralty House apparently were to allow nobody in.

The Royal Irish Constabulary was there under Mr Armstrong, and we appealed to him. He undertook to do his best for us. The crowd at the rear was pushing forward and the Navy decided to clear the place, so we were the first to be cleared, and that was just as the ship was tying up. Of course we reformed our forces, numbering all told something in the neighbourhood of twelve or *fourteen. But naval officers could not be persuaded to see commonsense. Some military officers were there, too – onlookers like many others.*

Eventually, through some intervention, an order was issued to admit the Press. A colleague working for the old Constitution, who was beside me, suggested that we (he and I) should remain outside as he believed those who went in would not have time to get stories. The survivors would be rushed through to the awaiting cars and conveyed to hotels, and as he put it, there was no use in trying to get stories from corpses.

Our best chance of getting anything was to get hold of likely-looking survivors outside the gates and accompany them to their hotels. Some stretcher cases were brought out and then came passengers. One of the first was a foreign-looking gentleman wearing a lifebelt. My friend made for him, got on the same car and disappeared to the hotel.

A STROKE OF GOOD LUCK

Soon after came a likely subject, a young man apparently in the thirties, accompanied by a little girl. I explained that I was a reporter seeking an interview. 'You a newspaper man?' he said. 'Yes,' I answered. 'I am another,' was the unexpected reply. 'Come along to the hotel and I'll tell you all about it'.

Here was a surprising piece of good luck.

We got to the Rob Roy, and after he put down a good stiff drink of whiskey, he gave me a dramatic story. He was a Mr Cowper, an Englishman, a native of the Liverpool area, and worked on an evening paper in that city. He then tried his luck in Canada, and got on very well. He was coming to Europe, accompanied by a proprietor of his paper, to write up war conditions in England.

He was after lunch, and was, if I remember aright, in his cabin or a writing-room preparing or revising 'copy' when he felt the ship rock. He knew instinctively that something had gone wrong and that probably she was hit. It was common knowledge that she was threatened and precautions had been taken to show all passengers their stations in case of danger. He went to his boat station, but that particular boat could not be got out.

As he was looking around for some other boat, a little girl, apparently lost in the crowd, asked him to save her, as he could not find her father and mother. A boat was about being lowered, and he put the little girl on board. When it was lowered some distance he noticed vacancies and asked he officer in charge if he could come himself. The officer said yes and Mr Cowper jumped for it. He injured his knee against some part of the lifeboat.

During the voyage many of the passengers were inclined to joke at the idea that a submarine could sink a ship like the Lusitania, and he left on me the impression that many more could have been saved of they made themselves thoroughly familiar with the lifesaving regulations and kept their heads when disaster came. The lifeboat on which he got could have taken some more, but there were none around to be taken when they started to lower it.

The little girl was taken in charge by the hotel staff, who did all they could to make her comfortable and happy. Her parents were lost, but some relatives arrived who took her with them after a few days.

The other survivors poured in, including a young Dublin doctor and a friend. They were athletic men of resource, and instead of rushing about in the crowd for a lifeboat, they got their lifebelts on and clambered down an anchor chain. They got on a raft after some time.

WORK UNDER PRESSURE

Time was passing rapidly and we had to catch the last train to Cork. I found most of my colleagues gathered at the Rob Roy comparing notes. They had soon discovered that there was no advantage in being on the landing stage. The passengers were rushed through and could not be interviewed. The reporters left and spread themselves out amongst the hotels, but found that the Navy had ordered the proprietors not to allow Pressmen to see the passengers. That was all very well for the Navy – but the reporters had to get stories – and did get them.

US Consul at Queenstown, Wesley Frost [left], with six-year-old American girl Helen Smith, and a man who may be Lewis Thompson, the US Vice-Consul. The girl was saved by a Toronto newspaper journalist, Ernest Cowper, to whom she appealed for help on the boat deck. Helen, who clutches a doll given to her by well-wishers, lost her father, mother, sister and brother in the tragedy.

The picture was taken outside the Rob Roy Hotel where both Cowper and Smith were accommodated, and where the newspaperman gulped down a whiskey before telling his story to the local newspaper men. Cowper said: 'As I was going about, a little girl asked me to get her out of the place. She was a pretty little child, about the same age as one of my own at home, and her appeal touched me. I put her on one of the boats that was being launched'.

Helen Smith, a little girl of six years, was a very pathetic person, but in herself most happy in that she was at Queenstown. For she with her parents was coming from New York to Liverpool on a visit to her grandmother. She is a charming little girl, and her confidence that her Mama and her Dada were going to join her in the Rob Roy Hotel excited only the deepest sympathy – for it was reported they are both drowned. She says she was playing on the deck before the explosion, after which she was taken into a boat by a gentleman, who asked her was she going to England. They were some time in the sea when they were picked up by a fishing boat and afterwards put on board a steamer, and 'here I am in Queenstown, to go to Liverpool with my mamma and dada and brother, who was playing on deck when the Lusitania sank'.

(CORK EXAMINER, 8 MAY 1915, P. 8)

LITTLE ORPHAN GIRL
QUEENSTOWN, SUNDAY

The little girl, Helen Smith, whose pathetic story has been already published, was the object of much attention on Saturday at Queenstown. A bright, winsome little lady, she had the sympathy of everybody, but amidst all the bustle she maintained the same cheerful demeanour, and is still quite sure that her 'Dada and Mama will come here'.

Outside the Rob Roy hotel, where she was put up by her rescuer, Mr Cooper [sic], her photo was taken by quite a crowd of photographers on Saturday. Someone presented her with a large doll, and this she hugged to her, and it very evidently gave her pleasure or at least a sense of companionship.

No trace could be found of her parents, but an aunt, Mrs Hubert Owens, who is amongst the survivors, finding where she was, took her in charge later in the day, and undertook to take her to her relatives at Liverpool.

CORK EXAMINER, 10 May 1915, p. 8

My friend of the Constitution was also fortunate in his 'victim', who turned out to be a French agent sent to America to buy medical supplies for the Government – we exchanged stuff. Tom Barker could not take photographs by night, so he turned interviewer and got some excellent stuff. All the others did well in face of exceptional difficulties.

A number of the survivors elected to come on to Cork on the same train that the reporters came. They gave interviews on the way up. By working in with one another and writing against time, we were able to supply the public of the South with graphic stories of the sinking of the Lusitania.

On Saturday morning the London contingent arrived and re-wrote our work in Cork or just 'lifted' it and put it on the wires. Some of them went to Queenstown and searched for new stuff, and there was a good deal of it to be obtained. For instance, Mr D. A. Thomas, later Lord Rhondda, was scathing regarding what he considered naval bungling. He retracted much of it later, but it fingered up Admiralty House.

A number of us went down again on Saturday and got more interviews or stories. There was unlimited material, though of course most of the stories were repetitions of other stories. The morgue under the Town Hall was filled with corpses, and many were placed in the premises of the Cork and Blackrock Railway Company. Undertakers were working at high pressure night and day to provide coffins. But hundreds of victims found graves in the broad Atlantic Ocean. There were 1,134 lives lost.

An inquest was formally opened and adjourned, but Queenstown lost whatever limelight a full blown inquest would bestow. The bodies of some victims had been landed at Kinsale, and Coroner J. J. Horgan fixed the inquest for the following midweek. The authorities had all their evidence prepared and the inquest was concluded in one day.

The principal witness was of course the Captain of the Lusitania. He told of the precautions that had been taken and the warnings and directions received from the Admiralty in London. For the first time it was revealed that the ship was travelling at reduced speed. The Captain wished to reach the mouth of the Mersey at a favourable state of the tide so as to run in at a high speed. It was expected that if an attempt was to be made to sink her it would be at the Mersey entrance.

The District Inspector of the RIC at Kinsale produced cuttings of advertisements published in New York papers warning passengers that if they travelled in British ships they did so at their peril. These advertisements were linked up with a noted German agent and with the German Embassy in Washington.

Looking back now, I am not sure if this was technically regular evidence, but that does not matter. The Kinsale jury found a verdict of wilful murder against the Kaiser. At this distance of time, that too seems to have been rather far removed from the functions of a Coroner's jury at Kinsale, but it certainly expressed public opinion then. Interest in the Queenstown inquest rather faded out. For days after the disaster the remains of victims were being removed for burial to distant places, including the United States. A number of them were buried at Queenstown, and a memorial to all the victims will be erected shortly in the town which is now known as Cove (D.J.R.).

(CORK EXAMINER, 7 MAY 1935, P. 8)

Wesley Frost

Wesley Frost, the American Consul in Queenstown at the time interviewed the survivors, preserving their accounts as a body of indictments for the State Department:

> Between midnight and morning, the principal official activities consisted in having the corpses – of which some 160 were brought ashore with the survivors – laid out in the three improvised morgues, and in arranging transportation for the living on the following day.
> ... One feature of the work at the Consulate on Saturday consisted in the loaning of small sums of money to Americans who needed it temporarily; and our inquiries as to the need were not too searching. We took the addresses and the personal promissory notes of the persons in-

Wesley Frost

volved, and disposed of about one hundred and forty pounds sterling. I think about one hundred pounds of this was eventually returned ...

The work of assisting survivors in ascertaining whether their relatives or companions on the lost vessel had been saved was the most distressing of our duties. We were quickly overwhelmed with inquiries about missing relatives, not only from Americans but from persons of British and other nationalities.

Widows, widowers, parents, orphans, brothers and friends of deceased victims crowded the Consulate steadily for three or four days; and in some cases appeared daily for weeks after the tragedy. When the relatives and friends from London and the continent reached Queenstown, and the cabled inquiries from America began to accumulate, the number of specific inquiries upon the Consulate, with descriptions of the missing persons, mounted up into the hundreds.

The personal visits from bereaved persons were often poignant to the last degree, particularly when such visits came to be repeated time after time, at intervals of hours of days, with increasing hopelessness and grief as the absence of news became tantamount to certainty of death.

He also had to accompany Americans reluctant to attempt identifications in the makeshift morgues – 'to see that they did not shirk this duty'. He saw 'five or six drowned women with drowned babies in their arms; and the corpse of one mother who had a dead infant clasped to each of the cold breasts which had so recently been their warm nestling-places'.

There was a curious effacement of social or mental distinction by death, and we often believed a corpse to be important when it turned out to be decidedly the opposite. The commonest expression was one of reassured tranquillity, yet with an undertone of puzzlement or aggrievement as though some trusted friend had played a practical joke which the victim did not yet understand ...

We contracted a temporary horror of any recumbent body, and especially of sleeping children, after a few days among these tiers of corpses.

Several weeks after the disaster, one night out at my home, I went into a bedroom with a lighted match and came unexpectedly upon the sleeping form of my own little daughter. I give you my word I recoiled as though I had found a serpent.

That innocent figure had thrust me back automatically into the presence of those poor livid little midget-corpses at which we had looked down so often among the Lusitania dead. Of course any one of those corpses might have been that of my young lady if we happened to be crossing at that time.

For that matter, any one of them might have been your daughter, reader, if your concerns had just then taken you onto the high seas, the common highway made by the Almighty for all nations.

Frost reported to his government on the destruction by submarines of 81 different ships in all, each carrying US citizens, during his time at Queenstown. 'I collected at first-hand much of the evidence upon which America entered the war', he later declared.

In 1917, Frost was recalled from his Irish post after the embittered admiralty officials at Queenstown complained of his handling of investigations of U-boat movements. He remained in America for four years, lecturing widely on the Lusitania disaster. He later served in Marseilles, Montreal, Rio de Janeiro and Santiago. He became US ambassador to Paraguay in 1942. He retired two years later and died in Florida, aged 83, on 9 January 1968.

Seen by a representative of the Free Press on Saturday afternoon, the American Consul (Mr Wesley Frost) said that the total number of survivors was 645, as far as he could ascertain, and the number of Americans saved about 58.

Asked as to the probable effect of this upon American opinion, he replied – 'It is very hard to say; but it is my opinion that there will be no declaration of war. In my opinion America will maintain peace at any price'.

'I gather from your reply,' he was asked, 'that you don't approve of that course?'

'No,' was the reply of the American Consul, 'I think it is time'. He added: 'If you don't break through the Dardanelles, you will lose it, and lose it very quick, in my opinion. I don't think you can break through them in France, they are so diabolically cute. And they are not unintelligent. Of course I am only giving you my own opinion'.

'Can you account at all for the fact that notwithstanding the warnings that had been given by the Germans in the American Press, so many Americans travelled?'

Mr Frost's reply was – 'It was the result of their confidence in British sea power. I wish to add that the naval and military authorities have been the soul of courtesy, and the citizens too. The Lord Mayor of Cork called on me this morning to tender to me on behalf of the citizens his sympathy, and made his customary generous and open-hearted offer of financial assistance.

'Fortunately this is not necessary, as we have been authorised by three separate authorities – the American Embassy, the American Relief Committee, and the Cunard Company – to spend all the relief necessary. American citizens will be provided for in every respect.

'The Vice Consuls of Dublin and of Cork, Mr Jenkins and Mr Thompson, have come down here to assist in arranging for the American survivors, and the military and naval attachés, Captain Castle and Captain Miller, have been dispatched from London'.

Asked as to whether he had received any reports from Washington, the Consul replied – 'I have received two; to report fully, and to go fully in the way of relief. A list of American survivors was cabled to the Department of State last night, and I will send the rest as they come along'.

'How did you first receive intimation of the disaster?' our representative asked.

'I received it from the Admiralty here,' he replied.

'Can you say definitely how many Americans have been saved?'

'No, but I can give you an approximate list of survivors'.

(CORK FREE PRESS, 10 MAY 1915, P. 5)

At a later council meeting, the Town Clerk read a letter from the consul:

Dear Sir – Please permit me to extend the most cordial appreciation on behalf of this Consulate for the resolution of sympathy passed by your honoured body on the 15th inst. with reference to the destruction of the *Lusitania*.

It is not too much to hope that the ties of blood and history to which you allude will enable the American public to comprehend fully the fine qualities of humanity evoked from the Irish people by such calamities. The communication advising this Consulate of the resolution in question has been

The coffin of a Lusitania victim being unloaded in New York having been shipped home. The body of Mrs Frances Washington Stephens, recovered later, was being sent home in September on the Hesperian *when the ship was sunk by the same submarine, U-20, which had taken her life on the Lusitania*

transmitted to the Secretary of State of the United States for the possible attention of the President.

Yours faithfully,
Wesley Frost,
American Consul.

(CORK FREE PRESS, 31 MAY 1915, P. 8)

HON. WESLEY FROST

Late US Consul, Queenstown, who for the past few years held office at Queenstown as American Consul. He has been promoted to an important administrative position in the States. His departure from Ireland is much regretted, for outside his unvarying courtesy and consideration, which much impressed all who met him either in commerce or in social life, his valuable work for this country in the matter of reciprocity of trade with America was of no small value to Ireland. He carries with him the best wishes of many thousands of Irish people.

(CORK EXAMINER, 1 JUNE 1917, P. 3)

Misreportage

All types of erroneous tales appeared in the contemporary press with early editions giving stories of people who hadn't even taken passage, including 'survivor' interviews with some who hadn't sailed.

DUBLIN GIRL ON BOARD

On board the Lusitania was an Irish girl named Miss Fahy, who had been on a visit to New York. Her friends in Dublin had expected her to reach Kingsbridge Station last night, and had arranged to meet her. They do not know yet whether she has been saved or not.

(DAILY EXPRESS, 8 MAY 1915, P. 5)

SUPPOSED LUSITANIA SURVIVOR

A report gained currency in New Ross on Friday to the effect that Mr William Ryder, son of Captain George Ryder, Marsh Lane, New Ross, who arrived home from Queenstown that morning, was one of the survivors of the dreadful disaster to the Lusitania.

The fact that Mr Ryder's wrist was injured lent colour to the report, and the supposed survivor was annoyed with questions. He however explained that his boat arrived at Queenstown from some part of America simultaneously with the arrival of the survivors of the Lusitania on Friday morning and he was home on short leave. The injury to his wrist was sustained on board his vessel.

(NEW ROSS STANDARD, 14 MAY 1915, P. 3)

Quite a fleet of Government and other ships were on the scene about ninety minutes later, and the survivors were transferred to them. One batch of some hundreds were landed on the Sovereign Islands, some miles off the Galley Head Light, and these were taken off by Government patrol boats and brought to Queenstown.

(DAILY EXPRESS, 8 MAY 1915, P. 5)

Hundreds of survivors were not landed on any islands, so were not taken off by patrol boats.

In another episode, passenger George Slingsby would later tell how he managed to find three lifebelts which he gave to Lady Marguerite Allan (wife of Canadian shipping magnate Sir Hugh Allan) and her teenage daughters Anna and Gwendolyn.

Slingsby survived, as did Lady Allan, but the daughters were listed as missing. He volunteered the next day to go to the morgue to search, and wrote that he was 'stopped in his tracks' along the rows of bodies by the sight of 'the two dear Allan girls', bloated and mottled and still wearing the life jackets he himself had put on them'. The lump in his throat threatened to choke him, he said.

With tears streaming down his face, he 'blundered out of that gruesome place' and blurted the news that the girls had been found to a doctor at Queenstown hospital, where Lady Allan was being treated.

The medical man passed on the sad tidings. But they were wrong. Neither body was recovered early, with Gwen only being recovered by the *Flying Fox* on 16 May, and Anna not at all. The remains of 16-year-old Gwendolyn now lie in Mount Royal cemetery, Montreal.

Lady Marguerite Allan with daughters Anna, left, and Gwendolyn, right

The Rescued

The passenger trade had collapsed since the outbreak of the war in August 1914, so many hotels and guesthouses in Queenstown had shut, only to have to open hurriedly to accommodate survivors.

Bookseller Charles Lauriat, Jr, of Boston wrote of his experience having been rescued by the *Flying Fish*:

When we went up the street in Queenstown it was filled with people willing to help and do anything in their power to relieve our sufferings. I have heard stories of Scottish hospitality, but I never saw anything more spontaneous or genuine and more freely given than the Irish hospitality of Queenstown …

We had quite a time finding a place to rest our weary heads and warm our chilled bodies. I kept away from the two main hotels, because I knew they were filled with the people who arrived on the first two steamers. When we got near the centre of the town I asked a native to tell us of some small place where we could get rooms. He directed us to the little hostelry 'Imperial Bar'. It was a perfectly appropriate name. The hospitality of the manageress was 'Imperial' and the 'Bar' was good.

Cunard Daily Bulletin.

FRIDAY MAY 7 1915   LUSITANIA   Presented Gratis.

REPORTS OF GERMAN VICTORY A HOAX

The Cunard Bulletin, the Lusitania's free on-board newspaper, carried this headline on the day of her sinking.

Prominent newspaper warnings placed in the American press by the Imperial German Embassy prior to the sailing of the Cunarder were dismissed as a hoax. These cautioned that vessels flying the flag of Great Britain or her allies were liable to be sunk in the war zone surrounding the British Isles. Passengers who embarked on the Atlantic voyage were told they did so at their own risk.

BRITISH HEROISM ON THE SINKING LUSITANIA.

DAILY SKETCH.

GUARANTEED DAILY NETT SALE MORE THAN 1,000,000 COPIES.

No. 1892   LONDON, SATURDAY, MAY 8, 1915   ONE HALFPENNY

LUSITANIA SUNK : AWFUL DEATH ROLL.

An early edition of the Daily Sketch for 8 May. When the other, more outraged, first editions came in, the sub-editors changed the headline to read: The Huns Sink the Lusitania, reflecting similar use of epithets by the Daily Mirror, which headlined: The Huns Carry Out Their Threat To Sink The Lusitania

Charles Lauriat

At the door we found Mr and Mrs K— [Keeble, saloon passengers]. He was badly injured. He had been brought to the hotel by the reserves on a stretcher. He was not in bad enough shape to go to a hospital, but he couldn't walk. The K—-s got the double room and McM— [Louis McMurray, saloon] and I took the other spare room.

He turned in and I turned out. I went down into the town, for I knew I could be of some help to the survivors. I got back at midnight and went to bed. I didn't have to lie awake and think about going to sleep, for I had been standing and moving around under a strain for some ten hours, so I just passed off into a dead, dreamless sleep. My clothes were almost dry, and I wasn't suffering from a chill.

We have always heard that Scottish hospitality is accompanied by a draught of the national beverage, and in justice to the old landlady I must say that she didn't omit to give me a draught of the Irish national beverage. She told me it was made by her old grandfather, and certainly he knows how to make Irish whiskey! I woke up McM—— and repeated the dose on him. He didn't cry at being waked up in a good cause!

Saturday morning I was up and dressed at six o'clock, and the dear old woman gave me a dish of tea and some bread and butter in the kitchen, and I started for the town to buy some raiment for people that I knew were practically destitute. I had dressed in the kitchen where it was warm and my clothes were dry.

My wardrobe was complete, even to my shoes, for I had not removed anything when I went overboard. The landlady had kept the fire going all night and had dried all our apparel, but as the other three were not going out as early as I was, she gave mine the preference, and I left the house feeling warm and comfortable.

As I walked down from our little hotel I shall never forget that beautiful morning in the quaint old town of Queenstown. The sun was shining warmly, and hardly a breath of air was stirring. As the day grew older and the people who had been rescued turned out into the street, it was as sad a sight as I ever care to see…

(THE LUSITANIA'S LAST VOYAGE – HOUGHTON MIFFLIN CO., 1915)

Lady Margaret Mackworth, a beautiful socialite, was the daughter of mining magnate D. A. Thomas. She wrote of her own post-survival experience on being reunited on the quayside with her father:

We went across the big dark quay to a tiny little brightly lit hut, a Customs Office, maybe a ticket office. Inside we sat down and hugged each other.

Some man asked what I wanted, and I said brandy. The man said brandy was rather dangerous when one was exhausted, but I said I would take the risk, and I got the brandy. Without it I do not know how I would have walked to the hotel, though it was only a few yards away. The hotel – I have forgotten its name – was, inappropriately enough, still kept by a German (his sister had been interned, but for some reason he had been left at large and in control of this quayside inn). It was by far the dirtiest place I have ever seen.

My father booked a room for himself there earlier in the evening, which he now gave up to me. It was on the first floor, and the steps of the stairs were shallow, but it was a big struggle to get up to it. I clung to the banisters, rested after every two steps, and felt very sick. Once in the room I got into bed, still wrapped in my blanket, which looked cleaner than the bedclothes.

There seemed to be no food in the hotel, but in the end they brought me biscuits and fizzy lemonade. At first I thought the skirting-board round the edge of the carpet was painted white, but I discovered later that it was really black, but covered inch-deep in grey dust …

One odd thing that had happened to us all was that we were exceedingly dirty. One might have supposed that four hours in the water might have washed one clean, but on the contrary I was covered with black-brown dirt (incidentally, why I didn't know, I was bruised from head to foot). I went to have a bath, but really that hotel bath was so filthy that it was a question whether one came out cleaner or dirtier than one went in.

… After dinner [the next day] my father and I went for a walk in the dark to have a look at Queenstown – a walk of which one incident recurs to me. A drunken inhabitant lurched up to us just after nine o'clock and confidingly inquired whether any pubs were still open (under wartime regulations there they were all obliged to close at nine). My father, still very irritable, gazed at him in revolted disgust: 'No, thank God!' he replied. The disappointed and startled drunkard vanished. I enjoyed that little interchange.

(THIS WAS MY WORLD – MACMILLAN & CO., 1933)

US Consul Frost later wrote: 'It is doubtless true that the quarters supplied at some of the lodging-houses was not quite what we were anxious to provide; but there is a limit to what a town of ten thousand people, nearly all working people, can provide in this direction upon less than six hours notice'.

Lady Margaret Mackworth

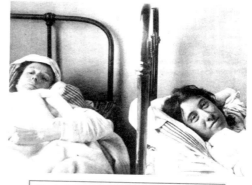

The bedridden survivor on the right may be
Margaret Mackworth

Lord Mayor of Cork city, Alderman Henry O'Shea, JP, congratulating a survivor in King's Square, Queenstown, now Pearse Square, Cobh. The two pubs in the background are now the Lusitania and Mauretania bars respectively, while the Lusitania memorial is today situated close to where the men are standing.
The man with his arms crossed is James H. Campbell, Town Clerk of Queenstown, 'who did much to succour the survivors'. The man to the right may be Mr Mullins, steward of the Cork Sailors' Home

The Dead

Queenstown was in shock. Hundreds of townspeople had done what they could, but the enormity of the destruction of human life threw up immediate and large-scale logistical problems. Doctors, nurses, beds, medicine, clothing and coffins had all been summoned or commandeered at short notice from miles around.

Then came the job of identifying the recovered, releasing and transporting those bodies wanted elsewhere, and burying the many who were left who needed speedy interral. By the time of the mass funeral, on Monday 10 May 1915, Queenstown had risen to the immense challenge with both energy and nobility.

The Funeral

A SAD PROCESSION
CORK'S SYMPATHY
WHOLEHEARTED MANIFESTATION

The public funeral took place at three o'clock from the Cunard Offices. It was an exceedingly sad procession, but an event which attracted the sympathetic interest of thousands of people from the City of Cork. Queenstown was in general mourning. All the shops were closed, and from one o'clock out people took every point of vantage to witness the dismal sight of the funeral proper of the victims.

Corpses were taken to the graveyard from midday in coffins covered with flags – the Union Jack – borne on lorries, Scotch carts, and all sorts of conveyances. Only at the cemetery could one get an even approximate idea of the full meaning of the terrible tragedy enacted.

Five private graves were opened; two of them were closed before the public funeral, which was of only three bodies, each borne on a hearse. But what was the vision in the graveyard?

Three graves remained open with ropes stretching across them, and Jack Tars standing by to lower the coffins into the last resting-place of the victims; and a short distance to the west three large pits, 40 feet x 20 feet, and about 10 feet deep. In these were all the horrors of the calamity mirrored.

One of them contained 65 coffins and a total of 67 bodies – two babes had been interred with their mothers. The next yawned its full length, breadth and depth, and so also with the third grave of

the Catholics. The vast majority of the remains were unidentified, and one pathetic incident was the re-opening of the lid of a coffin in the huge tomb to assist a distracted relative seeking for the bodies of his friends. It was all too ghastly to comprehend, and too sickly to dwell on.

The route of the funeral – West Beach, East Beach, Harbour Hill, Chapel Hill, and on to the cemetery – was lined with detachments of the Connaught Rangers and 600 of the Royal Dublin Fusiliers, and on every point of vantage people congregated to witness the sad spectacle.

Requiem Mass was concelebrated in St Colman's Cathedral, which three years earlier had performed the same solemn rites in memory of the many victims of the Titanic.

The sloping hills on the right of the road were dotted with people, who there found a natural grandstand to witness the procession; to the left persons crowded the high ditches, and all felt the grief which the appalling catastrophe brought in its wake.

Entrance to the graveyard was strictly prohibited, and the Press representatives have to acknowledge the kindness and courtesy of Captain Dickie, who gave them every facility to do their work; and as the Royal Garrison Artillery shouldered the coffins into the cemetery a sea of faces lined the walls. It was all deeply impressive and most pathetic.

The Lord Bishop of Cloyne, followed by clergy, recited prayers on the way to the grave of the Catholic victims, and their solemn intonations awakened the very saddest emotion. This procession in itself was most impressive. The Bishop, wearing his Canonical robes and mitre, was headed by a cross-bearer, acolytes with lighted tapers, and incense bearers. They then formed up around the huge grave, and after the final prayers the Benedictus was chanted.

The ceremonies at the Protestant graves, which contained 67 bodies and 14 respectively, were conducted by Rev. Archdeacon [William] Daunt, who opened the services. The lesson and some prayers were recited by Rev. R. [Richard] S. Swann Mason, and the anthem was recited by Rev. T. Kane, RN.

The order of the funeral was – Mounted police, band of the Royal Dublin Fusiliers, clergy, hearses, mourners, carriages, public bodies, military, navy, military officers, naval officers and rearguard. As it wended its way it attracted the saddened attention of thousands of visitors as well as the townspeople. It was an exceedingly dismal happening, but the magnitude of its misery was attenuated by reason of the fact that for over three hours were the corpses being conveyed from the morgues.

However the funeral gave the people of Cork generally and many other cities and counties an opportunity to manifest their heartfelt sympathy with the victims of an outrage, the horrors of which have astounded the world.

(CORK EXAMINER, 11 MAY 1915, P. 5)

On every point of vantage the people congregated … Part of the main funeral procession at the junction with the lane leading to Old Church Cemetery, where 148 bodies were interred on Monday, 10 May 1915

The order of the procession was:

Mounted Police
Royal Dublin Fusiliers Band and buglers
Clergymen of all denominations
Three hearses, with remains
Private mourners (some survivors)
The Captain, Officers and Crew of the
  ss *Wayfarer*
The Bishop of Cloyne (in motor car)
The Cork Harbour Board
The Cork Corporation
Queenstown Urban Council
Eight officers of the National Volun-
  teers
Military
Navy
General public.

The prayers over the Protestant graves were per-
formed by royal navy chaplain Richard Swann
Mason, who had previously survived the sinking of
HMS Ocean. It has been claimed that a group of
Catholic schoolgirls nearby were given orders by a
nun to cover their ears when these prayers began.
Religious distinction was observed even in the case
of the three mass graves in Queenstown. Bishop
Robert Browne at the Catholic pit, below

Today Queenstown took on her best garb. A
warm sun shining from a perfect sky kissed the
glistening leaves of the trees, radiated silvery
streaks on the placid waters of the harbour, and
bathed the natural beauties of the port in unsur-
passing loveliness.

All this rich wealth in magnificent nature
served to accentuate the deplorable events which
were passing – events which were dismal and
sad in the extreme. Everywhere one turned the
same unaffected expressions of sympathy and
ejaculations of dread horror of the experiences
of the immediate past were heard.

That the town has assumed its normal quiet
– nearly all the survivors have left – increased
the sorrow which circumstances made Queens-
town to share.

The gloom which overhangs Queenstown,
which shared so largely and with credit to itself
in the immediate consequences of the torpedo-
ing of the Cunard liner Lusitania, was in-
tensified today in the last acts when it became the unhappy lot of the townspeople to perform, or to
be witnesses of, the burials of over 100 human beings – men, women, children and infants – which
were carried out just shortly after 12 o'clock.

One could not gaze on the steam of cars and lorries and hearses to the Old Churchyard without
a pang of deep sorrow. The solemn services at the gravesides brought tears to many eyes, and even
the most stoical could not look on the mournful happenings of the day unmoved.

It was all a cruel awakening to the stern realities of Germany's desperate prosecution of a wild
policy of terrorism, and brought home with striking force to a peace-loving people the abominable
horrors of what war really is, as also what war may mean even to persons and subjects not remotely
concerned with the interests of the nations involved.

(CORK EXAMINER, 11 MAY 1915, P. 5)

Digging the Graves

Sixty men from the Fourth Royal Rifles were sent to dig the mass graves in the Old Church cemetery outside Queenstown on the day after the disaster. The next day, Sunday, they were relieved by 100 more as three deep pits were laboriously opened. The weather in Queenstown that weekend was extremely warm, making the task of excavating the tons of earth by shovel power all the more exhausting.

Coffins were placed in the mass graves before the arrival of the solemn funeral procession on the Monday, which featured a token three coffins but comprised the main civic and religious obsequies.

Even as the thousands-strong cortege was approaching the cemetery gates, a coffin in mass grave A had to be opened 'to satisfy the pent-up feelings of a distracted relative'.

Identified Bodies Buried at Old Church Cemetery, Cobh

NAME	BODY	DETAILS	GRAVE
Abercromby, Ralph Frank	23	male, 2nd-class passenger	(Removed)
Aitken, Mr James	14	male, 2nd-class passenger	Common C
Anderson, Mrs Margaret Armstrong	29	female, age 30 years, 2nd-class passenger	Common C
Arthur, Mr George Herbert	97	male, 2nd-class passenger	Common C
Barr, Mrs Catherine Symington	115	female, age 40 years, 2nd-class passenger	Common C
Barrow, Mrs May	34	female, 3rd-class passenger	Common C
Beattie, Rev James Anderson	9	male, age 54 years, 2nd-class passenger	476
Booth Jones, Miss Ailsa Georgina	213	female, age 8 years, 2nd-class passenger, buried with her mother (No 189)	487
Booth Jones, Mrs Millichamp L.	189	female, 2nd-class passenger, buried with daughter, Ailsa (No 213)	487
Bruno, Mr Henry Augustine	212	male, 1st-class passenger, age 45 years	590
Bruno, Mrs Annie Thompson	147	female, 1st-class passenger, age 45 years	Common B
Buchanan, Miss Mary	3	female, age 30 years, 2nd-class passenger	Common A
Bull, Mrs Elizabeth	78	female, 2nd-class passenger	Common C
Butler, Mrs Margaret	31	female, age 40 years, 2nd-class passenger	Common C
Cain, Thomas	177	male, crew, age 54 years, fireman	Common A
Cameron, Mr Charles W.	105	male, crew, bandmaster (orchestra)	580
Canigan, Miss Margaret	74	female, age 28 years, 3rd-class passenger	Common A
Casey, Patrick	39	male, age 48 years, crew, fireman	Common C
Chambers, Mrs Ethel Paull	165	female, age 30 years, 2nd-class passenger	Common B
Chirgwin, Mrs Maud Gertrude	88	female, 2nd-class passenger	Common C

Lusitania Interments in Old Church Cemetery, Cobh (Section B)

27	26	25	24	23	22	21	20	19	18	17	16	15	
937	900	863	826	790	754	718	683	648	613	578	543	508	38
936	899	862	825	789	753	717	682	647	612	577	542	507	37
935	898	861	824	788	752	716	681	646	611	576	541	506	36
934	897	860	823	787	751	715	680	645	610	575	540	505	35
933	896	859	822	786	750	714	679	644	609	574	539	504	34
932	895	858	821	785	749	713	678	643	608	573	538	503	33
931	894	857	820	784	748	712	677	642	607	572	537	502	32
930	893	856	819	783	747	711	676	641	606	571	536	501	31
929	892	855	818	782	746	710	675	640	605	570	535	500	30
928	891	854	817	781	745	709	674	639	604	569	534	499	29
[A 23 — mass grave]				780	744	708	673	638	603	568	533	498	28
				779	743	707	672	637	602	567	532	497	27
				778	742	706	671	636	601	566	531	496	26
				777	741	705	670	635	600	565	530	495	25
				776	740	704	669	634	599	564	529	494	24
922	885	848	811	775	739	703	668	633	598	563	528	493	23
921	884	847	810	774	738	702	667	632	597	562	527	492	22
920	883	846	809	773	737	701	666	631	596	561	526	491	21
919	882	845	808	772	736	700	665	630	595	560	525	490	20
918	881	844	807	771	735	699	664	629	594	559	524	489	19
917	880	843	806	770	734	698	663	628	593	558	523	488	18
[B 52 — mass grave]				769	733	697	662	627	592	557	522	487	17
				768	732	696	661	626	591	556	521	486	16
				767	731	695	660	625	590	555	520	485	15
				766	730	694	659	624	589	554	519	484	14
				765	729	693	658	623	588	553	518	483	13
911	874	837	800	764	728	692	657	622	587	552	517	482	12
910	873	836	799	763	727	691	656	621	586	551	516	481	11
909	872	835	798	762	726	690	655	620	585	550	515	480	10
908	871	834	797	761	725	689	654	619	584	549	514	479	9
907	870	833	796	760	724	688	653	618	583	548	513	478	8
[C 69 — mass grave]				759	723	687	652	617	582	547	512	477	7
				758	722	686	651	616	581	546	511	476	6
				757	721	685	650	615	580	545	510	475	5
				756	720	684	649	614	579	544	509	474	4
902	865	828	791	755	719								3
901	864	827											2

SECTION B

= *Lusitania* [MASS GRAVES]
= *Lusitania* [WITH HEADSTONE]
= *Lusitania* [WITHOUT HEADSTONE]

Grave 651 contains the body of first-class passenger George Ley Vernon, right, as well as the ashes of his wife, Inez, who shot herself in her New York apartment two years later. Their tombstone says they were 'young, gifted and beautiful' and both 'victims of the Lusitania crime'.

Coady, James	153	male, crew, age 53 years, fireman	Common A
Coughlan, Miss Margaret	62	female, age 2½ years, 3rd-class passenger. buried with unknown male child (No 68)	Common B
Crompton, Master John David	192	male, age 6 years, 1st-class passenger	482
Crompton, Master Peter Romelly	214	male (infant), age 9 months, 1st-class passenger	482
Crompton, Mr Stephen Hugh	134	male, age 17 years, 1st-class passenger	482
Crosby, Miss Ellen	133	female, age 36 years, 2nd-class passenger	Common C
Davis, Miss Annie	32	female, age 52 years, 2nd-class passenger	Common C
Driscoll, Cornelius	67	male, age 20 years, crew, 3rd-class waiter	Common C
Enderson, Mrs Anna	71	female, age 45 years, crew, Matron	Common C
Feeley, Mrs Teresa	4	female, age 34 years, 3rd-class passenger	Common A
Fentiman, Miss Nellie	148	female, age 26 years, 2nd-class passenger	Common B
Ferguson, Master Edward	154	male (infant), age 11 months, 3rd-class passenger	Common B
Ferrier, Miss Sheila	123	female, age 1 year, 2nd-class passenger	Common C
Finch, Mrs Eva Eliza	85	female, age 29, 2nd-class passenger	Common C
Ford, John	55	male, age 45 years, crew, fireman	Common C
Gardner, William George	20	male, age 45 years, crew, 2nd-class waiter	Common C
Gill, Mrs Catherine	1	female, age 40 years, 2nd-class passenger	Common C
Gilroy, Charles Stuart	124	male, age 22 years, crew, 2nd-class waiter	Common C
Dingley, Mrs Catherine S.	70	female, age 38 years, 2nd-class passenger	591
Grandidge, Miss Eva Mary	155	female, age 3 years, 2nd-class passenger	Common B
Grant, Mrs Chastina Jane	47	female, age 36 years, 1st-class passenger	Common C
Greenshields, Mr A. J.	217	male, 3rd-class passenger	Common B
Groves, Mrs Clara	166	female, age 27 years, 2nd-class passenger	Common B
Hannah, Thomas	173	male, crew, waiter	Common B
Hanson, Mr Samuel	44	male, age 51, 2nd-class passenger	Common C
Hanson, Mrs Mary	72	female, age 49 years, 2nd-class passenger	Common C
Hare, Miss Bessie	95	female, age 27, 2nd-class passenger	622
Henn, Mr Ernest George	144	male, 2nd-class passenger	Common B
Henn, Mrs Edith Mabel	8	female, age 27 years, 2nd-class passenger	Common C
Hine, John Benjamin	171	male, age 24 years, crew, vegetable cook	Common B
Hodges, Mrs Sara	209	female, 1st-class passenger	Common B
Hopkins, Miss Alice Eliza	187	female, age 33 years, 2nd-class passenger	Common B
Hopkins, Miss Kate Mary	5	female, age 35 years, 2nd-class passenger	Common C
Horton, Mrs Elizabeth	77	female, age 51 years, 2nd-class passenger	Common C
Howdle, Mrs Jane Ellen	183	female, age 33 years, crew, stewardess	Common B
Hunt, Miss Isabella Gertrude	205	female, age 37 years, 2nd-class passenger	Common B
Jacobaeus, Mr Sigurd Anton	84	male, age 55 years, 1st-class passenger	Common C
Jacobs, Mrs Liba Bella	33	female, age 55 years, 3rd-class passenger	Common C
Jones, Miss Margaret Drutler	89	female, 1st-class passenger	Common A
Jones, Miss Mary Elizabeth	30	female, age 43 years, crew, stewardess	Common C
Jones, Richard Ellis	22	male, age 31 years, crew, junior 4th engineer	583
Kelly, Miss Margaret S.	125	female, age 34 years, 2nd-class passenger	Common B
Kelly, Miss Marie Annie	87	female, age 32 years, 3rd-class passenger	Common C
Kewley, Ernest Alexander	206	male, age 38 years, crew, 1st-class waiter	649
King, Mrs Martha Frances	7	female, age 58 years, 2nd-class passenger	602
Lakin, Miss Martha Maria	182	female, age 40 years, 2nd-class passenger	Common B
Lancaster, Mr Francis William	12	male, age 50 years, 2nd-class passenger	Common A
Lapphane, Charles	119	male, age 19 years, crew, 3rd-class waiter	Common C
Lawrence, Miss Ella Woods	145	female, age 50 years, 2nd-class passenger	493
Lee, Daniel	219	male, age 50 years, crew, fireman	Common A
Linton, Isaac	65	male, age 48 years, crew, fireman	Common C
Lockwood, Miss Lily	69	female, age 7 years, 3nd-class passenger	Common B
Logan, Master Robert	42	male, age 3 years, 3rd-class passenger	Common C
Longden, Mrs Matilda	157	female, age 30 years, 2nd-class passenger	Common B
Loynd, Mrs Alice	75	female, 2nd-class passenger	Common C
Lucko, Mr Timofej	96	male, age 20 years, 3rd-class passenger	Common C
Madden, John	197	male, crew, age 43 years, fireman	Common A
Mainman, Mr John V.	118	male, 2nd-class passenger	Common B

Three women framed in the doorway of the Customs and Mercantile Marine Building gaze at flag-decked coffins from a colossal catastrophe. The large noticeboard nearby certainly relates to the Lusitania. A boy appears to be saluting the passing remains, as he has seen soldiers and RIC men do. There are more coffins stacked outside a funeral home further up the street (Lynch's Quay)

British army soldiers under a regimental sergeant major place the Union Jack over three coffins, including that of 19-year-old third-class waiter Charles Lapphane (marked No. 119) on a cart. Lapphane was buried in mass grave Common C (see p. 108)

Name	No.	Description	Burial
Marsh, Mr Thomas	80	male, 3rd-class passenger	Common C
Martin-Davey, Mrs Elizabeth	35	female, age 53 years, 2nd-class passenger	Common A
Mason, Mr Stewart Southam	59	male, 1st-class passenger	Common B
McDermott, Dr James Farrell	200	male, age 37 years, crew, ship's surgeon	474
McKenzie, Kenneth	140	male, age 25 years, crew, waiter	Common C
McNulty, Mr Stephen	19	male, age 27 years, 3rd-class passenger	Common C
Meaney, Mr George Peter	45	male, age 30 years, 3rd-class passenger	Common C
Mitchell, Walter Dawson	122	male, age 6 months, 2nd-class passenger	Common C
Murphy, John Henry	136	male, age 32 years, crew, 1st-class waiter	Common C
O'Hare, Owen	193	male, crew, age 42 years, Engineers' stores	Common A
Padilla, Mr Frederico G.	175	male, Consul-General for Mexico, 1st-class passenger	587
Palmer, Master Albert	179	male, age 6 months, 2nd-class passenger, buried with Mrs Annie Palmer	Common B
Palmer, Master Edgar	184	male, age 7 years, 2nd-class passenger	Common B
Palmer, Mrs Annie	179	female, age 33 years, 2nd-class passenger	Common B
Parsons, Archibald Ernest	106	male, age 30 years, 2nd-class passenger	Common B
Press, Miss Mary Jane	116	female, age 34 years, 2nd-class passenger	Common C
Pye, Miss Marjorie	239	female, age 18 months, 2nd-class passenger, buried with No 240	545
Quirk, William Edouard	233	male, age 33 years, crew, seaman	Common B
Roach, James	49	male, age 24 years, crew, fireman	Common C
Robb, Joseph	51	male, age 27 years, crew, fireman	Common C
Roberts, Miss Annie Jane	60	female, age 35 years, crew, stewardess	Common C
Ronnan, George	53	male, age 16 years, crew, ship's baker	Common C
Scott, Mrs Alice Ann	50	female, age 25 years, 3rd-class passenger	Common B
Seccombe, Miss Elizabeth Ann	164	female, age 40 years, 1st-class passenger	Common B
Sheedy, Mr Patrick	13	male, age 30 years, 3rd-class passenger (deported)	Common A
Smith, Mrs Minnie	110	female, age 28 years, 3rd-class passenger	Common C
Spillman, Mr John Bowen	26	male, age 33 years, 2nd-class passenger	Common B
Stankiewicz, Mr Anthony	198	male, age 46 years, 3rd-class passenger	Common B
Stevens, Mr Charles Henry	241	male, age 57 years, 2nd-class passenger	654
Stewart, Thomas Edgar	41	male, crew, age 23 years, steward on SS *Cameronia*	Common C
Thom(p)son, Mr John	196	crew, trimmer	Common B
Thomas, Mr Ernest	235	male, age 33 years, 2nd-class passenger	475
Thomas, William Stanford	138	male, age 44 years, crew, 2nd-class bedroom steward	Common C
Thompson, Mr Albert	141	male, age 37 years, 2nd-class passenger	Common B
Tiberghien, Mr Georges	191	male, 1st-class passenger. later buried in France	(Removed)
Tierney, Miss Nina	102	female, age 5 years, 2nd-class passenger	Common C
Tierney, Mrs Mary Ann	2	female, age 26 years, 2nd-class passenger	Common C
Toole, James	232	male, age 38 years, crew, fireman	Common A
Vernon, Mr George Ley P.	201	male, 1st-class passenger	651
Wallace-Watson, Mrs William	132	female, 1st-class passenger	(Removed)
Weir, Mrs Margaret	40	female, crew, age 51 years, stewardess on SS *Cameronia*	Common C
Welsh, Christopher	64	male, age 36 years, crew, trimmer	Common A
Wickham, Mrs Ann	54	female, age 50 years, 2nd-class passenger	Common C
Williams, Mr James	108	male, age 30 years, 3rd-class passenger	Common B
Witherbee, Master Alfred Scott	243	male, age 4 years, 1st-class passenger	616
Wood, Henry Edward	90	male, age 35 years, crew, pantry steward	Common B
Wood, Mr Arthur John	126	male, age 37 years, 1st-class passenger	Common C
Yeatman, Mr Charles A.	107	male, age 37 years, 2nd-class passenger	1630
Yeatman, Mrs Cora	131	female, age 36 years, 2nd-class passenger	1630

Males: 85 Females: 84
Overall: 169, including 45 unidentified

A coffin on a jaunting car on the Queenstown seafront at West Beach. It may have just come from the Cunard wharf on Lynch's Quay where bodies were laid out.
Local dignitary Clayton Love, owner of one of the shops in the background, served on a Queenstown inquest jury in connection with the disaster, but had to be excused after the sudden death of his wife when she learned that a relative had gone down with the Lusitania

The coffin of Lusitania Staff Captain James Anderson moves off from outside the American Saloon at East Beach, Queenstown, on 11 May 1915 as townspeople line the streets and watch from upper windows

The list of Cobh cemetery burials on previous pages is a compilation by Luke Cassidy, Geoff Whitfield and Noel Ray; gratefully acknowledged.

Descriptions of the 45 unidentified bodies interred at Old Church Cemetery, Queenstown (Cobh)

Body Number

6) Female, 60 years, dark complexion.
    Property – one plain gold wedding ring (22 carat) no initials.
    Common grave C.

10) Male, 35 years, apparently a seaman. Tattooed star on back of right wrist.
    Property – none
    Common grave C.

15) Male, 24 years, apparently member of crew. Wore serge suit with brass buttons.
    Property – one penknife, one handkerchief.
    Common grave C.

21) Male, 55 years, apparently fireman or seaman.
    Property – none.
    Common grave A.

27) Female, 50 years, fairly stout, hair turning grey, large face.
    Property – lady's 18 carat keyless Geneva watch with red dial, watch engraved inside 'Remontoir Cylindre 10 rubies Medaille d'Or, No. 220063'; one pair eyeglasses, gold and platenoid brooch, pendant set with rose diamonds, size reduced by inside half ring; gold band ring set with onyx (English make); one pearl earring; long gold watch guard, carbuncle and crystal; coins bearing Chinese marks and square hole.
    Common grave A.

38) Female, 35 years, brown hair, medium build, height 5'6".
    Property – one plain gold band bangle, initial 'G' on gold chain attached.
    Common grave A.

43) Female, 50 years, grey hair, stout build, height 5' 8".
    Property – one antique gold ring with motto slightly defaced, possibly '*I like my chance too well to change*'.
    Common grave B.

68) Boy of about two and a half years.
    Property – none.
    Buried in coffin with child Margaret Coughlan (body no. 62) in Common grave B.

73) Female, 50 years.
    Property – one silver enamelled brooch, one gold plate eyeglass chain holder (button shape) made by Kellchan & McDougall, New York (patented Feb 24/03 and Apl 26/06) one button, one 14 carat gold ring, stones missing; one 22ct gold wedding ring (English).
    Common grave B.

81) Female, 45 years, black hair, medium height and build.
    Property – one 18 carat half hoop white paste ring with 3 stones; one diamond and ruby gypsy ring, 22 carat (English); one wedding ring (English); one 5-stone sapphire half hoop ring; one gold marquise white paste and sapphire ring; one gold amethyst pendant brooch; one twist wire gold knot ring.
    Common grave C.

British soldiers of Irish regiments bearing coffins at Westbourne Place, Queenstown – these coffins may be empty as the photograph appears posed and the road leads out of town in the direction of Cork city, where few victims were buried

The sole family to survive the disaster intact were the Rileys, who were on a visit to England from their home in Boston. Young Sutcliffe Riley, left, appears still shaken by his experiences, unlike his cheery sister Ethel. Parents Annie and Edward, aged 29 and 30 respectively, were travelling with their children in third-class

82) Male, 30 years, apparently seaman, clean shaven, fair hair, brown canvas clothes.
Property – none.
Common grave C.

83) Male, 28 years, apparently seaman, fair hair medium build height 5' 7".
Property – none.
Common grave C.

86) Female, 32 years, fair hair, green dress, height 5' 5".
Property – one 9 carat signet ring, one enamelled gilt brooch with initials *RMS Aquitania*.
Common grave C.

100) Female, 38 years, dark hair, height 5' 5". Wore grey woollen jacket.
Property – one gold plated star brooch with white paste; one plated ring with three green stones.
Common grave C.

101) Female, 34 years, dark hair, slight make, height 5' 4".
Property – one gold curb padlock bracelet, one 9 carat square locket (engraved), one 22 carat gold wedding ring, one 18 carat gold plain ring with heart, one 9 carat signet ring with initials MH and one 9 carat gold necklet.
Common grave C.

103) Female, 35 years, fairly stout build, dark hair, height 5' 6". Wore heavy black fur coat.
Property – one gold curb padlock bangle (large pattern), one 14 carat gold wedding ring, one half hoop 5 stone diamond ring, one 9 carat gold garnet ring, one 18 carat gold sardonyx ring with rose diamonds, one metal safety pin, one leather folding purse inscribed 'Compliments of W. F. Lunt, Insurance, 95 Wick Street, Boston', one linen bag, one pair plated links (bearing photo of four funnelled Cunard steamer) one plated stud.
Common grave C.

104) Female, 54 years, hair turning grey, pointed nose.
Property – one silver plated white paste brooch, one brass safety pin, one plated ring with green and white paste, one plated gold ring, one metal safety pin.
Common grave C.

109) Female, 40 years, broad face, dark complexion.
Property – one wristlet gold watch and one gold ring.
Common grave B.

112) Female, 50 years, hair turning grey, stout build.
Property – none.
Common grave B.

113) Female, 35 years, medium build.
Property – four £1 Treasury Notes; one 14 carat gold wedding ring, one 9 carat gold garnet and diamond ring (one stone missing), one silver brooch with 'Windmill' engraving, and word 'Nantucket', one fancy linen purse, one small leather purse.
Common grave B.

120) Female, 33 years, fair hair.
Property – none.
Common grave C.

121) Female, 12 months.
Property – none.
Common grave C.

Unidentified

128) Female, 35 years, brown hair, ordinary nose, front upper teeth missing, slight build, height 5' 4".
Wore blue cloth dress, fancy shoes, corsets and white cotton blouse.
Property – one small button badge brooch with picture of *Lusitania*.
Common grave C.

130) Female, 55 years, dark hair turning grey, long nose, inclined to be Roman, all teeth gone except three in upper jaw and one in front lower jaw, slight build, height 5'. Wore strong laced boots, blue dress, cotton striped petticoat, corsets made of black material, white singlet 'Winchester, 38 Mills, Maker' and brown worsted stockings.
Property – four $1 bills, one $2 bill, two gold plated keeper rings, three shillings in silver, one key 'Eagle Lock Co. No 178'; two and half pence in coppers, one 5 centimes piece, one purse, inscribed 'A present from the Isle of Man'.
Common grave C.

135) Male, 25 years, apparently deck hand, light fair hair, regular nose, medium build, height 5' 7". Had tattoo marks on right arm, 'Union Jack', 'Stars and Stripes', Heart in centre with hands clasped across heart all worked into a device. Wore leather belt, old shirt and trousers, but no boots. Circumcision scar.
Common grave C.

146) Male, 27 years, brown hair, clean shaven, height 5' 7". Wore blue clothes and black tie.
Property – one gold watch with leather guard, seven shillings in silver, nine foreign coins, one penknife, one stud, two links, one fountain pen (Waterman – medium pointed nib), one hand-kerchief, also unfinished letter commencing 'Dear Ted – we hit New York at 7.30 in the morning, and after seeing to our luggage we made our way to Bronx Park to see some friends of mine ...'
Common grave B.

149) Male, 40 years, apparently fireman, dark moustache, short thick nose, strong build, height 5' 9". Wore blue trousers, cotton shirt, no other clothes.
Property – one pair spectacles.
Common grave A.

161) Female, 28 years, dark hair, fresh complexion, pointed nose, false teeth in both jaws, slight build, height 5' 7". Wore black coarse serge dress, three-quarter coat, dark lining, three buttons, crepe bound braided loops, dark serge skirt, black stockings, black satin blouse, black alpaca underskirt, white linen camisole.
Property – none.
Common grave B.

167) Female, 30 years, grey eyes, brown hair, short thick nose, round face, stout make, height about 5' 1". Wore white silk blouse and cream dress, patent leather boots with cloth uppers.
Property – one brooch with five stones (one centre and 4 outer), one wedding ring (18 carat) No. 9095 scratched inside, maker's name evidently 'Hemsley', one engagement ring with three white and two blue stones, one keeper ring with three green stones and two white, three rings and one metal brooch with five stones.
Common grave B.

178) Male, 50 years, apparently member of crew. Dark hair turning grey, regular pointed nose, medium build, height 5' 11". Wore blue serge suit and plaid shirt.
Common grave A.

185) Boy, 3 or 4 years, fair complexion, fair hair. Wore blue suit knickers of serge check, striped vest with four pearl buttons, two white under-flannel vests and drawers, two common safety pins in front vest, toe-cap boots, seven buttons, white woolly collarette round neck.
Property – *Lusitania* brooch badge.
Common grave B.

186) Female, 32 years, pregnant, stout strong build, fair complexion, round face, good looking, long light brown wavy hair, height 5' 9". Wore blue serge dress with red jersey underneath jacket, blue check bodice, black button boots, cashmere hose.
Property – gold wedding and keeper rings
Common grave B.

204) Male, 24 years, apparently fireman. Slight build, clean shaven, dark hair, tattoo marks: cross with reef with words *In memory of my mother* done on left arm; on right arm, laurel with bunch of flowers and word *Sarah*. Height 5' 9". Wore brown trousers and grey woollen shirt.
Common grave A.

207) Male, 35 years, apparently trimmer or seaman, clean shaven, round regular features, dark hair, medium build, dark eyes, height 5' 8". Wore light brown trousers.
Common grave A.

221) Boy, 5 or 6 years, round full face, broad, high forehead, small mouth, blue eyes, well shaped features. Wore white woollen singlet and white cotton combinations, check jacket and knickers of same pattern, pink woollen jacket outside with dark ivory buttons, black button boots and black socks, black patent belt.
Property – gold ring with initials 'JWP' worn on second finger of right hand.
Common grave B.

222) Infant male, 12 to 18 months, round chubby fat face, hair inclined to be red, small short nose, sunken eyes, prominent forehead, sucking tube fastened round neck with cord. Wore white woollen wrapper, white cotton bodice having red and blue stripes round edges, blue cotton overall fastened at back with white buttons and plaited down front, embroidered with dotted squares, coarse grey woollen outside jacket with four ivory buttons, black stockings, shoes and straps.
Common grave B.

224) Female, 23 or 24 years, round full face, nose broad at top, full eyes, fresh complexion, good plump build, good teeth, centre tooth in upper jaw set with gold. Height 5". Wore woollen singlet with lace collarette, dark blue jacket, double row of buttons on right side with plaited braid, skirt same material, black cotton stockings, brown button boots with high heels, three twisted cord loops, connecting six acorn pattern buttons on body of dress.
Property – wedding ring, brooch, silver enamelled brooch, English and French flags crossed.
Common grave B.

225) Infant female, 4 to 5 months, fair hair, large sloping forehead, well nourished. Wore cotton wrapper, cotton bodice, white cotton front, white cotton overall or jacket with sleeves, white coarse knitted woollen stockings with two tassels on top and two on vamp, pink thread top of stocking and pink threaded lines extending downwards from top of stocking about two inches, cotton overall embroidered at edges, three white buttons at back of bodice, sucking tube attached to clothes.
Common grave B.

226) Female, 35 to 36 years, appeared to be pregnant, full round face, small short nose, large forehead, dark brown hair, blue eyes, large mouth, stout build, height about 5' 3". Wore blue skirt, woollen singlet, white corset, grey woollen cardigan jacket with 5 grey buttons at front, black stockings, black laced boots.
Property – one 22 carat plain gold ring with letters 'SH' engraved (sunk into ring, may be maker's initials) ring cut apparently when being taken off finger, one small brooch with brown sparkling stone, one rubber teat, one safety pin.
Common grave B.

227) Female, 40 years, height 5' 4". Wore black skirt, black pony shorn coat, and boots with lavender cloth uppers.

'A large number of coffins were sent down from Cork by the trains on Saturday night, and others followed by every train on Sunday. The coffins were taken to the Cunard Company's premises, and all through the day the bodies were being placed in them'
CORK EXAMINER, 10 MAY, P. 7

The local Cunard office was eventually left with a large surplus of unused coffins because fewer than the expected number of bodies came ashore. These were difficult to sell, even at a discount, because no one wanted 'second-hand' coffins

Lily Lockwood, aged seven, whose body was recovered and buried in mass grave B in Queenstown. Her brother Clifford, three years older, right, was also lost, as was their mother, Florence, but neither of these bodies was recovered. The Lockwoods were travelling third-class.

Their father, Dick Lockwood, of Harrison, Illinois was not aboard. He remarried and died in 1935.

Property – one large gold bangle, one diamond ring with three rubies, one gold wedding ring, one silver and coral ring, one safety pin, one handkerchief.
Common grave B.

236) Male, 30 years, apparently fireman, unrecognisable. Round face, clean shaven, medium build, black hair cur short, nose pointed slightly to left side, apparently result of old accident, height 5' 8". Wore dungaree trousers, kept on by leather strap around waist. Military blue woollen drawers and shirt, red woollen socks, trousers, no coat, vest nor boots.
Common grave A.

238) Male, apparently steward, unrecognisable.
Property – one pair sleeve links, one stud.
Common grave B.

240) Infant female, aged 12 to 18 months.
Buried in coffin with infant Marjorie Pye (body no. 239) in grave No. 545.

242) Male, unrecognisable, supposed to be Russian. Wore blue serge trousers and vest, cotton drawers, blue stripe cotton undershirt and cotton shirt.
Property – one clasp leather purse with two pockets containing the following: four Russian rouble bills, two unknown silver coins, one half dollar piece, one 5-cent piece and four cent pieces, two cuff links (brass), one shirt stud (brass), one pocket knife, two linen handkerchiefs, five Russian 100 rouble bills in canvas bag with paper slip around bills marked $500, piece of ordinary white paper on back of one of Russian bills with some names scribbled on same. Printed on said canvas bag were the following 'Zimmerman and Forshay, Bankers and Brokers, special and foreign bank notes, letters of credit, drafts on all parts of the world, 9–11 Wall Street, New York'.
Common grave A.

244) Male, 25 to 35 years, unrecognisable, apparently fireman, recovered by trawler *Standard* off Old Head. Clean shaven, very fair hair, strong build, height 5' 10". Wore blue trousers, black cotton stockings, cotton drawers, blue and yellow stripes, cotton singlet. Buried in grave 619.

A crew memorial and a Mass Grave stone in Cobh

The solid granite boulders were placed on the mass graves as part of a major refurbishment programme undertaken in 1986. Unfortunately when the bronze faceplates were unveiled, they were found to read 'Luisitania', and the misspelling of the vessel's name meant they had to be melted down and re-cast.

The cost of maintaining of the *Lusitania* graves has been transferred from Cunard to the Cobh Town Council. A crew memorial was erected by the Commonwealth War Graves Commission (*above left*)

Mrs Gladys Crompton of Philadelphia and her six children, along with her husband, Paul, and the children's nanny, Dorothy Allen, were all drowned.
Three bodies of the Crompton children were recovered and are buried together in grave 482 in the Old Church Cemetery in Cobh. They comprise babe-in-arms Peter, six-year-old John, facing the infant, and teenager Stephen, standing behind his mother.
The other children, from bottom left, clockwise, are Catherine (10), Paul (9), and Alberta (13).
The Cork Examiner reported that the Crompton children were the nephews and nieces of Alfred Booth, Chairman of the Cunard Company, owners and operators of the RMS Lusitania

This photograph is the most emblematic of the Lusitania disaster, its depiction of the Stars and Stripes encapsulating the United States' dilemma on whether to enter the 'European War'. In the event, that vast nation would not do so until April 1917, nearly two years after this image was captured.

This may not be an adult body being carried from the quayside to a temporary morgue. Instead it seems to show the body of an American child (or children) being carried past the Soldiers Home and Sailors Rest, where a party of royal navy bluejackets are respectfully saluting. It would also seem to be a transfer from the Town Hall temporary morgue, where many children's bodies were laid out, to the Cunard yard where coffins were stockpiled, according to the following:

The bodies of American citizens who are identified are wrapped in American flags, and the others in Union Jacks. Bodies from the other temporary morgues were transferred through the day on stretchers to the Cunard shed, according as batches of coffins were received.

(CORK EXAMINER, 10 MAY 1915, P. 7)

BORN
JUNE 27TH 1911
DIED MAY 7TH 1915

A VICTIM OF THE LUSITANIA
FOULLY MURDERED BY
GERMANY

Bearing a coffin aloft to its final rest. Soldiers and sailors gathered around Rev. Swann Mason at the edge of Mass Grave common C, with its freight of no fewer than 69 coffins

Alfred Scott Witherbee, Jr, aged nearly four. His tombstone in the Old Church cemetery notes that he was 'A victim of the Lusitania, foully murdered by Germany.' His was the last body interred here, on 16 June 1915. Grave plot 616, see map, p. 126

Descriptions of 19 Unidentified Lusitania Bodies interred elsewhere in Ireland

Aran Islands

4) Female, 45 years, recovered at Straw Island, very decomposed. Wore blue linen dress, black boots and stockings, hair short, turning grey.
Property – one gold ring with three stones (two blue, one supposed diamond), one expanding bracelet and watch (latter damaged) apparently gold, initials 'J. C. C'.
Buried in Kilronan graveyard, Inishmore.

12) Male, body washed ashore at Inisheer, Aran Islands, 20 July. Greatly decomposed and identification impossible. No clothing except singlet, drawers, and tie bearing name 'W. Weldon, Hosier and Glover, Scarborough' and on drawers 'S. Grafton & Sons, Manchester'.
Buried Kilronan graveyard, Inishmore.

Clare

5) Male, unrecognisable, recovered at Ballaghaline, Doolin, wearing heavy grey woollen jersey, pyjamas, one light cotton sock, dark striped trousers.
Property – one gold cased watch, No. 488994 engraved 'Dennison Watch Co.'., two $1 bills.
Buried in Killilagh churchyard, Doolin.

11) Female, body washed ashore at Ross, Carrigaholt, 20 July. Body very decomposed, breast bones, legs and arms missing, teeth in upper jaw were sound and regular, except two molars on left side which were gold filled. There were three teeth missing in left side and one on the right side, which had been extracted before death. The two front teeth had been knocked out since death. Besides the body there was a corset, maker's number 6110955 with letters 'N. H'. marked on it in ink. Pieces of white silk underclothing were adhering to the body, on one of these was printed 'Niagara Maid' probably maker's trade mark, on another piece the letter 'J' and other letters not decipherable were marked in black thread.
Buried at Kiltrillig graveyard, Carrigaholt.

14) Female, body washed ashore at Lahinch on 20 July, very decomposed. Clothing missing, with exception of a corset, part of a chemise, and part of a dress.
Buried in workhouse graveyard, Ennistymon.

17) Male, body washed ashore at Carrowmore North, Co. Clare, 20 July. Very decomposed, head and hands missing, no clothing on body, except waist of the trousers, pair of braces, small portion of a flannel shirt, pair of buttoned boots and stockings, watch found in a small pocket in the waist of trousers marked 'Ingersoll Watch Co. No. 26682630, Made in USA'.
Buried at Clohan's graveyard, Carrowmore.

19) Male, body recovered at Quilty, Co. Clare, 23 July. Unrecognisable, skull and bones of face were bare, forearms from elbows were missing, four teeth in upper jaw gold cased and four gold filled, similar lower jaw. Part of pair of laced shoes and part of socks covered by them on feet, part of underpants, part of inside undervest, the neckband and a fragment of the shirt were adhering to body. Neckband and shirt portion were of linen with blue stripes having the following laundry mark in black indelible ink on inside of band (V)X 176. Band was 15 size. Band was closed in front with dark brown stud, set in plain metal, all of which may have been gold washed when new. Stud at back similar to front (set in white ivory). Under-vest of pale white colour bore laundry mark (V)X. The underpants were similar in texture and colour to the undervest and bore maker's name 'American Silk Reis, underwear, Pat. V. finish'
Buried at Leitrim Cemetery, Doonbeg.

21) Male, body washed ashore at Murrough, Fanoremore, 30 July. Decomposed. Remnant of trousers and left foot on. Rubber sole and heel. Boot marked 'Franklin's Special Shoe'.
Interred in Craggagh burial ground, Murrough.

22) Male, body recovered at Murrough, 23 July. Portion only from hip to feet, left shin bone was protruding, flesh being torn away, length of legs 34", portion of waist appeared to be a man of medium build. Only clothing found on body consisted of a pair of trousers and boots.
Buried in Glenina Burial Ground, Murrough.

Cork

158) Male, 40 years, apparently steward, dark hair, clean shaven, good teeth in front of upper and lower jaws, bald in front of forehead, height 5' 9". Wore black serge clothes (no coat), brass buttons on vest.
Property: One bunch of keys, whistle marked 'S. Auld, Glasgow, No, 143091', fountain pen (Waterman, with clip cap holder), penknife, nine keys, one large key, with figure 8 in Roman character.
Buried in Jewish cemetery, Mount Desert, Cork city.

172) Male, 40 years, apparently fireman, dark brown hair, brown moustache, blue eyes, thick nose, regular heavy eyebrows, regular face, medium make, 2 teeth in upper jaw, bald in front of head, height 5' 4". Wore grey shirt and black trousers only.
Buried in Jewish cemetery, Mount Desert, Cork city.

174) Male, 42 years, apparently greaser, blue eyes, regular nose, fresh complexion, sandy moustache, full face, stout build, dark hair, height 5' 11". Wore dark jacket and grey shirt, boots and socks.
Property – pipe and penknife.
Buried in Jewish cemetery, Mount Desert, Cork city.

246) Male, apparently steward, brought ashore at Ballyally, no means of identification, head and arms gone, height about 5' 7". Clothing mostly gone but wore vest with white ivory buttons, small foot, laced boots, leather laces and toe caps, white shirt, cotton socks, white cotton drawers.
Buried at the Abbey, Skibbereen.

247) Male, apparently fireman, picked up by trawler *Bempton*, 24 June, and brought to Castletownbere, height about 5' 9". Wore dungaree pants, blue serge drawers, blue serge singlet, boot on left foot branded 'Globe', right foot missing, no stockings or papers.
Buried St Finian's cemetery, Castletownbere.

Galway

9) Male, washed ashore at Cleggan, 11 July, almost a skeleton and unrecognisable. Wore new tennis boots, black cloth trousers and vest, woollen singlet marked 'Devonshire', fleece drawers, light woollen cotton shirt with blue stripes, dark socks, buckles on braces marked 'Shirley President', a coloured handkerchief, no coat on body, trousers, vest and boots of American make.
Buried Ballinakill graveyard, near Cleggan.

Kerry

249) Male, body washed ashore at Gortgower, Valentia, Co. Kerry, 14 July. Head, arms and feet missing. Dressed in blue serge trousers, flannel shirt, black and white stripe, woollen singlet and drawers, wore a leather belt to which was attached a bunch of keys, two gun metal and five steel. The drawers bore mark D75 in red thread. On trouser buttons was the name 'S. B. Cole Swindon'; medium build, measured 31 inches round waist, wore braces.
Buried Kilmore graveyard, Valentia.

250) Male, body washed ashore at Rossleigh [*Rossbeigh?*], near Glenbeigh, 15 July. Description, headless trunk, supposed sailor or labourer, no identification marks except 'WG' or 'SM' or 'W8' on some shreds of clothing.

Property – three £1 Treasury notes, one sovereign, one florin, nine shillings, one sixpenny piece, two half pence, watch and chain, leather belt.
Buried in Curra graveyard, Glenbeigh.

253)   Male, body washed ashore at Kilcummin, 17 July, very decomposed and face unrecognisable.
Property – pocket book marked 'Compliments, Savings Dept, The Union Trust Co. Ltd, Toronto', penknife, notebook, cigarette picture of M. Maeterlink, four plain cigarette holders, one ten cent Canadian coin and two lead pencils.
Buried on beach above high water mark, Kilcummin strand, Brandon Bay.

260)   Male, body washed ashore at Ballyheigue, Tralee, Co. Kerry, 26 July. Very decomposed, all flesh gone off head, six teeth gone from upper jaw, lower jaw completely gone, both arms from elbow down gone, right leg complete. Wore blue serge trousers over suit of flannelette pyjamas, large black buttons around waist of trousers, black leather belt with brass buckle around waist, coat and waistcoat gone, pyjama jacket gone from waist, four white ivory buttons in jacket, pyjama trousers much torn, 173687W and 460 on waistband of pyjamas, cashmere sock on right foot with the letter 'K' worked in red wool.
Property – penknife.
Buried in Ballyheigue graveyard.

Other *identified* victims of the *Lusitania* buried in Ireland, exclusive of Old Church Cemetery, Queenstown

NAME	BODY	DETAILS	GRAVE
Bistis, Leonidas M.	251	male, 1st-class passenger	Killury Churchyard, near Tralee, Co. Kerry
Blackburn, George A.	259	male, 3rd-class passenger	Beach at Teer, Brandon Bay, Co. Kerry
Bretherton, Miss Betty	156	female (infant), 2nd-class passenger	Ursuline Convent, Blackrock, Cork City
Brownlie, Mr Thomas	8*	male, 2nd-class passenger	Belmullet Protestant Cemetery, Co. Mayo
Busvine, Mr William Robert	18	male, 2nd-class passenger	Jewish Cemetery, Mount Desert, Cork City
Chamberlain, Richard	5+	male, age 57, crew, night watchman	St Multose's Church, Kinsale, Co. Cork
Cranston, George	4+	male, age 63 years, crew, night watchman	St Multose's Church, Kinsale, Co. Cork
Crooks, Mr Robert William	93	male, 1st-class passenger	Jewish Cemetery, Mount Desert, Cork City
		(Disinterred and sent to New York via ss *Saxonia*, 19 June 1915)	
Emond, Mr Wilfred Alfred	20*	male, 1st-class passenger	Doonbeg Graveyard, Co. Clare
Harvey, Mr William	7*	male, age 53 years, 3rd-class passenger	Gleninagh Cemetery, Ballyvaughan, Co. Clare
Learoyd, Mr Charles A.	257	male, 1st-class passenger	Kilmore Graveyard, Valentia, Co. Kerry
Leverich, Mrs Rosina Thomas	254	female, 2nd-class passenger	Killury Churchyard, near Tralee, Co. Kerry
Matthews, Lt Capt Robert	1+	male, 2nd-class passenger	Cork (Collins Barracks)
Miller, Capt James Blaine	13*	male, 1st-class passenger	Ennistymon Workhouse Cemetery, Co. Clare
		(Disinterred and sent to Erie, PA, via ss *Cymric*, 4 December 1915)	
Ordyniez, Mr Andrej	1*	male, age 48 years, 3rd-class passenger	Killilagh Churchyard, Doolin, Co. Clare
Samoilescu, Mr David	9	male, 2nd-class passenger (David Samuels)	Jewish Cemetery, Mount Desert, Cork.
Shineman, Mr James	18*	male, 2nd-class passenger	Kiltrillig Graveyard, Carrigaholt, Co. Clare
Shineman, Mrs Margaret	3+	female, 2nd-class passenger	St Multose's Church, Kinsale, Co. Cork

Stackhouse, Mr Joseph Foster	211	male, 1st-class passenger	Society of Friends Burial Ground, Quaker Road, Cork City
Thompson, Mr Robert Joseph	15*	male, 2nd-class passenger	Avery Island
Twigg, Mr Frederick Alexander	10*	male, 2nd-class passenger	Louisburg, Co. Mayo
Wheelhouse, A.	258	male, crew (Junior 7th Engineer)	Kilmore Churchyard, Lixnaw, Co. Kerry
Winter, William	228	male, 1st-class passenger	Dublin
Woolven, Mrs Nellie	3*	female, 2nd-class passenger	Kilronan Graveyard, Inishmore, Co. Galway

[*Doolin and Aran Islands body list + Kinsale body list] *Acknowledgments to Luke Cassidy, Noel Ray and Geoff Whitfield*]

Almost no photos were taken of Lusitania bodies in situ. Top shows bodies from the 1904 disaster in New York to the General Slocum *awaiting removal. Bottom: A generic illustration. One washed-up body was initially presumed to be from the* Lusitania *and included in the list of victims (No. 248) but proved to be from the* Falaba, *torpedoed on 28 March. Leon Thresher, an American found on 11 July, is buried in Stradbally graveyard, Castlegregory, Co Kerry.*

A Pathetic Sight

The bodies washed ashore on the western coast of Ireland, curiously enough, appeared late in June and early in July, long after the searching operations had been discontinued.

Apparently the corpses remained below the surface of the sea for several weeks, and only floated again in sporadic instances after decomposition had made considerable progress. More than nine hundred corpses, of course, were never recovered at all.

The bodies first recovered made a very strong appeal through their lifelikeness – a sort of an unearthly aura of personality lent them by the rigor mortis. But this appeal was one to stimulate meditation and sentiment. The bodies recovered later on perhaps had a still more powerful effect upon the observer, because of their revolting condition; but in this case the reaction was emotional, almost physical.

The rigidity relaxed into an inebriate flabbiness, and the features broke down into a preposterously animal-like repulsiveness. I was present as official witness to an autopsy performed on one body seventy-two days dead, but other corpses equalled it in the ravages they displayed.

The faces registered every shading of the grotesque and the hideous. The lips and noses were eaten away by sea-birds, and the eyes gouged out into staring pools of blood. It was almost a relief when the faces became indistinguishable as such. Toward the last the flesh was wholly gone from the grinning skulls, the trunks were bloated and distended with gases, and the limbs were partially eaten away or bitten clean off by sea-creatures so that just stumps of raw bone were left projecting.

This was the final phase of the disaster as we saw it at Queenstown; and I have given it to you without mincing words because it seems a peculiarly appropriate termination for the Lusitania 'incident'.

The picture of a proud ship on a sunny day in lovely waters, beautiful even in her death throes, is not what the word Lusitania calls up in my mind. I see, and every American ought to see, scores and hundreds of corpses of men and women and little folks – some rotting in pools of blood in unnamed deal coffins, some staring wearily up past me from the damp floor of the old Town Hall, and some lying with vile disfigurements in shreds of clothing soaking with the salt ocean. But always corpses. That is what the Lusitania means to me – corpses.

(Wesley Frost, German Submarine Warfare, Appleton, 1918)

Inquest at Kinsale

The small fishing port of Kinsale, like Queenstown, attracted international attention in 1915. The town had its own burials of *Lusitania* victims, and survivors to look after, but it was the first to institute an inquest into the deaths – due to the drive of local coroner John J. Horgan.

Horgan had the captain of the *Lusitania* giving his story on the stand, and sobbing at the recollection of it, before the admiralty in London could put a stop to it. The inquest jury at Kinsale brought in a historically memorable verdict of wilful murder against the officers of the submarine, the government of Germany, and the kaiser himself.

Visitors to Kinsale can see the room where the inquest was held in what is now the town museum – it also has a number of *Lusitania* artefacts. Some victims are buried in the church of St Multose, 50 yards from the museum, and a modern memorial on the Old Head of Kinsale commemorates the calamity on the nearest point of land to the sinking.

Coroner J. J. Horgan

THE FUNERALS AT KINSALE
(FROM OUR CORRESPONDENT) KINSALE, MONDAY NIGHT

The funeral of three of the victims of the Lusitania *disaster – George Cranston, Richard Chamberlain, and an unknown female about 35 years of age – took place at the St Multose churchyard today, amid many manifestations of regret and sympathy.*

The sad procession was formed at the Barrack Square, being headed by the band of the Connaught Rangers. Then came the hearses containing the coffins, followed by a few of the crew, the members of the Urban Council, and the Harbour Board.

The local constabulary next followed, under District Inspector Wansborough, and about 150 officers and men of the Connaught Rangers under Colonel L. A. C. Lewen.

The attendance of the general public was extremely large, and as the funeral cortege drew near the town the business establishments were closed and the blinds drawn. The route to the burial ground was lined throughout by the townspeople to show their sympathy and pay their tribute of respect to the dead. All business was suspended in the town during the evening.

The Rev. Dr Pearson conducted the service, the choir singing Hymn 385, Nearer My God to Thee, *and as the coffins were borne on the shoulders of the men of the Connaught Rangers to their last resting place, Mrs N. Goggin played the* Dead March in Saul *on the organ.*

The coffins were covered with beautiful wreaths sent by the following – Mrs S. L. Goggin, Mr and Mrs D. H. Acton, Miss Sheila Acton, Master Bob Acton, Mrs Tonson Rye, Mr and Mrs J. H. Crowley, Miss Wellis, Misses Daunt, Rev Dr Pearson and family, Mr and Mrs H. T. Daunt, Mrs Herrick, Mrs Popham, Mrs Warren Perry, Misses Pratt, Miss Herrick, Mr and Mrs E. E. Wolfe, Mr and Mrs R. A. Williams and Mrs Bleazby.

(CORK EXAMINER, 11 MAY 1915, P. 5)

The Captain's Tale
Kinsale Inquest Resumed

Another landmark was added to Kinsale's history yesterday when a coroner and jury inquired into the cause of the death of five victims who lost their lives in consequence of the barbarous system of warfare followed by the government of the German empire.

The story of the *Lusitania* is occupying the minds of the whole civilised world at the moment, and he would be a prophet indeed who could forecast with certainty the results that will arise from this deliberately planned piece of destruction.

Most of the leading newspapers of the three Kingdoms were represented at the inquest, and thousands of journals all over the world will publish full accounts of all that transpired. No wonder then that the townspeople should manifest the keenest interest in the event, and that the courthouse and its vicinity should be crowded.

Expectation ran high when it became known that the principal witness would be Captain Turner, the Commander of the ill-fated *Lusitania*. Perhaps it was the best thing that could be done to satisfy the natural eagerness to ascertain the real facts as to what occurred, to produce Captain Turner as a witness. Numerous passengers gave the story of their personal experiences, but none of these could know what was happening prior to the disaster as the Captain.

Various rumours were going about, and various comments made as to the action of the authorities and so on. A number of persons seemed to have got scraps of information on different points, but as usually happens in such cases the true facts turned out differently.

It was eleven o'clock when Mr Coroner J. J. Horgan, solr., resumed the inquest at the Courthouse on the five bodies lying in the mortuary at Kinsale military barracks.

District Inspector [Alfred] Wansborough said that the first witness he intended to examine that day was the Captain of the liner.

The Coroner – He has attended on my instructions.

District Inspector Wansborough – I now propose, sir, to call the Captain of the *Lusitania*.

The Coroner – Captain Turner now please.

Captain William Thomas Turner then deposed – I was acting as Captain of the *Lusitania* on her voyage –

District Inspector Wansborough – What we want the Captain to do is throw light on the wreck, and we will leave it to him to give facts as regards the occurrence.

The Coroner (to witness) – When did you leave New York, Captain? On the 1ˢᵗ May.

Had you personally received any warnings? No, only by the papers – that is all.

Did anything happen on the voyage that you wish to mention? Nothing whatever.

It was a voyage without incident up to the time of the tragedy? Quite so.

You were aware that threats had been made that this ship would be torpedoed? Fully aware of it.

Was she armed? No, sir.

What special precautions did you take in connection with those threats? I had all the boats served out and bulkheads and doors closed where they were likely to get at them.

That was when the ship came into the danger zone? Yes.

What time did you pass the Fastnet? About 11 a.m. on Friday I should think, sir.

Between that time and the time of the accident, did you see any submarines? None whatever. There was no sign of them.

I believe, Captain, there was some kind of a fog or a haze off the Irish Coast when you came to it? There was a fog near the Fastnet.

Captain Turner

Kinsale Town Hall

Dist. Insp Wansborough

Did you slow down speed then? Yes, I slowed her down to 15 knots.

I take it, Captain, that you were in wireless communication with the shore all the way across? Yes, all the way across. We received, but we did not send, you know.

Did you receive any message in reference to submarines being off the Irish Coast? Yes.

What was the nature of those messages, Captain? I respectfully refer you to the Admiralty, sir, about the answering of that question.

I will put it to you this way, Captain – Did you receive any message as to the sinking of a ship off the Old Head of Kinsale? No, sir.

District Inspector Wansborough – The *Earl of Latham* was the name of that vessel, sir.

The Coroner – Did you receive any special instructions? Yes, sir.

Are you at liberty to tell us what those instructions are? No, sir.

Did you carry them out? Yes, sir, to the best of my ability.

Tell us in your own words, Captain, what happened after you passed the Fastnet? The weather cleared up, and we had run a speed of 18 knots. I was on the port side of the lower deck, and I heard the second officer call out –

What is the name of the second officer? His name is Mr Hefford.

What did the second office call out? He called out: 'There is a torpedo'.

What did you do? I ran over to the other side and just saw the wake of it approaching the vessel, and it struck.

District Inspector Wansborough – What was the position of the vessel at the time – where were you? Fifteen miles south of Kinsale, I think.

The Coroner – Would you describe what happened next? There was an explosion and smoke and steam went up between the third and fourth funnels – and there was a slight shock to the vessel.

Would you tell us what speed the vessel was travelling at that particular time? Eighteen knots.

You could not say at what depth was the torpedo in the water? It would be almost on the surface. You could see that by the gush in the water.

Was there another explosion afterwards? Yes, directly after the first there was another report, but that might have been an internal explosion. The order was given to lower all the boats down to the rails and to get all the women and children into them.

Who gave that order, Captain? I did, and I wanted to stop the ship and could not do so, as the engines were out of commission. Therefore, it was not safe to lower the boats on account of the speed. It could not be done until the speed was off.

Was she stopped as a matter of fact? Not altogether. There was a perceptible motion on her when she went down.

When did she go down? The moment she was struck she listed to starboard, and –

District Inspector Wansborough – Where she was struck between the third and fourth engines [*sic*], was that where the engine room was situated? Yes.

The Coroner – I believe you remained on the bridge all the time, Captain? Yes, sir, and she went down from under me.

How long after she was struck did she sink? About 18 minutes I should imagine. It was a quarter past two by my watch when the explosion took place.

Give us the time when it stopped? It stopped at 2.36 and a quarter.

A Juror – That corresponds with the time in the watch found on one of the dead bodies and produced on Saturday last.

The Coroner – Yes, it does.

District Inspector Wansborough – You were picked up afterwards, Captain? Yes, about 2 hours or 3 hours. I was picked up from amongst the wreckage and was placed on a trawler.

The Coroner – At the time of the collision was there any warship convoying you? None whatever, and I did not see any. In fact there was none reported to me as having been seen.

Did you pick up any warship at the time that you came to the Irish coast? Not that I know of, sir.

Of course you would know of it if it were so? I did not see any.

District Inspector Wansborough – Were there many other passengers or people in the water around where you were picked up, Captain? No, I did not see anyone, only bodies around.

There were no live ones as far as you could see? No.

Would you know any of the five persons we are inquiring about today? I don't recognise any of them.

Do you know Capt. Richard Matthews who was a passenger on the *Lusitania*? No, sir.

There is therefore no use in showing you any of the pictures of these bodies? I don't think so, sir. I might have seen them, but I would not know them by name.

It has been said that the periscope of a submarine was seen? It might have been said, but I did not see it.

Is 18 knots, which you were travelling at, the normal speed of your vessel? No; in ordinary time she goes 25 knots.

Had you any special reason for only going 18 knots? In time of peace we go 25 knots, but in war times that has been reduced to 21 knots. I was going straight ahead to Liverpool for the purpose of arriving at the Bar.

The Coroner – You wanted to get to the Liverpool Bar for high water? Not exactly for high water, but two or three hours before full water, without stopping for a pilot.

Were those your instructions? Yes, sir, those are part of my instructions.

District Inspector Wansborough – Was there a lookout being kept on the *Lusitania* for submarines, having regard to the previous warning? There were double lookouts kept specially for submarines.

The Coroner – Is it true to say that you were going a zig-zag course at the time of the accident? No, sir.

District Inspector Wansborough – You had fair weather and you could see a long way? That is so, sir. You could see full range on the horizon, and there was smooth water.

You could see the land? Oh yes. We were about 15 miles from the Old Head, as far as I could judge.

As an experienced officer, do you think it possible, having regard to the lookout and the conditions of the weather, for a submarine to be there without being seen? Oh quite.

The Coroner – I believe, Captain, a submerged submarine is quite impossible to see? Yes, except in quite clear weather.

District Inspector Wansborough – In the evidence given on Saturday it was stated that there was an impossibility of launching the boats on the port side, and that they were only lowered to the rails on the starboard side? Owing to the list of the ship.

Of course if the boats were lowered on the port side they would be carried away by the motion of the ship? Quite so.

Can you say if any boats got into the water uninjured – how many boats were launched safely?

I cannot say that.

Were any boats launched safely? Oh yes, there were some, and one or two on the port side as well.

Were your orders promptly carried out according to your instructions, and was there any panic on board? Very little panic at all. All was calm.

All your orders were promptly obeyed and carried out? Yes. I could not find fault with anyone.

How long after you immersion did the rescuing vessel arrive in your opinion? I could not form any opinion. I have no opinion as to the lapse of time at all.

The Coroner – How many passengers had you on board, Captain? About 1,500, I think. And how many of a crew? I could not tell you, but I think it was about 600.

The Coroner – Thank you, Captain. I can quite understand that you cannot answer about all these things offhand.

A juror – Captain Turner, in face of the warnings you heard before you left New York about the vessel being torpedoed before she reached her destination did you make any particular application to the Admiralty for an escort? No, I did not. I leave that to them. It is their business. I simply carried out my orders to go, and I went, and I would do it again.

The Coroner – I am glad to hear you express yourself in that way, Captain, and I am sure you would do your duty again.

A juror (Mr Gleeson) – Is there any truth in the report, Captain, that you got a wireless to steer the vessel in a more northerly direction? No.

The Foreman – Did you alter the course of the vessel after being torpedoed? I headed right straight for the land, but the engines refused to work and it was useless.

Were the watertight compartments closed? They were all ordered to be closed, and also the doors previous to this.

Another juror – I suppose the explosion opened them again? It opened something, evidently.

The Coroner – And sank the ship.

A juror – In addition to all the precautions you have enumerated I take it that lifebelts were given to all the passengers? Yes.

Was any order given approaching the coast about danger, and if so, was it acted on? There was none.

The Foreman – When you gave the order to the crew about getting lifebelts for the passengers, was it obeyed? Yes. The order went round, and the passengers got the lifebelts.

The Coroner – Every cabin had lifebelts.

A juror (Mr Murphy) – I would like to know if the Captain is quite clear about no information being received by him before the terrible crime was committed.

The Coroner – Captain Turner, was any warning given to you before the submarine sent the torpedoes into you? None whatever, sir. It was straight and done with, and the whole lot went up in the air. It was straight and done and finished.

A juror – What is your opinion, Captain, as to whether there were any patrol boats on the look-out for you? That is a matter for the Admiralty.

If they had been there, would they have been of assistance? It might have helped, or it might not. You cannot tell what might have happened. They might have been torpedoed themselves.

The Coroner – It is a matter on which we cannot form an opinion.

Witness – That is so, sir.

The Coroner – We all sympathise with you, Captain, and the Cunard Company in the terrible crime that was committed against your vessel, and I also desire to express our appreciation of the great courage you showed – it was worthy of the traditions of the service to which you belong. We realise the deep feelings you must have in the matter.

Captain Turner, who was visibly affected – he wept for a brief time – acknowledged these expressions by bowing his head.

The Coroner – I also thank you for coming here and giving us such assistance in this inquiry.

Captain Turner – I am very much pleased, sir. I was glad to come and help in any way.

In accordance with the directions of the coroner, the jury returned the following verdict:

That the said deceased died from prolonged immersion and exhaustion in the sea eight miles south south-west of the Old Head of Kinsale, on Friday, May 7th, 1915, owing to the sinking of the *R. M. S. Lusitania* by torpedoes fired without warning from a German submarine.

We find that this appalling crime was contrary to international law and the conventions of all civilised nations, and we therefore charge the officers of the said submarine and the Emperor and Government of Germany, under whose orders they acted, with the crime of wilful and wholesale murder before the tribunal of the civilised world.

We desire to express our sincere condolence and sympathy with the relatives of the deceased, the Cunard Company, and the United States of America, so many of whose citizens perished in this murderous attack on an unarmed liner.

(CORK EXAMINER, 11 MAY 1915)

The jury was as follows – Michael Slattery (foreman), James Barry, Michael Murphy, John Murphy, Thomas Anglin, Michael Herlihy, John Cowhig, Charles J. Barry, John Barrett, Joseph H. Barry, Francis Kiernan, William Kelly, Francis Gleeson, and Richard Forde, Jr (14 members). The original jury issue paper, with its historic finding, was sold to the National Maritime Museum in Greenwich for £3,000 in 1997 by the family of Coroner John Joseph Horgan. The money went to the Royal National Lifeboat Institution.

'A Ramshackle Chamber'

The following brief report, teeming with contempt for everything Irish, appears in the *Evening News*, London, on the Inquest held on five victims of the *Lusitania* held at Kinsale. It is regrettable that such a peculiarly sad occasion should be used as a lever to ventilate false impressions of the south of Ireland:

> In a little courthouse here, an ancient building with still more ancient and primitive furniture, the first official inquiry into the Lusitania disaster was continued today.
>
> In this old ramshackle chamber in the Irish village, Captain Turner, who was in command of the Lusitania, gave to the world his account of the disaster, his audience comprising of a few fishermen and a jury of Irish peasants.

(CORK COUNTY EAGLE, 22 MAY, 1915, P.11)

Aftermath

The German Question

LETTER TO THE CHIEF SECRETARY OF IRELAND (in National Archives):

May 18th 1915

Dear Sir,

I have a German governess whom I wish to get rid of, to send her back to England, and if necessary on to Germany. I want to find out how I can do this, as if it was local police it may take so long and I want to get rid of her as soon as possible.

Can you give me any information as to what steps to take? My husband, Brigadier General Caulfield is in England working, and I don't want a German in the house. I am sorry to trouble you, but I don't know whom to apply to.

Truly yours,
Alice Caulfield.

Mrs Caulfield and her brigadier general husband lived at Inishannon House, Inishannon, Co. Cork. The chief secretary's office advised her to write to the under secretary of state at the Home Office.

ALIEN MANAGERS OF IRISH HOTELS
TO THE EDITOR OF THE DAILY EXPRESS

Sir – Now that the Government is taking steps to intern enemy aliens, it is to be hoped that amongst these will be included a number of German hotel managers and proprietors who live in this country. I myself know of a hotel in the south of Ireland, situated in a district which I am told is a 'prohibited area', where not only is the proprietor a German (though naturalised), but the manager is also a German and not naturalised.

It seems strange that, with so many military officers frequenting this and other hotels, the authorities do not yet seem to be informed of the state of affairs. Do they know that in one hotel, which is managed by a German, the spy Lody once stayed?

Yours etc.,
A Constant Reader

(DAILY EXPRESS, 15 MAY 1915, P. 10)

QUEEN'S HOTEL, QUEENSTOWN
PROPRIETOR'S NATIONALITY
QUESTIONS IN PARLIAMENT

In the House of Commons yesterday Mr Joynson Hicks asked the first lord of the Admiralty whether he was aware that the proprietor of the Queen's Hotel, Queenstown, overlooking the harbour and the Navy anchorage was a German and could not speak English properly; and whether, having regard to the presence of enemy submarines off Queenstown he would take immediate steps to have this German removed?

Dr McNamara replied in a written answer that a German naturalised in 1905 had for some years managed the Queen's Hotel, Queenstown. His wife is English. He has been under supervision since the outbreak of war, but up to the present there has been nothing against him. Nevertheless the question contained in the closing part of the question will be considered.

(CORK EXAMINER, 20 MAY 1915, P. 4)

Hotelier Otto Humbert did three things when he heard of the sinking: he ordered rooms prepared for the survivors, cancelled the string orchestra booked for the Saturday night and retired to his wine cellar.

GERMANS IN DUBLIN

TO THE EDITOR OF THE *IRISH TIMES*

Sir – It may not be generally known to the public that Germans are still employed in Dublin. Yesterday I was surprised to find a German assistant working in a first-class establishment in the city. After the recent outrages of the Huns, surely it would be a good thing if all persons made it a rule to give their patronage only where Germans are not employed? – Yours, etc.

R. G. Alexander, Major.
Newtown, Straffan, Co. Kildare, May 12th 1915.

(IRISH TIMES, 13 MAY 1915, P. 7)

A German woman being taken to a police station for safety after Lusitania rioters in Britain wrecked her bakery.

THE LUSITANIA MASSACRE

Sir – Following a horrifying list of atrocities, a deliberately-planned and skilfully executed murder of some 1,500 defenceless people has been perpetrated by the German Navy almost at our very door.

With characteristic savagery these butchers have not discriminated in favour of either woman or child; there was neither pity nor hesitation; there can be neither defence nor denial.

In our city, and in other cities and towns throughout Ireland, many Germans reside, who are permitted to carry on their trades, professions and occupations and to enjoy practically the same freedoms as we do ourselves. So far as I am aware, they have not either individually or as a body made a public protest against the inhuman outrages perpetrated by their fellow countrymen.

Are we to assume from their silence that they tacitly approve of these acts, and if so, is it right of us not only to tolerate in our midst, but to actively support, the compatriots of the murderers of our kith and kin?

Yours etc,

T. J. O'Callaghan

73 Grand Parade, Cork.

(Cork Constitution, 11 May 1915)

THE SERVANT QUESTION

In the largest of the servants' agencies it was stated yesterday that German servants had been dismissed almost everywhere and that the German cook was rare in English families.

In one of the German women's associations, on the contrary, it was said that though German servants were dismissed at the beginning of the war, many applications were afterwards received from Englishwomen, overwhelmed by the servant difficulty, for German cooks, and these women, unless they have been dismissed as a result of the present outcry, are perhaps the only German women in British employment.

(The Times, 13 May 1915, p. 10)

Patriotic British people will be glad to know that the valuable drug sold under the German trade name of Aspirin is now being prescribed and supplied by chemists under the British trade name of Helicon. Its chemical constitution is identical in every particular.

(The Illustrated London News, 13 October 1914)

The Lusitania's Mails

The Postmaster-General announces that only about eighty bags of mails were despatched by the Lusitania, *the bulk of the United States mail having been forwarded from New York by the American liner* New York, *which sailed the same day as the* Lusitania.

(Cork Examiner, 10 May 1915, p. 8)

A US mailbag washed ashore from the wreck is on permanent display in Kinsale museum. One of the *Lusitania*'s lifeboat davits, snared by a fishing vessel, lies outside. The collection includes a ship's deckchair.

A church in Castletownsend has an oar, while a 90-year-old 'Ixion' ship's biscuit, taken from a recovered *Lusitania* lifeboat on Sunday 9 May 1915 (by one J. Law of Templebreedy) is preserved in the museum at Scot's Church, Cobh.

The National Museum at Collins Barracks in

Dublin holds an oar branded with the ship's name, recovered on the Clare coast near Kilkee on 20 August 1915. Also on display here (out-of-storage room 2, first floor; cabinet 4, shelf 5) is a *Lusitania* lifebuoy picked up by the Dublin steam trawler *Dean Swift* on 21 May 1915, some 72 nautical miles NNW of the Fastnet Rock.

Money in Death

Offers of a reward of £1 have been made by the Cunard Company for each body recovered and £2 by the American Consul if it should prove to be an American. For the recovery of the body of Mr [Alfred Gwynne] Vanderbilt, a reward of £200 is offered.

(THE TIMES, 14 MAY 1915, P. 5)

VANDERBILT'S BODY
SUPPOSED TO BE WASHED ASHORE AT CLARE
THURSDAY

A body, believed to be that of Mr Vanderbilt, the American millionaire, who was lost in the Lusitania, *was ashore last night on the Clare coast, north of Moher cliffs. The pockets contained gold and also a gold watch, with monogram corresponding to Vanderbilt's initials.*

(THE KERRYMAN, 12 JUNE 1915, P. 8)

In fact, Mr Vanderbilt's body was never recovered. His fortune was estimated at $75 million in 1915, which should be multiplied by 15 for its value at the beginning of the twenty-first century.

US Consul Wesley Frost wrote: 'Mr Walter Webb Ware, representing the Vanderbilt estate, spent a fortnight at Queenstown and along the south-western coast; and his pains-taking management of the search for Mr Vanderbilt's body was of general value to all the relatives interested in having the coast inhabitants aroused to the desirability of searching for and reporting corpses.

'Mr Ware offered, through the Consulate, a reward of four hundred pounds for the re-covery of Mr Vanderbilt's remains, a sum equally as potent to the minds of the Kerry fishers as would have been four hundred thousand pounds'.

Meanwhile the London insurance houses estimated they had paid out £100,000 on 350 life policies by the beginning of June – meaning an average of around £300 for each in-dividual.

The rewards being offered by families or an individual's company led to parties of speculators scouring the coves and headlands of Ireland, with the Vanderbilt body under-standably seen as the Holy Grail.

One team of Kerry body-finders, William O'Connor, Pat Donoghue and Pat Leen, dis-covered the body of Lindon Bates, a New York financier and first-class passenger. His re-mains were washed up near Tralee on 19 July. There was a reward of £150.

Lindell Bates was arrested at Kinsale in the company of an American friend while searching the coast for his brother's body. Wet-trousered, they had been mistaken for German U-boat officers who were coming ashore. The pair were eventually released after strenuous representations by the US consul.

The day after finding Bates, the team discovered the body of a man of fine physique, of about 50 years, at Meeagahane, Causeway, Co. Kerry. The corpse had visiting cards bearing the name of Harry J. Keser, and a gold watch with the same initials. Mr Keser was a vice president of the National Bank of Phila-delphia, another first-class passenger. He also had a life insurance policy on his

Lindon
Bates

body. The remains of his wife, Mary, had already been found on another strand 120 miles away.

The bodies of both Bates and Keser were forwarded to New York on the ss *St Paul*, sailing from Queenstown on 31 July.

'Many were out on the headlands, north, south, east and west, others up at cock-crow next morning in search of the millionaires ...'

So wrote Muiris Ó Súilleabháin in his book about Blasket Island life entitled *Fiche Bliain ag Fás* (*Twenty Years A-Growing*). He also wrote of his father and uncle putting off in a currach to retrieve a body from the sea:

> They had it tied now, and were turning home. We stayed as we were till they came towards the Point. 'On my oath, Liam, it is a human body. Do you see it standing straight down in the water?'
> 'You are right, for that is a lifebuoy under its head'.
> Shortly afterwards, with a pull from the rope, the pale face turned towards us in the sunlight. We ran down to the quay.
> It was a terrible sight, the eyes plucked out by the gulls, the face swollen, and the clothes ready to burst from the swelling of the body.
> 'What's that you had?' said Eileen to my father when they came home.
> 'A dead body'.
> 'And what will you do with it?'
> 'Oh, we will bring it home,' said he, smiling.
> I went out to the door. I saw a currach making for the quay, and I thought it was peelers were in it. I ran back in excitement.
> 'The peelers are come to the quay,' I cried, and my father got up from the table.
> He went to speak to the sergeant. It was arranged to take the body to Dunquin, so that the peelers could take care of it till its people would take it.
> They went down to the quay, and I slipped into the currach, my father, my uncle and myself in one of them, and the peelers in the currach from Dunquin. When we reached the Great Cliff, the body was taken out and stretched on the quay.
> The sergeant began searching the pockets, all of us looking on, but soon he drew back again. The smell was too strong. No one had the courage to go near it.

> But there was one old man called Mick of the Hill standing beside us with his hands in his pockets. He walked up and stood over the body. He put a foot on each side of it, took his hands from his pockets, looked first at us and then at the body. He went down on his knees and began to open the coat.
> When he had the coat and vest open, he put his hand in one of the pockets and drawing out a small diary, he handed it to the sergeant.
> In the other pockets were found a watch and gold chain, a comb, a mirror and three sixpences. 'Keep the sixpences yourself', said the sergeant. 'You have earned them well'. 'Musha, God leave you your health, my son,' said Mick, putting them in his pocket.
> They all helped to carry the body to the top of the cliff. Then they laid it in the sergeant's motor car and went off with it to Ballyferriter.

Royal Irish Constabulary men on a coastal patrol in Connemara in 1915

Kinsale Memorial

A memorial stone was unveiled at the Old Head of Kinsale on 7 May 1995, the eightieth anniversary of the disaster. The circular block of Kilkenny limestone faces the entrance to the Old Head golf course, leading to the lighthouse where the calamity was witnessed by watchkeepers. Brian Little carved the stone and it features a stylised representation of the sinking by British artist Stuart Williamson. A local committee raised the necessary funds, the stone was donated by the golf course developer, and local farmer Dan Buckley donated the plot of land.

The original notes made of the sinking by the lighthouse men were stolen from the archives of the Commissioners of Irish Lights after a foreign individual had sought access to the material for research purposes some years ago. They were later sold in America.

At the unveiling by Minister for the Marine Hugh Coveney, Courtmacsherry lifeboat placed a wreath on the sea over the location of the wreck and fired a signal flare to honour the dead.

The Old Head of Kinsale lighthouse is eleven miles south of the town. The tower stands 98ft high (30 metres), and the light beam has an intensity of 800,000 candles. The light can seen for 25 nautical miles. The *Lusitania* was taking a four-point navigational fix on the Old Head when she was hit.

At the time of the sinking, the lighthouse bore two red bands instead of the black bands seen today. The beam provided a double flash every ten seconds, worked by a clockwork apparatus. In 1972 the light was converted to electric, and fully automated by 1987, resulting in the withdrawal of keepers. It is now in the care of a part-time attendant, thus necessitating that visitors make an appointment with the Commissioners of Irish Lights. Those who pre-arrange access will be rewarded with a demanding climb and spectacular views to the place where the *Lusitania* went down.

The vicinity of the wreck also provides fishing for conger and pollack, and a day trip to the location can be arranged privately through Kinsale boat owners.

The Lusitania *passing the Old Head of Kinsale on a westbound voyage, circa 1911*

Legacy and Memory

When the bodies were buried and the pits filled in, the population of Queenstown could go back to their normal lives – for a while. The war still raged, and many more survivors would soon be landed in the port from other sinkings. The next most prominent sinking after the *Lusitania,* was the *Arabic,* which had the unwanted distinction of becoming the first White Star liner sunk in wartime.

The *Arabic* was torpedoed on 19 August 1915, some 50 miles from the Old Head of Kinsale. She sank faster than the *Lusitania* – in eleven minutes at most – but only 44 lives were lost as she settled evenly by the stern. A total of 390 were rescued and landed at Queenstown, three months after the *Lusitania* survivors had trudged the same streets.

Like the *Lusitania,* the *Arabic,* followed by the *Laconia* and others, prompted diplomatic notes of outrage from the Wilson administration to Germany, yet the great power to the west chose still not to enter the war.

Meanwhile salvaged lifeboats were being sold off in Queenstown, and as the graves began grassing over, there was already talk of erecting a permanent *Lusitania* memorial.

Six *Lusitania* lifeboats were corralled in the harbour at Queenstown within hours of the tragedy. They were boats number 1, 11, 13, 15, 19, and 21 – and they quickly became the playgrounds of small boys, dimly aware that something momentous had happened.

The odd numbers show that it was only the starboard lifeboats that were successfully launched and taken in tow or brought in by rescue vessels. A further ten lifeboats and life rafts were eventually salvaged – among them rafts that were lashed to the deck, designed to float off a sinking ship.

The subsequent disposal of these lifeboats and life rafts led to an extraordinary letter emanating from the Cunard Company:

> Cunard Steam Ship Company, Queenstown
> 25th March 1916
>
> A. Hanlon Esq.
> Receiver of Wreck
> Baltimore.

Top: exercising Lusitania's lifeboats before the liner left New York
Below: some little boys playing in the Lusitania lifeboats on the Queenstown waterfront in the wake of the tragedy

> Dear Sir,
> We beg to apply for refund of £8, Lloyds expenses and commission, paid you in connection with the salvage of 'Lusitania' boats etc picked up in your district. We also beg to apply for relief in connection with the sum of £2 4/-which you inform us in yours of 14th ult. is still outstanding.
>
> As you are aware, this property when sold did not realise anything like the combined cost of salvage and expenses: and the recovery, instead of being any benefit, became a heavy loss. It would have been much better, had we known the wretchedly poor prices obtainable, to have handed the articles over to the salvors.

Under the circumstances, of which you are already fully aware, the property salved was worse than valueless, and consequently no commission or expenses should, in our opinion, be charged.

Trusting to receive a favourable reply, and with apologies for trouble, we are, yours faithfully, The Cunard Steam Ship Company.

A life raft recovered on 10 May had been valued at £20, and the salvor paid £3. But at the sale by the Receiver of Wreck it only realised £1.5s, which was cancelled out for Cunard by a commission payment and Lloyd's fees.

Another raft, valued at £40, saw £6 salvage paid. It was subsequently sold for only £2 10s, with fees wiping out all but 5s for the company.

The company meanwhile paid another £6 bounty for a lifeboat recovered on 12 May and also valued at £40. It later sold for £5, but £2 5s came out of that in charges. A life raft found the same day saw £3 salvage paid, and was sold for £2, with £1 2s 6d to pay in sales costs.

A 'slightly damaged' life raft attracted the same charges, and in the next case there was no sale, despite the salvor getting £3 on a £20 valuation. By 26 May, the company was paying only 10s for one salvaged raft, while another had been adjudged 'not worth moving'. A further craft was handed over *gratis* by the Cunard agent to the salvor as valueless.

In a report to the Board of Trade in light of Cunard's application for relief from fees, the Receiver of Wreck noted sympathetically:

> Cunard had arranged with Messrs Palmer, Cork, to remove the rafts at Baltimore on which salvage and commission had been paid, but the steamer sent to remove same was unable to hoist them on board. She then took lifeboat 33* alongside, and during the night the boat came ashore at Baltimore and was much damaged. (*Number refers to droit 33, not boat 33 – a droit is an entitlement to wreck under admiralty law.)

The Customs and Excise, in a submission from the South Munster district, agreed that Cunard was entitled to some refund, pointing out that the fees had been charged on estimated values which turned out to be hopelessly optimistic.

The local Cunard agent had informed them, said Customs, that the company 'have lost considerably over the property salved from this ship, *Lusitania*, and that the charges have been considerably greater than the amount realised by sale'. It was 'consequently submitted that where these fees have been paid, that they be returned'.

But in May 1916 the Board of Trade adhered to legal advice that repayments might set a dangerous precedent, and Cunard's application was refused.

Some of the *Lusitania*'s lifeboats undoubtedly had a new life with local fishermen and water enthusiasts. A large *Lusitania* lifeboat, in perfect order, was washed ashore at Clogher, Ballyferriter, Co Kerry, on Friday 23 July 1915, according to the next day's issue of the *Cork County Eagle*.

Another lifeboat was converted into a ferry-vessel that brought pilgrims from shore to Our Lady's Island in Co. Wexford. It lasted well into the 1930s.

Other craft, meanwhile, were more immediately deployed in propaganda stunts. *Lusitania* boats were displayed through Cork, London and other cities and towns.

The *Cork Examiner* of 22 March 1916, carried two photographs of such a procession, reporting that 'Doctor Macaura intends to visit the principal cities and towns of England to solicit funds for the heroes who are engaged in the perilous work of mine-sweeping ... He will speak to his audiences on the story of the *Lusitania*, and will show one of the rafts that came ashore on the South Coast of Ireland. Yesterday the raft was paraded in procession through Cork, military bands, the Macaura silver band taking part, the military authorities, the Boys Brigade, and the Boy Scouts providing guards of honour'.

A Lusitania *model paraded through the streets on London on* Lusitania Day, *1916. (The* Sphere*) Lent by the Cunard Company, the model was drawn on a draped lorry from Westminster to Hyde Park. Some survivors of the disaster are among those members of the public immediately following.*

A raft from the Lusitania *on which ten bodies were washed ashore on the Irish coast will be driven through the chief streets of London on a lorry and will be offered for sale in the early part of the afternoon at Messrs Woods' Riding School, Brompton Road. The raft came into the possession of Mr Macaura who has used it for some time in a recruitment campaign in Ireland.*

(THE TIMES, 18 OCTOBER 1916, P. 11)

The raft was bought by Mr Don Mason who took it to Broadstairs, Kent, where it was donated to a school.

The Cobh Lusitania Memorial

The magnificent *Lusitania* memorial in Cobh today is a fitting tribute to those who died. But it was not completed before a long-running saga of neglect had blighted the enterprise.

Sculptor Jerome Connor (1876–1943) was commissioned to carry out the work by an American committee which included Franklin D. Roosevelt. The original idea was to inscribe the name of all the victims on the base, although they numbered nearly 1,200.

Connor returned to Ireland from the United States in 1930 to begin the ambitious project, but the London newspapers reported that shopkeepers in Cobh objected to the design on the grounds that it would 'obstruct their fronts too much'.

It took a further six years – until 1936 – before full-size wax models were ready for casting in bronze. Only the base of the monument, devoid of names, had been prepared before the Second World War intervened. By the time it was over, the sculptor had died and the money run out. The memorial then stood unfinished for another 20 years.

'A storm blew up yesterday over a bid to end the 52-year-old controversy of the unfinished *Lusitania* memorial', reported the *Sunday People* in December 1966. The newspaper reported a spokesman for the Arts Council, which was seeking to complete the work, as saying: 'Few people in Cobh seem particularly interested in the memorial. No one wants to accept responsibility for it. They have let it fall to pieces. The fishermen's hands are damaged and all of the metal inscription has been picked off the base. People don't seem to realise that this memorial is the most impressive example of Connor's genius to be found anywhere'.

A file in the Irish National Archives shows that the struggle to complete the memorial had taken on new urgency in 1964, with the looming of the fiftieth anniversary of the sinking in May 1965.

Sculptor Domhnall Ó Murchada (Donal Murphy) had managed to save the original casts for what was to be a crowning Angel of Peace atop the structure. He wrote a letter to the Department of External Affairs in Dublin, emphasising that the project was on a par with Michelangelo's *David* in Florence – and demanding action. This is his argument:

The *Lusitania* Memorial at Cobh, when completed, would be Ireland's only major contribution to the art of European sculpture since Edward Smith and the nameless masters of the figured High Crosses.

[Jerome Connor's] work is unique in these islands and one seeks comparative artistic achievement in the old cultures of Europe. Certain of the twentieth century French masters may surpass him in artistry at times, to be surpassed by him in turn in his greater humanity.

The present condition of this memorial shows little appreciation of its importance either historically or aesthetically. A certain amount of carelessness, occasioned by the memorial surround and base lying unoccupied by its figures over the war years, is perhaps understandable. But the loss of a forefinger from the youthful bronze figure some time after its erection calls for investigation and vigilance.

Were it realised that a treasure as remarkable in our century as the *Book of Durrow* or *Kells* in their time lies open to wanton destruction on a public street, some positive action would be taken. The problem is not unknown elsewhere. The Fonte Gaia in Siena has been removed to the civic museum while a copy replaces it across the street. Similarly the Florentines in the last century removed Donatello's *St George* and Michelangelo's *David* to the Bargello and the Academy respectively, replacing them out of doors with copies.

Some public protection and care should be afforded a masterpiece in a public place. In the case of this memorial, its lamps should be lighted, its inscription replaced, and any pointing necessary for the preservation of the stonework surround carried out immediately.

The replacement of the inscription might enlighten American and other visitors and prevent them annoying the local shopkeepers! Then the Angel of Peace should be cast into bronze and erected on its pedestal above the carved frieze of seagulls.

The completed plaster model for the figure of the Angel was in the sculptor's studio at his death in 1943. It was saved from being carted to the city dumping ground when vacant possession of the studio was sought by the new tenant through my overhearing a conversation about the delays involved. I took over the figure, have held it since, and shall continue to do so.

To friends who come to see it I can only say that I store it out of pride, as a national treasure, in the hope that one day the nation may awake to its greatness. However the life of plaster cannot be guaranteed.

Domhnall Ó Murchada, Assistant Professor of Sculpture,
National College of Art; Lecturer on the History of Art.

Even this complaint to the government, laced with conscientious indignation, might not have had the desired effect were it not for a fortuitous turn of events that underscored the importance of the points at issue.

A second letter arrived with the authorities soon thereafter, addressed to the Taoiseach, 'Seán Lemass, Prime Minister of Eire', from an ordinary American citizen. The gentleman in question, Thomas J. Fox, had fired his torpedo at just the right moment.

52 Robin Road
West Hartford, Connecticut.
April 1965.

Mr. Sean Lemass,
Prime Minister, Eire,
Your Excellency,

a letter sent by me to several American newspapers, enclosed, a copy of which, I believe, is self explanatory.

I took the liberty of writing you as I believed you would be interested in the matter. Is there anything that can be done to keep alive the memory of these poor souls.

Perhaps some way could be found to have the inscription cut into the stone base of the monument permanently.

I am a native of Ballyshannon, Donegal, who emigrated in March 1888 at the age of two years.

Please accept my thanks for any interest you may be able to take in this matter.

Very respectfully yours,
Thomas J Fox

Fox enclosed a letter he had sent to several American newspapers complaining of the unfinished memorial. It read:

Dear Editor,

At the waterfront of Cobh (formerly Queenstown), Ireland, there is a beautiful statue of two exhausted seamen struggling onto the beach. A stranger is puzzled to understand its significance. The bronze letters have been removed by souvenir hunters or vandals.

The monument commemorates the one hundred sixty-eight unidentified victims of the steamship *Lusitania* whose bodies were recovered and buried in the churchyard on the hilltop overlooking the harbor, after the ship was torpedoed and sunk May fifth [sic] 1915, by a German submarine in the nearby waters.

I visited the cemetery a few years ago when I stopped overnight in Cobh. It was noontime; the sun broke through clouds as the church bells tolled the Angelus. The wavelets sparkled in the bay below me; the hills beyond were green with the foliage of subtropical County Cork. The scene was quiet, peaceful and beautiful beyond my ability to describe. It was very lonely and extremely sad, the last resting place of so many unidentified Americans known only to God.

An ocean stretched between them and their homeland. No starry flag waved above them. A stone marker was inscribed '*Lusitania*, May 5 1915'. [sic – marker says May 7, date of the sinking] Three other stone tablets on the separate plots enumerated 'Fifty', 'Fifty', and 'Sixty Eight'. The sod is neatly mown and the boxwood is carefully trimmed.

There they rest in peace, forgotten, unvisited by the thousands of Americans who pass through this port yearly. Should they not be remembered next May fifth, the fiftieth anniversary of their deaths? Have we forgotten that we went to war for them?

Fox's letter produced immediate results. The Taoiseach asked for the views of the Minister for External Affairs on the 'dilapidated condition of the *Lusitania* memorial at Cobh'. The minister said he was of the opinion 'that the incomplete and neglected condition of this memorial will continue to give rise to adverse criticism in the United States and other countries, and I consider that it would be politic to arrange for its completion and proper maintenance. Such a step would enhance Ireland's good name abroad, and would also be appreciated, not only in the Cork area, but in Ireland as a whole'.

The minister advised that in the special circumstances of the case, the Arts Council should be asked to arrange for the completion of the monument in accordance with the sculptor's design, the monument then to be entrusted to the care of the Office of Public Works.

In a letter to the Taoiseach's office, the minister's private secretary noted sardonically: 'Both the Cobh Urban District Council and *Bord Fáilte* [The Irish Tourist Board] are anxious that the memorial be completed, but neither body is prepared to undertake any expenditure in this regard'.

The Department of the Taoiseach ordered the Arts Council to oversee completion of the monument, and other bodies to cooperate. Nothing could be done however in time for the fiftieth anniversary, and 7 May 1965 came and went.

In early June, however the Arts Council wrote to the Taoiseach's private secretary to say that it now had an estimate for the casting of the Angel in bronze so that the memorial could be completed. It confirmed that: 'Bord Fáilte has undertaken to renew the lighting system and the three inscriptions, point the stonework, clean the surfaces, and open a recess in the pedestal at a cost of £300'.

But it went on to report that 'conversations with artistic interests in Cork City and business interests elsewhere failed to interest them in the completion, but after a long correspondence with Cobh Urban District Council, that body agreed to accept responsibility for the care and maintenance of the memorial if and when presented to them in a completed state'.

The council reported that it had instigated the creation of a local fundraising committee in Cobh in February 1965 under the chairmanship of J. J. Wilson, 17 Casement Square. But

> in order not to encourage any laxity in fund collection on the part of the local committee, this office has not informed the committee or the local authority of the exact terms of the Art Council's decision which authorised me as Secretary to incur 'such necessary expenditure from the Council's funds as may be necessary to restore and complete the memorial in the manner intended by the sculptor'.

The committee managed to raise only £50 towards the £300 target. Perhaps news of the Arts Council's secret commitment to complete funding had leaked out. The Secretary, Mervyn Wall, told the Taoiseach that the Arts Council would 'see to it' that the monument was 'brought to a successful conclusion'. That eventually happened by 1970.

The Sculptor

The single theme of his *Lusitania* work was to be the Angel of Peace, but sculptor Jerome Connor petitioned the American sponsors to approve his own idea of depicting mourning fishermen who had worked to recover the living and the dead. This was agreed, but it had to accompany the angel, not replace it.

Jerome Connor

Connor eventually found the face of his angel in Annie Stephens, who lived near his workshop in Dublin. He took a plaster mask of her features – and Annie would blame the process for giving her eczema for years afterwards. The bust for the statue, incidentally, came from a cast made of Annie's daughter Patricia.

Connor was declared bankrupt in 1938, by which time his wife had left him, taking their daughter. The sculptor died in poverty five years later. He is buried in Mount Jerome cemetery.

The inscriptions on the memorial read *Siochán in Ainm Dé* (Peace in God's Name) and *Laborare est Orare* (To Work is to Pray).

Unfinished Lusitania *memorial at Cobh*

Right: The face for the Angel: Annie Stephens of Dublin. Also Annie's great granddaughter, Lorna Little, holding the original facial cast for the statue

Rediscovery and Exploitation

The idea of finding and salvaging the *Lusitania* may have occurred during the Great War, but no civilian plan could be put into effect during hostilities. After a few years of peace, however, the notion began to rise.

In 1922, the *Nationalische Volkes Partei* or National People's Party of Germany proposed an international scientific exploration to establish whether the vessel was indeed laden with the military materiel that might have justified her sinking as a man-of-war. There was little enthusiasm among the neutrals urged to undertake the task, and the idea was eventually dropped. That same year, however, the *Belfast Weekly News* reported:

> THE LUSITANIA
> PROPOSAL TO RAISE HER
> PHILADELPHIA, 9TH MAY (1922) –

An expedition for salving the Lusitania *and a number of other ships sunk during the past few years will start from here on 25th inst. The steamship* Blakeney *has been chartered for the purpose by the* Lusitania *Salvaging Company. It is not expected that there will be great difficulty in raising the* Lusitania, *as her exact position is known.*

REUTER

This front page report was startling in its claim that the Cunarder's exact position had been determined. If the *Blakeney* had found her, then the *Lusitania* Salvaging Company could have tested its assertion that there would not be any great difficulty in raising the 30,000 ton vessel from 50 fathoms. It seems likely these claims were aimed at drawing in financial backing for the Philadelphia-based enterprise, but there is no evidence that a vessel was ever commissioned for such a mission.

Three years later, ten years after the sinking, a diver named B. F. Leavitt of Brooklyn, New York, inserted the following classified advertisement in the columns of the *Times*:

Lusitania: *I am open for financing to salvage* Lusitania. *Complete system, holding world's deep sea salvage, lighting, diving records from actual operations. Proof available.*

(THE TIMES, 29 AUGUST 1925, P. 1)

Little came of this proposed expedition, although Leavitt set up a *Lusitania* Salvage Club of starry-eyed backers and engaged in some correspondence with the admiralty in 1926, to be disappointingly told that there was no bullion aboard.

The next effort was to be far more substantial. Late in 1931 two American

Popular Mechanics Magazine
WRITTEN SO YOU CAN UNDERSTAND IT
Vol. 57   FEBRUARY, 1932   No. 2

LUSITANIA TREASURE *to be* RAISED

DOWN a steel-incased stairway inside a 200-foot tube, deep-sea divers expect to descend soon to the wreck of the historic "Lusitania," sunk in 240 feet of water eight miles off the Irish coast, in 1915, by a German submarine. From the end of this ocean stair, the divers propose to step onto the decks of the ill-fated liner and, with the aid of powerful submarine searchlights, will search every foot of the vessel, salvaging all articles of historic and intrinsic value, including the purser's safe and its contents.

The salvaging expedition is under the direction of Simon Lake, maker of submarines and inventor of the tube that is to be used, which was tested recently in the English channel. By employing this

Above, Top of "Stairway" Leading Down into Atlantic; Below, Lowering Powerful Submarine Lights

tube, Mr. Lake asserts the venture has been made as simple as "going down in an elevator" and less hazardous and difficult than other salvaging operations that have been carried out successfully.

entrepreneurs, Hilton Railey and Simon Lake, decided to find, photograph and salvage the *Lusitania*. Lake was a diving expert, while Railey later played a role in Admiral Byrd's expeditions to the Antarctic. Papers in the Irish National Archives show that Lake and Railey costed their operations carefully and sought help and advice from the Free State government.

Sponsors were brought in who made cash contributions in the hope of benefiting from the subsequent publicity, including the *New York Times*, the North American Newspaper Alliance, and a subsidiary of the Paramount motion picture company, as well as Westinghouse Lamps, who would provide the illumination for pioneering underwater photography.

The objectives of the mission were to achieve pictures at undreamt-of depths, and to salvage the purser's safe on A Deck, other safes, and anything else that appeared worthwhile. Lake and Railey obtained a contract for the dive from the Liverpool and London War Risks Insurance Association, which owned the remains, having been the insurer for her final voyage.

The explorers agreed not to penetrate the holds of the vessel and not to concern themselves with the question of contraband. It was their stated intention to 'avoid the international political issues' of the wreck. The expedition was to begin in the early months of 1932.

Captain Railey went to Kinsale to scout for skilled crew, accommodation and ship repair facilities. The Irish government, approached through its high commissioner in London, indicated it had no objection to the work, although any artefacts landed in the country would immediately become the legal property of the Receiver of Wrecks.

The Department of Industry and Commerce recommended that the Americans approach Ralph Palmer of Palmer Bros, Ship Owners and Repairers, of Marlboro Street, Cork, and Richard Wallace, Chairman of Cork Harbour Commissioners. It said they would give 'every assistance towards establishing a base for the expedition and executing any repair work that may be necessary'.

In February 1932, *Popular Mechanics* magazine reported:

Ralph Palmer, left, and Richard Wallace, right.

> Down a steel-incased stairway inside a 200-foot tube, deep-sea divers expect to descend soon to the wreck of the historic *Lusitania*, sunk in 240 feet of water eight miles off the Irish coast in 1915 by a German submarine. From the end of this ocean stair, the divers propose to step onto the decks of the ill-fated liner, and with the aid of powerful submarine searchlights, will search every foot of the vessel, salvaging all articles of historic and intrinsic value, including the purser's safe and all its contents.

The magazine said that Simon Lake, the maker of the steel tube, had already tested it in the English Channel. It quoted him as stating that the venture had been made 'as simple as going down in an elevator', and less hazardous than other salvaging operations that had been carried out successfully.

Hilton Railey, left, and Simon Lake. Believed they could dive and photograph the Lusitania wreck in 1932 using steel pipes and even a metal-enclosed staircase. They liaised with the Irish government

Inevitable delays came about, but on 14 April 1932 (the twentieth anniversary of the *Titanic* hitting an iceberg) the *Cork Examiner* reported:

The *Lusitania*
Hopes of Salvaging Valuables

New York, Wednesday – Captain Hilton H. Railey of the Lake Railey *Lusitania* Expedition, who hopes to salvage valuable portions of the cargo of the *Lusitania* by descending to the decks of the vessel through a steel tube, left New York last night in the *Bremen* with a number of commissions from private individuals anxious to recover personal property.

One woman lost a pearl necklace valued at 100,000 dollars which has been lying in one of the safes of the *Lusitania* since 1915. Captain Turney (*sic*), who was in command at the time of the sinking, has asked Captain Railey to recover his sextant from the chartroom.

Captain Railey expects to find the vessel in an upright position and the hull intact. The construction of the tube with an interior ladder down which the salvage party will descend is not expected to be completed for three months, says a *London Times* telegram, *per* Press Association.

It quickly became apparent however that the ambitious steel tube, designed to house a staircase for the divers, was not long enough. Hilton and Railey had wrongly believed the *Lusitania* was standing almost upright on the ocean floor, with the tops of her stacks 'only 175 feet below the surface'. In fact she was lying on her starboard side and had become considerably compressed. The elaborate tube, designed to withstand 85lbs of pressure, with an 8ft-wide observation room at one end, was never up to the job. By 1933 the project was dead.

A year later came new excitement:

The Lake/Railey tube system was literally a shortsighted idea, as it could not be lengthened to meet the Lusitania's unexpected depth. Instead of climbing a stairway to the surface, divers would have to work on the wreck in unwieldy metal suits when she was finally privately explored in 1935

SALVAGE SHIPS
PREPARATIONS IN PROGRESS OFF THE SOUTH COAST
OPERATIONS NEAR THE GALLEY HEAD

Our Clonakilty correspondent writes: Preparations for salvage work on an extensive scale along the south coast line between the Galley Head and the Old Head of Kinsale are in progress, judging by the results of some enquiries made today.

People residing along the coast-line are following the movements of the salvage ships with considerable interest. The first man with whom I had a conversation told me that the two vessels understood to be engaged in the work paid several visits to this portion of the coast during the past week and placed buoys on at least four different points. Asked what ships the buoys were likely to represent, he thought the one directly in front of where we were standing on a promontory of the Seven Heads was most likely, as far as he could judge, to be directly over the spot where the ss Sierra Leone was sunk during the war. The vessel is believed to have contained, in addition to cotton, a quantity of copper, and a considerable amount of drugs.

'I was out fishing and within easy distance of the spot', said another when I referred to the position of the ill-fated Lusitania. 'I can point to its exact location,' he added, 'and the salvage people have placed a buoy within a quarter mile of the spot'. He did not think however that they were immediately concerned with this ship, but with another of which he could not recall the name, believed to have been torpedoed in the same waters.

The two salvage ships were last seen at work on Saturday last, when they spent the day to 5 p.m. along the coast.

When one comes to think of it, this portion of the coast, i.e. from the Galley Head to the Old Head of Kinsale, must be responsible, in proportion to its length, for more shipping losses than any other portion of the coast of the entire British Isles.

COALING AT COVE

The Italian salvage ships Artiglio and Capione, which have been carrying out sweeping operations off the Galley Head for some time past in an effort to salvage vessels sunk during the Great War, were reported to be making for Cove last night. On arrival at Cove they will take coal on board and will then return to the position off the Galley Head, where they recently discovered the wreck of a vessel.

(CORK EXAMINER, 10 APRIL 1934, P. 8)

The wreck was later identified as that of the *Spectator*, a 3,800 ton steamer torpedoed by a U-boat on 19 August 1917, six and a quarter miles south-west of the Seven Heads. The *Artiglio* salvaged the copper cargo, just as it had recovered gold bullion from the P&O liner *Egypt* in a famous recovery in 1932.

The Italian expedition also probed the case of the *Ludgate*, a 6,182-ton vessel torpedoed by U-boat on 26 July 1917. She lies two miles south of Galley Head, and had been carrying over 1,000 tons of copper. Captain Bruno of the *Artiglio* denied he was interested in the *Lusitania*, but said they were certain of getting the *Enterprise*, a Harrison liner homeward bound with a cargo of copper. They also intended to search for the *Lincolnshire*, carring 2,000 tons of brass.

The *Lusitania* breakthrough came the next year when deep sea diver Jim Jarratt of Byfleet, Surrey, wearing a flexible new diving suit, spent half an hour on the hull of the vessel on 27 October 1935. The following recounts a memorial service that immediately followed the rediscovery:

TORPEDOED OFF CORK COAST
SINKING OF LUSITANIA RECALLED
MEMORIAL SERVICE
POIGNANT STORY TOLD BY SURVIVORS.
(BY A SPECIAL REPRESENTATIVE)

Since that tragic day, 7 May 1915, when the Cunard liner Lusitania was torpedoed off the Cork coast with a loss of 1,196 lives, many tributes have been paid to the dead the sea claimed on that occasion.

A 1930s artist impression of wreck diving. In reality divers
had practically no illumination and the sea was pitch black.
The first diver known to set foot on the wreck, Jim Jarratt
(right), had to feel his way along the hull. Working blind, he
thought the Lusitania was lying on her port side and that he
was standing on her starboard, whereas it was actually the
other way around. The all-metal suits, with reservoirs of oil
for the joints, were heavy and unwieldy with no sensitivity.
Jarratt could tell very little about the ship. The side where the
torpedo struck is buried in mud making final answers elusive
even today.

Ships passing by the ocean near the Old Head of Kinsale have dipped their flags in salute to the hundreds who lie buried in the hulk of the vast Lusitania, and at times, too, wreaths have been dropped overboard from passing boats. American tourists have gazed overboard towards the sea as liners passed by, and many a silent prayer has gone across the waves from the lips of relatives or friends of those who went down on that fateful May day, and at many other times, under many circumstances, the sinking of the Lusitania has been remembered, always solemnly and sadly.

Yesterday I sailed from Kinsale to join in the most solemn and sad of all those many tributes, for yesterday, for the first time since the sinking of the liner, a memorial service for the dead was held right over the position which her hulk now holds in the bed of the ocean.

Nearly twelve miles off the Old Head of Kinsale she lies – 11.2 miles S. by 3 E., to be exact – on her starboard side, embedded in four feet of sand, under 51 fathoms of water, and yesterday was the first occasion upon which her location was definitely known to those who were participating in the service.

UNIQUE TRIBUTE

Many tributes have no doubt been paid approximate to the spot, but the fact that the Lusitania definitely lay beneath us in a steamer yesterday was known because the steamer was the Clyde-built salvage boat Orphir, and the Orphir located the Lusitania on 6 October.

After nearly four months of roaming the sea around the Old Head covering during that time an area of 120 square miles, the Orphir's instruments on 6 October located the wreck of a large vessel which is now definitely known to be the Lusitania, and now before any salvage work was carried out, the salvagers were paying an unique tribute to those lost in 1915.

Shortly after 10 a.m., the Orphir left Kinsale with a full crew and a large number of guests invited from the City and County of Cork to join in this first tribute to the dead over the vast tomb which they occupy 50 fathoms beneath the Atlantic.

Those on board included: – Rev. P. McSweeney, CC Kinsale; Rev. Mr Beresford Poer, Rector, Kinsale; Rev. Mr Welman, head of the Jewish Church in Cork; Messrs. L. R. Woods, US consul at Cork; E. O'Neill, TD; J. Crosbie, BL; H. E. Donegan, solr., Cork.

SURVIVORS ON BOARD

An air of constraint hung over the boat as she ploughed her way through a choppy sea towards the tragic spot, marked by buoys from the Orphir. Men spoke in subdued voices, and conversation was mainly confined to the subject of the sinking of the Cunarder.

One man on board the Orphir looked sadly out to the spot where twenty years previously he had seen hundreds of human beings perish. He was Mr Robert Chisholm, the steward of the Orphir, a survivor from amongst the crew of the Lusitania. On the voyage out he told heartrending tales of the horrors and heroism witnessed on that day – how a lady passenger was thrown to the ground in one passage as the boat lurched, and how the carpeting of the passage, becoming loose, wrapped itself around her, pinioning her hands to her side until her screams were drowned by the inrushing water.

He told, too, how a group of men, women and children were trapped in a saloon when the boat lurched upwards on the beginning of her plunge to the sea-bottom; how water surged down the stairways to drive back those who were racing upwards and carrying them back to a horrible grave in the saloon.

Those and other tales, told by a few who helped in the tragic work of recovering the dead on the shores of County Cork, were recounted as the Orphir steadily bore towards the spot where the Lusitania lies. As the shoreline grew dim behind us, the buoys rose and fell on the ocean in front. A solemn moment arrived when the ship, with engines silent, came to a stop exactly between the buoys. Up in the control room the Orphir's echo-sounding apparatus showed that just beneath us lay the Lusitania, and guests and crew were requested to proceed to the after-deck, where the service was to be held.

THE SERVICE

Assembled here – the crew gathered in a little group on one side, the guests on the other, and in the centre the Master (Capt. H. B. Russell), with the clergymen of three denominations, Catholic, Protestant and Jewish, standing behind him – we paid our sad and solemn respects to the memory of the 1,169 who met death on this very spot in the hazy sunshine of a May afternoon twenty years ago. It was, in fact, just about at this hour that the waters, so deserted now, had closed over hundreds of doomed men and women, for it was now 1.35 p.m. and the Lusitania was struck by the torpedo about 1.15 p.m. on the day of the tragedy.

Captain Russell of the search vessel Orphir presides at an on-board memorial service over the Lusitania wreck in 1935. Lusitania survivor Robert Chisholm is the man with his arm extended, near the captain

The tolling of the Orphir's bells and the screaming of a few wheeling seagulls were the only sounds which broke the silence as the flags were half-masted, and then the Master, speaking slowly and with emotion, spoke a few words.

'Shortly after this hour,' he said, 'on 7 May 1915, the great ship Lusitania, bound from New York to Liverpool, with 1,959 passengers and crew aboard, was torpedoed by an enemy submarine and sank at this spot. Of her complement, 1,195 souls lost their lives in the disaster.

'Many of you will remember the wave of horror and pity that swept the world when the tidings of the tragedy were received. On that I do not wish to dwell. It profits us not at all to recall such unhappy things, but now that the resting place of the Lusitania, for so long unknown, has been located, we feel that it is only fitting that we should pay this humble tribute to the dead.

'Of those who perished, the bodies of only 288 men, women and children were recovered from the sea. The ocean claimed 907. Many of them lie beneath us, and this simple service is to pay them tribute.

'We are gathered to offer our respects to the dead, not only of our own people, but also to those of many other nationalities. On that fateful day, 589 Britons, 123 citizens of the United States, four Greeks, five Swedes, two Belgians, two Mexicans, two Frenchmen, one Dane, 42 Russians, three Dutchmen, one Argentine, one Italian, one Swiss, two Finns, one Hindu and nine Persians, in addition to 404 members of the crew, died in company.

'In the two minutes' silence which will follow the sounding of the Last Post let us remember them, fervently trusting that such happenings shall be no more', concluded Captain Russell.

THE LAST POST

The strains of the Last post greeted the end of the Master's remarks – strangely impressive they sounded out there with the sea all round us – and then, with bare heads, the gathering observed the two minutes of silent prayer.

Mr Chisholm stood with the rest of the crew, his eyes cast overboard, and what were his thoughts none could fathom. Perhaps they went back twenty years, and perhaps this was why his eyes held more emotion than those of any others amongst the crew.

One again the bugle broke the silence – this time to the strains of the Reveille, and at a word from Captain Russell, four beautiful wreaths were sent overboard – two from the crew of the Orphir, one from the American Minister in Dublin, and one from Mr E. E. Wolfe of Kinsale. Just then a rainbow broke an arch in the sky, and it seemed something beyond coincidence that its varied colours came to an end just behind the Orphir – between the two buoys marking the Lusitania's resting place.

Its rays painted the wreaths in bright colours as they rose and fell on the waves for a minute. With a long-sustained blast of her whistle the Orphir went full steam ahead for the shore, leaving *behind it in the distance the wave-tossed wreaths and the rising and falling buoys which guard the Lusitania's grave.*

ORPHIR TO LEAVE
The members of the Orphir's crew are sworn to strict secrecy regarding the expedition, and no information as to the progress of salvage work was forthcoming in Kinsale yesterday. It is believed however that the boat will leave Kinsale for England in two days' time and no more work will be undertaken until the weather improves.

(CORK EXAMINER, 7 NOVEMBER 1935, P. 6)

The *Lusitania* had been found, and the company behind the venture, Argonauts Ltd, sought to raise money for a full-scale expedition. Public investment was invited, but nothing was in place by 1939, and in September the Second World War broke out, ending the plans forever.

Latter Developments

Some years after the war ended, interest in the once-mighty Cunarder resurfaced. The gulf of time since the sinking had turned her into a folk memory, but plenty of gossip and speculation remained. There was a theory that royal navy vessels had returned to the site immediately after the Second World War to depth charge what remained. The implication that they were destroying a munitions cargo is obvious, but it ignores the nature of depth-charges, which are unsuitable for fixed wrecks. That may not have mattered if the wreck was being used as a target for anti-submarine practice, as was also theorised.

In the early 1960s a diver claimed that the *Lusitania* had inward blast holes in areas not likely to have been struck by the U-20 torpedo. These claims may hold some truth or derive from the murkiness of the water itself and the unreliability of research work at those depths and at that time, but they were later given some credence.

The British naval vessel *Reclaim* was reputed to have visited the site in 1948, although there is no contemporary record of this. The admiralty denies that the ship was ever there and further denies that the royal navy has ever undertaken any blasting, target-practice or salvage operations on the *Lusitania* since she sank.

The salvage vessel *Artiglio* had been nosing around the wreck before the war and routinely deployed explosives in its salvage of sunken vessels. But the *Artiglio* came to an incendiary end – she was sunk in the Bay of Biscay by an underwater blast that went wrong, taking the lives of several divers and crew.

It appears that a British salvage company named Risdon Beazley may have visited the wreck in 1950. It has been claimed that diving operations were carried out under contract to the admiralty, and that divers working from a ship named the *Recovery* placed explosives, lowered from a derrick, against the hull. The firm denies it was ever there.

What is accepted is that the first civilian dive on the *Lusitania* since wartime occurred on 20 July 1960, when a 27-year-old native of Boston, John Light, became the second man known to have reached the hull. The former US navy diver would make over 100 trips to the *Lusitania*, but little information was reliably gleaned because of site difficulties and the fact that breathing compressed air at such depths made divers susceptible to narcosis and distorted perception.

In 1967 the Liverpool & London War Risks Association Ltd, wartime insurers of the ship, auctioned off the rights to the wreck. John Light bought title to the wreck and its appurtenances for £1,000 sterling. In 1968, he established a speculative partnership with F. Gregg Bemis, Jr, of Santa Fe, New Mexico, who would 'inherit' certain rights to the *Lusi-*

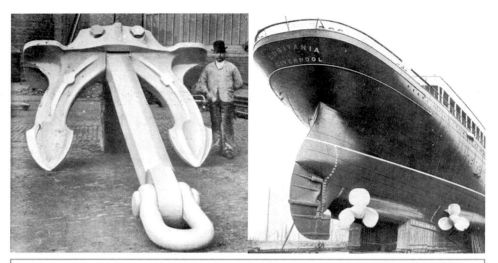

A giant anchor of the Lusitania at the John Brown shipyard on the Clyde, where she was built. Four of these anchors were raised by salvors, who also lifted three of the vessel's huge propellers. Each anchor weighed ten and a quarter tons, while the cable was 125 tons. The propellers were 17 feet in diameter and each weighed a staggering 21 tons. Still, they were hauled to the surface

tania's remains (not without legal dispute from Light's widow), and who eventually became the recognised owner in the Irish courts.

Light claimed to have found extensive evidence of blast damage and cutting operations, although the wreck had by now become wreathed in fishing nets and trawler gear. He also claims to have seen a gun barrel, although no evidence of its existence has since emerged.

Light made numerous dives on the *Lusitania* during the 1960s, and appeared to have interested legendary marine explorer Jacques Cousteau in conducting a full investigation of the wreck. The project fell through, and financial troubles later resulted in the seizure of the *Kinvarra*, the vessel used as a dive platform.

With developments in deep-sea diving and salvage techniques, the *Lusitania* became increasingly vulnerable. Her uncertain legal position was underlined in 1972 when the Irish government resisted calls for it to deploy naval service vessels to ward off scavengers.

In 1982, a nadir was reached when a consortium named Oceaneering International used cutting equipment or explosive to remove and raise three of the *Lusitania*'s four bronze propellers. Two of the massive screws were eventually melted down for scrap, some of the metal supposedly turned into golf clubs. The other propeller is now a sentry outside the Liverpool Maritime Museum.

Operating from the Norwegian charter vessel *Myrevag*, Oceaneering International deployed the first remotely operated vehicle (ROV) on the wreck. Film from the ROV *Scorpio* led to suggestions that the torpedo strike and secondary explosion may both have happened forward of the bridge, in the vicinity of the main storage hold. Highly unstable gun-cotton was alleged without real evidence to have been stowed in this area.

The ROV had a robotic arm, which was used to cut away the *Lusitania* bell from the crow's nest. Seaman Thomas Quinn had used this bell to sound the alarm when he spotted the track of the torpedo in 1915. The bell was eventually sold at a Sothebys auction to a private buyer in May 1991.

All four of the *Lusitania*'s giant anchors were removed by divers using the support vessel *Archimedes*. They also recovered a cargo of copper ingots, and indeed sauce dishes, gold watches, cutlery, window frames and the ship's whistle.

In 1988, after years of inaction, Taoiseach Charles Haughey declared the extension of

Irish territorial waters from three miles to twelve, thus including the wreck, which lies 11.5 nautical miles from the closest point of land. The Maritime Jurisdiction Amendment Act 1988 was lodged with the UN Convention on the Law of the Sea.

In 1993, the discoverer of the *Titanic* eight years previously, Robert Ballard, carried out an expedition to photograph and explore the wreck by ROV, pledging to recover no artefacts. *National Geographic* magazine backed him, and funding of the project extended to a payment to Bemis, the claimed owner. That expedition led to a television documentary, video and coffee table book, bringing the *Lusitania* once more to widespread attention.

There was a separate expedition in 1994, and items were taken from the site. A subsequent court case heard that diving notes prepared by the British team leader, Polly Tapson, had advised members to 'keep any irresistible item well hidden'.

On 25 January 1995, the Minister for Arts, Heritage, Gaeltacht and the Islands, Michael D. Higgins finally placed an Underwater Heritage Order on the *Lusitania*, The wreck was thereby accorded the status of a submerged National Monument 'on account of its historical importance'.

The law now required that a licence be obtained from the state to dive on wreck. Any item retrieved in such a dive must be handed over to the local Receiver of Wreck under the provisions of the Merchant Shipping (Salvage and Wreck) Act.

The Irish high court meanwhile decided a year later in May 1996 that Gregg Bemis was the owner of the wreck of the *Lusitania*, a decision later confirmed on appeal to the supreme court.

The Irish state continues to assert ownership to the cargo and personal effects. The result of the extensive legal action is that anyone now wanting to dive on the *Lusitania* must receive the written permission of both Mr Bemis and the Irish government.

Bemis had a stated objective that artefacts should be recovered, with some given to museums in Cork and Kinsale and the remainder taken on a travelling exhibition. The Irish government, in continuing discussions with Bemis, remains opposed to artefacts leaving the jurisdiction. Gregg Bemis announced his intention to personally dive the wreck, using scuba equipment, in 2004. At the time of the announcement he was aged 75.

Ireland's only underwater national monument lies in latitude 51° 24.7' N., longitude 8° 32.8' W. Unlike most of the country's other sites of outstanding heritage, she has no nearby interpretative centre or visitor facility. Even the Old Head of Kinsale, where her death throes were witnessed, is now a golf course, with no public right of way.

Artwork on the Lusitania *memorial that was erected on the Old Head of Kinsale through private donations and maritime society subscriptions*

Epilogue

Everywhere in Cobh today are vestiges of the *Titanic*, from a bar and restaurant of that title to a fine 1998 memorial to the emigrants who boarded from here. Less marketed, and less marked, is the town's extraordinary connections to the single incident that ushered in 'total war' for a sanguinary century.

The world's second-most-famous shipwreck has been steadily forgotten. It is an irony of history that Queenstown is generally remembered as the last port of call of a ship destined for disaster more than 2,000 miles away – and not for the 1,200 lives obliterated by a ship's destruction in the immediate vicinity.

The *Lusitania* is a symbol not just of America's entry into the war – that came on 6 April 1917 – but of the entry of war into the heart of ordinary Irish men and women who found themselves directly threatened for the first time. The fondly imagined rules of engagement had just been torn to pieces, and no one has ever put them back together.

Peace in God's Name reads the legend in the Irish language at the base of the *Lusitania* memorial in Cobh, but Ireland instead went on to have her own years of recurring conflict.

Yet in 1915 a French agent and a British mercantile marine officer could stand together in an Irish square and grin at the vicissitudes of life. Nearly 40 Russians, along with Persians Greeks, and a myriad other nationalities stumbled injured through the streets – and found both a warm-hearted and an open Irish welcome.

A new millennium brings a fresh appraisal. The *Lusitania* is as much a part of Irish history as it is an anchoring point in the annals of the sea and a landmark in modern warfare and diplomacy. In looking again at the past it is possible to embrace in generous spirit that same spirit of bygone days that brought some good out of immense horror.

The *Lusitania* was an Irish, as well as an international, tragedy. She remains a rich treasure of Irish heritage, even if her grave is the unmarked, featureless sea.

The Lusitania *burying her bows into the waves south of the Old Head of Kinsale on a warm summer's day in May 1915 (The Sphere)*

Appendix 1

U-20's War Record

The 30,396 ton *Lusitania* was the largest ship sunk by the U-20 and her greatest success – if such is measurable by displacement and the number of casualties.

Prior to that act, the U-20 had sunk eight vessels over 500 tons. They were:

1) *Ikaria*	30 January 1915
2) *Oriole*	30 January 1915
3) *Tokomaru*	30 January 1915
4) *Bengrove*	5 March 1915
5) *Princess Victoria*	9 March 1915
6) *Florazan*	11 March 1915
7) *Candidate*	6 May 1915
8) *Centurion*	6 May 1915.

The U-20 heading out on patrol, and below, the same vessel wrecked by her crew after she became embedded on a sandbank off Jutland in 1916

Inside a U-boat – Illustierte Zietung, Leipzig, 1916.

Above: *where the torpedo struck the Lusitania*
Below: *damage to the* ss Belridge *from a torpedo that penetrated the bow, but failed to detonate*

The casualty rate before the *Lusitania* was low – numbering just 22 fatalities. There were 21 casualties when the General Steam Navigation Company's *Oriole*, on a voyage from London to Le Havre, was torpedoed in the English Channel and sunk with the loss of all hands. The other loss occurred when the *Florazan* was sunk in the Atlantic.

After the sinking of the *Lusitania*, the U-20 continued waging war against British shipping. She sank a further thirteen ships of 500 tons or more, by torpedo or gunfire, before her own destruction:

10) *Ellesmere*	9 July 1915
11) *Meadowfield*	9 July 1915
12) *Roumanie*	2 September 1915
13) *Hesperian*	4 September 1915
14) *Dictator*	5 September 1915
15) *Duoro*	5 September 1915
16) *Caroni*	7 September 1915
17) *Mora*	8 September 1915
18) *Ruabon*	2 May 1916
19) *Cymric*	8 May 1916
20) *Aaro*	1 August 1916
21) *Thelma*	26 September 1916
22) *Ethel Duncan*	18 October 1916.

The largest vessel sunk subsequently was the White Star Line's *Cymric*, 13,370 tons, while on a voyage from New York to Liverpool. Her sinking, and the deaths of five crew members, came a year and a day after the destruction of the *Lusitania*.

The Allan liner *Hesperian*, en route from Liverpool to Montreal with 653 passengers and crew, suffered 32 casualties when she was torpedoed 85 miles south-west of the Fastnet rock. There were three deaths on the *Aaro* and one each on the *Ellesmere* and *Meadowfield*.

The U-20's own end came on 4 November 1916, when she stranded at Harbooere on the west coast of Jutland. Attempts to refloat her proved useless and the crew abandoned her and blew up her internal gear the next day.

U-20's torpedo officer, Raimund Weisbach, in later years became a friend of Irish maritime authority John de Courcy Ireland. Weisbach (in 1916 commander of the submarine U-19 which delivered Roger Casement to Ireland for the Easter Rising), told his friend how Commander Schwieger had told him to load one of only two gyro torpedoes he had left, neither of which were very powerful, for the attack on the Cunarder.

After he was ordered to fire, Weisbach pressed the trigger button. Schwieger then called him to the periscope to watch his tinfish on its journey. Weisbach was definite that a second explosion followed immediately the torpedo's impact, and was totally convinced that the second explosion was what had sunk her so fast. The torpedo alone might have been enough to sink her, but it would have done so much more slowly, he said.

De Courcy Ireland said the German 'struck us all as being strictly reliable'. Weisbach said the explosion that followed the torpedo strike was 'extremely powerful' (*ausserordentlich stark*). His war ended as commander of the U-81 when a British destroyer forced it to surface and surrender in 1917.

Weisbach wrote out his account of the *Lusitania* sinking in German in 1966 at de Courcy Ireland's request, and said it could be published after his death. Weisbach died four years later, on 16 June 1970. His account was published in 'An Irishman's Diary' in the *Irish Times* on 31 July 1970:

I am indebted to Dr John de Courcy [Ireland], of the Irish Maritime Institute, for a copy of an original document of considerable historic importance. It came from the hand of the German Naval Captain Raimund Weisbach, who died in Hamburg recently.

Captain Weisbach had been the commander of the submarine U-19, which put Roger Casement ashore at Banna Strand in April 1916. He visited Ireland during the Fiftieth Anniversary commemoration of the 1916 Rising in 1966, and at that time made it known to some members of the Maritime Institute that he had been torpedo officer of the submarine U-20, which sank the Lusitania off the Old Head of Kinsale on 7 May 1915.

At their request, he wrote the following account of the Lusitania sinking for the Institute's archives, on the undertaking that they would not publish it until after his death. The account below is, of course, a translation.

Captain Raimund Weisbach

POWERFUL EXPLOSION

'U-20 was off the south-west coast of Ireland, not far from the Old Head of Kinsale. The U-boat had been sailing for a long time in very thick weather without sighting a single steamer. It suddenly cleared, and on the horizon the four funnels and high masts of a very big ship were seen. The commander at once gave the order: 'Dive!'

'From then on, I am able to observe no more, as the commander stayed at the periscope and organised the attack on the ship. He did not know what ship he had before his eyes. After the U-boat had proceeded for a long time under water, came the order to fire a torpedo (only one).

'The distance for the shot was – so far as I can remember – quite considerable – more than 500 metres. The explosion was exceptionally powerful. After some minutes, the commander called me to the periscope.

'I observed the ship with a marked list, the lifeboats were hanging crookedly, or pointing vertically downwards. Now you could see the name Lusitania sharply outlined. The U-boat stayed a little longer in the vicinity, and then steered underwater seawards, as a heavy swell set in, in the direction of Queenstown.

'The unusually powerful explosion following the torpedo's impact led us to the conclusion that the Lusitania had taken on board ammunition'.

FORGED MEDALS

Captain Weisbach's statement goes on: 'The so-called Lusitania medals (in the Maritime Institute's 1916 exhibition) are an outright English forgery. The crew of U-20 never got any medals for the sinking, and in fact the sinking was very much of a shock to the (German) High Command. The Commander of U-20 (Schwieger) had a very unfriendly reception at headquarters. Those medals were definitely never minted at Leipzig'.

Readers interested in naval history may remember that there was a long controversy about the Lusitania medals in the correspondence columns of the Irish Times in the summer of 1965. Captain Weisbach's statement would seem to settle it once and for all.

(IRISH TIMES, 31 JULY 1970, P. 11)

It was also alleged that an Alsatian member of the U-20, Charles Voegele, refused to serve having learned she had sunk a passenger ship. He was later court-martialled and sentenced to life imprisonment, but released as soon as the war ended. Voegele died in 1920.

The bell of the U-20 was auctioned at Christies in London, in May 1998. It went to a Japanese buyer for £14,800 sterling.

Appendix 2

LOSS OF THE STEAMSHIP 'LUSITANIA'

REPORT of Formal Investigation into the circumstances attending the foundering on 7 May 1915, of the British Steamship 'Lusitania', of Liverpool, after being torpedoed off the Old Head of Kinsale, Ireland.

Presented to both Houses of Parliament by Command of His Majesty.

REPORT OF THE COURT

The Court, having carefully enquired into the circumstances of the above-mentioned disaster, finds, for the reasons appearing in the annex hereto, that the loss of the said ship and lives was due to damage caused to the said ship by torpedoes fired by a submarine of German nationality whereby the ship sank.

In the opinion of the Court the act was done not merely with the intention of sinking the ship, but also with the intention of destroying the lives of the people on board.

Dated this seventeenth day of July, 1915.

MERSEY,

Wreck Commissioner.

We concur in the above Report,

Admiral Sir F. S. Inglefield, KCB; Lieutenant-Commander H. J. Hearn; Captain David Davies; and Captain John Spedding, Assessors.

Lord Mersey

INTRODUCTION

On the 18th May, 1915, the Board of Trade required that a Formal Investigation of the circumstances attending the loss of the 'Lusitania' should be held and the Court accordingly commenced to sit on the 15th June.

There were six sittings, some of which were public and some of which were in camera. Thirty-six witnesses were examined, and a number of documents were produced. Twenty-one questions were formulated by the Board of Trade, which are set out in detail at the end of this annex.

THE SHIP

The 'Lusitania' was a Turbine steamship built by John Brown & Co., of Clydebank, in 1907, for the Cunard Steamship Company. She was built under Admiralty Survey and in accordance with Admiralty requirements, and was classed 100 A1 at Lloyd's. Her length was 755 feet, her beam 88 feet, and her depth 60 feet 4 in. Her tonnage was 30,395 gross and 12,611 net. Her engines were of 68,000 h.p. and her speed 24 and a half to 25 knots. She had 23 double-ended and two single-ended boilers situated in four boiler-rooms.

The ship was divided transversely by eleven principal bulkheads into twelve sections.

The two forward bulkheads were collision bulkheads without doors. The remaining bulkheads had watertight doors cut into them which were closed by hand. In places where it was necessary to have the doors open for working the ship they could be closed by hydraulic pressure from the bridge. A longitudinal bulkhead separated the side coal bunkers from the boiler-room and engine-rooms on each side of the ship.

The 'Lusitania' was a passenger as well as an emigrant ship as defined by the Merchant Shipping Acts. She fulfilled all the requirements of the law in this connection and had obtained all necessary certificates.

She had accommodation on board for 3,000 persons (including the crew).

The lifeBoats and life Saving Appliances

The ship was provided with boat accommodation for 2,605 persons. The number of persons on board on the voyage in question was 1,959.

The number of boats was 48. Twenty-two of these were ordinary lifeboats hanging from the davits – eleven on each side of the boat deck. These had a total carrying capacity of 1,323. The remainder (26) were collapsible boats, with a total carrying capacity of 1,282. Eighteen of these collapsible boats were stowed under eighteen of the lifeboats. The remaining eight were stowed four on each side of the ship abaft the lifeboats.

In addition the ship was provided with 2,325 lifejackets (125 of which were for children) and 35 lifebuoys. All these were conveniently distributed on board.

The boats, the lifejackets and the lifebuoys were inspected at Liverpool on the 17th March, 1915, by the resident Board of Trade Surveyor, and again on the 15th April, 1915, by the Board of Trade Emigration Officer. Both these gentlemen were called before me and satisfied me that the condition of the different appliances was in every way satisfactory.

The boats were also examined by the ship's carpenter at New York on the commencement of the homeward voyage on 1st May and found to be in good order.

The Captain, the Officers and the Crew

The Captain of the ship, Mr William Thomas Turner, had been in the service of the Cunard Company since 1883. He had occupied the position of Commander since 1903, and had held an Extra Master's Certificate since 1907. He was called before me and gave his evidence truthfully and well.

The 'Lusitania' carried an additional Captain named Anderson, whose duty it was to assist in the care and navigation of the ship. He was unfortunately drowned when the ship went down, and I can only judge of his capacity by the accounts given to me of the work he did. Several of the officers gave their evidence before me and gave it well. I am quite satisfied that the two Captains and the officers were competent men, and that they did their duty. Captain Turner remained on the bridge till he was swept into the sea and Captain Anderson was working on the deck until he went overboard and was drowned.

It appears that since the commencement of the war the Cunard Company has lost all its Royal Naval Reserve and Fleet Reserve men, and the managers have had to take on the best men they would get and to train them as well as might be in the time at their disposal. In connection with this training prizes have been given by the Company to induce crews to make themselves proficient in handling the boats, and efforts in this direction seem to have been successful in the case of the 'Lusitania's' crew. Mr Arthur Jones, the First Officer, described the crew on this voyage as well able to handle the boats, and testified to their carrying out the orders given to them in a capable manner.

One of the crew, Leslie N. Morton, who, at the time the ship was torpedoed was an extra look-out on the starboard side of the forecastle head, deserves a special word of commendation. He had been shipped in New York. He was only 18 years of age, but he seems to have exhibited great courage, self-possession and resource. He was the first to observe the approach of the two torpedoes, and before they had touched the ship he had reported them to the bridge by means of a megaphone, calling out 'Torpedoes coming on the starboard side'. When the torpedoes struck the ship, Morton was knocked off his feet, but, recovering himself quickly, he went at once to the boats on the starboard side and assisted in filling and lowering several of them. Having done all that could be done on board, he had, as he expresses it, 'to swim for it'. In the water he managed to get a hold of a floating collapsible lifeboat and, with the assistance of another member of the crew named Parry, he ripped the canvas cover off it, boarded it, and succeeded in drawing into it fifty or sixty passengers.

He and Parry rowed the lifeboat some miles to a fishing smack, and, having put the rescued passengers on board the smack, they re-entered the lifeboat and succeeded in rescuing twenty or thirty more people. This boy, with his mate Parry, was instrumental in saving nearly one hundred lives. He has cause for being proud of the work he did. Morton had a good opportunity of judging how the crew performed their duties in the short time which elapsed between the explosion of the torpedoes and the foundering of the ship.

He saw the crew helping the women and children into the boats; he saw them distributing lifebelts to the passengers. He heard the officers giving orders and he observed that the crew were obeying the orders properly.

Some of the passengers were called, and they confirm this evidence. They speak in terms of the highest praise of the exertions made by the crew.

No doubt there were mishaps in handling the ropes of the boats and in other such matters, but there was, in my opinion, no incompetence or neglect, and I am satisfied that the crew behaved well throughout, and worked with skill and judgment. Many more than half their number lost their lives.

The total crew consisted of 702, made up of 77 in the Deck Department, 314 in the Engineering Department, 306 in the Stewards Department and of 5 musicians.

Of these, 677 were males and 25 were females. Of the males, 397 were lost, and of the females, 16, making the total number lost, 413. Of the males 280 were saved, and of the females, 9, making the total number saved, 289.

I find that the conduct of the masters, the officers and the crew was satisfactory. They did their best in difficult and perilous circumstances and their best was good.

The Passengers

The number of passengers on board the 'Lusitania' when she sailed was 1,257, consisting of 290 saloon, 600 second cabin, and 367 third-cabin passengers.

Of these, 944 were British and Canadian, 159 were American, and the remainder were of seventeen other nationalities. Of the British and Canadian, 584 perished. Of the American 124 perished, and of the remainder 77 perished. The total number [of passengers] lost was 785, and the total number saved was 472.

The 1,257 passengers were made up of 688 adult males, 440 adult females, 51 male children, 39 female children, and 39 infants. Of the 688 adult males, 421 were lost and 267 were saved. Of the 440 adult females, 270 were lost and 170 were saved. Of the 51 male children, 33 were lost and 18 were saved. Of the 39 female children, 26 were lost and 13 were saved. Of the 39 infants, 35 were lost and 4 were saved.

Many of the women and children among those lost died from exhaustion after immersion in the water.

I can speak very well of the conduct of the passengers after the striking of the ship. There was little or no panic at first, although later on, when the steerage passengers came on to the boat deck in what one witness described as 'a swarm', there appears to have been something approaching a panic.

Eva Mary Grandidge, second class passenger. Aged three. Buried Queenstown, 13 May; Grave B, sixth row, lower tier. Property sent to the New York office of Cunard, per ss. Carpathia, 17 July, and handed over to her father, Mr Arthur Grandidge, 161 Stanley Avenue, Yonkers, N.Y., 30 July

Some of the passengers attempted to assist in launching the boats and, in my opinion, did more harm than good. It is, however, quite impossible to impute any blame to them. They were all working for the best.

Lusitania crewmen and boys carrying bundles of their wet clothes. The youth on the left is wearing a pair of trousers several sizes too big for him, and is still in his bare feet, outside Aherne's lace shop, King's Square

Newsreel footage of crew heroes, taken outside Fitzgerald's confectionery shop on West Beach, Queenstown. The man on the left of the trio is assistant purser William Harkness, who pulled people from the water into his lifeboat. He also picked up toddler Barbara Anderson on the boat deck, and leapt with her into a lifeboat. Anderson became the longest living survivor, and was still alive in 2004.
In the background of this photograph is Wilson's chemists. The Cork Examiner of 8 May 1915 reported: 'Those in need of immediate help were quickly taken in hand by some kind volunteer workers, Mr [John] Wilson, chemist, rendering splendid help in supplying restoratives, and only for his prompt and kindly action many might have suffered greatly from their nerve-wracking experience'

The Cargo

The cargo was a general cargo of the ordinary kind, but part of it consisted of a number of cases of cartridges (about 5,000). This ammunition was entered in the manifest. It was stowed well forward in the ship on the orlop and lower decks and about 50 yards away from where the torpedoes struck the ship. There was no other explosive on board.

The Ship Unarmed

It has been said by the German Government that the 'Lusitania' was equipped with masked guns, that she was supplied with trained gunners, with special ammunition, that she was transporting Canadian troops, and that she was violating the laws of the United States. These statements are untrue: they are nothing but baseless inventions, and they serve only to condemn the persons who make use of them. The steamer carried no masked guns nor trained gunners, or special ammunition, nor was she transporting troops, or violating any laws of the United States.

THE VOYAGE

The Departure from New York

The 'Lusitania' left New York at noon on the 1st of May, 1915. I am told that before she sailed notices were published in New York by the German authorities that the ship would be attacked by German submarines, and people were warned not to take passage in her. I mention this matter not as affecting the present enquiry but because I believed it is relied upon as excusing in some way the subsequent killing of the passengers and crew on board the ship.

In my view, so far from affording any excuse the threats only serve to aggravate the crime by making it plain that the intention to commit was deliberately formed and the crime itself planned before the ship sailed. Unfortunately the threats were not regarded as serious by the people intended to be affected by them. They apparently thought it impossible that such an atrocity as the destruction of their lives would be in the contemplation of the German Government. But they were mistaken: and the ship sailed.

The Ship's Speed

It appears that a question had arisen in the office of the Cunard Company shortly after the war broke out as to whether the transatlantic traffic would be sufficient to justify the Company in running their two big and expensive ships – the 'Lusitania' and the 'Mauretania'. The conclusion arrived at was that one of the two (the 'Lusitania') could be run once a month if the boiler power reduced by one-fourth. The saving in coal and labour resulting from this reduction would, it was thought, enable the Company to avoid loss though not to make a profit. Accordingly six of the 'Lusitania's' boilers were closed and the ship began to run in these conditions in November, 1914. She had made five round voyages in this way before the voyage in question in this enquiry. The effect of the closing of the six boilers was to reduce the attainable speed from 24 to 21 knots. But this reduction still left the 'Lusitania' a considerably faster ship than any other steamer plying across the Atlantic. In my opinion this reduction of the steamer's speed was of no significance and was proper in the circumstances.

THE TORPEDOING OF THE SHIP

By the 7th May the 'Lusitania' had entered what is called the 'Danger Zone', that is to say, she had reached the waters in which enemy submarines might be expected. The Captain had therefore taken precautions. He had ordered all the lifeboats under davits to be swung

PROMENADE DECK

SHELTER DECK

← Dotted line →
represents
approximate
height of water
& debris thrown
up by the explosion

Approximate size
of vast hole caused
by Torpedo

Torpedo

← Area affected (Rivets started Etc) →

G H DAVIS
1915

The original caption to this illustration declared it to
be the 'damage wrought by the first torpedo'. In fact
there was only one, but it suited the British to inter-
pret the second explosion, soon after the first, as being
another torpedo. If a single U-boat could not re-fire
so quickly, that only meant that there were two or
more submarines 'lying in wait' for the giant Cunarder. In fact the sinking was an opportunistic kill for
the U-20, which had already commenced her return
journey to Germany at the end of her patrol.

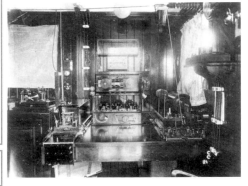

Interior of the wireless room of the Lusitania, from
which Robert Leith sent urgent appeals for assistance

out. He had ordered all bulkhead doors to be closed except such as were required to be kept open in order to work the ship.

These orders had been carried out. The portholes were also closed. The lookout on the ship was doubled – two men being sent to the crow's nest and two men to the eyes of the ship. Two officers were on the bridge and a quartermaster was on either side with instructions to look out for submarines. Orders were also sent to the engine-room between noon and two p.m. of the 7th to keep the steam pressure very high in case of emergency and to give the vessel all possible speed if the telephone from the bridge should ring.

Up to 8 a.m. on the morning of the 7th the speed on the voyage had been maintained at 21 knots. At 8 a.m. the speed was reduced to 18 knots. The object of this reduction was to secure the ship's arrival outside the bar at Liverpool at about 4 o'clock on the morning of the 8th, when the tide would serve to enable her to cross the bar into the Mersey at early dawn. Shortly after this alteration of the speed a fog came on and the speed was further reduced for a time to 15 knots. A little before noon the fog lifted and the speed was restored to 18 knots, from which it was never subsequently changed.

At this time land was sighted about two points abaft the beam, which the Captain took to be Brow Head; he could not, however, identify it with sufficient certainty to enable him to fix the position of his ship upon the chart. He therefore kept his ship on her course, which was S. 87 E. and about parallel with the land until 12.40, when, in order to make a better landfall he altered his course to N. 67 E. This brought him closer to the land, and he sighted Old Head of Kinsale.

He then (at 1.40 p.m.) altered his course back to S. 87° E., and having steadied his ship on that course began (at 1.50) to take a four-point bearing. This operation, which I am advised would occupy 30 or 40 minutes, was in process at the time when the ship was torpedoed, as hereafter described. At 2 p.m. the passengers were finishing their mid-day meal.

At 2.15 p.m., when ten to fifteen miles off the Old Head of Kinsale, the weather being then clear and the sea smooth, the Captain, who was on the port side of the lower bridge, heard the call, 'There is a torpedo coming, sir', given by the second officer. He looked to starboard and then saw a streak of foam in the wake of a torpedo travelling towards his ship.

Immediately afterwards the 'Lusitania' was struck on the starboard side somewhere between the third and fourth funnels. The blow broke number 5 lifeboat to splinters. A second torpedo was fired immediately afterwards, which also struck the ship on the starboard side. The two torpedoes struck the ship almost simultaneously.

Both these torpedoes were discharged by a German submarine from a distance variously estimated at from two to five hundred yards. No warning of any kind was given. It is also in evidence that shortly afterwards a torpedo from another submarine was fired on the port side of the 'Lusitania'. This torpedo did not strike the ship: and in the circumstance is only mentioned for the purpose of showing that perhaps more than one submarine was taking part in the attack.

The 'Lusitania' on being struck took a heavy list to starboard and in less than twenty minutes she sank in deep water. eleven hundred and ninety-eight men, women, and children were drowned. Sir Edward Carson, when opening the case, described the course adopted by the German Government in directing this attack as 'contrary to International Law and usages of war', and as constituting, according to the law of all civilised countries, 'a deliberate attempt to murder the passengers on board the ship'.

This statement is, in my opinion, true, and it is made in language not a whit too strong for the occasion. The defenceless creatures on board, made up of harmless men and women, and of helpless children, were done to death by the crew of the German submarine acting under the directions of the officials of the German Government. In the questions submitted to me by the Board of Trade, I am asked, 'What was the cause of the loss of life?' The answer is plain. The effective cause of the loss of life was the attack made against the ship by those on board the submarine. It was a murderous attack because it was made with a deliberate and wholly unjustifiable intention of killing the people on board.

German authorities on the laws of war at sea themselves establish beyond all doubt that though in some cases the destruction of an enemy trader may be permissible there is always an obligation first to secure the safety of the lives of those on board. The guilt of the persons concerned in the present case is confirmed by the vain excuses which have been put forward on their behalf by the German Government as before mentioned.

One witness, who described himself as a French subject from the vicinity of Switzerland, and who was in the second-class dining-room in the after part of the ship at the time of the explosion, stated that the nature of the explosion was 'similar to the rattling of a maxim gun for a short period', and suggested that this noise disclosed the 'secret' existence of some ammunition. The sound, he said, came from underneath the whole floor. I did not believe this gentleman. His demeanour was very unsatisfactory. There was no confirmation of his story, and it appeared that he had threatened the Cunard Company that it they did not make him some compensation, he would have the unpleasant duty of making his claim in public, and, in so doing, of producing 'evidence which will not be to the credit either of your Company or of the Admiralty'. The Company had not complied with his request.

It may be worth while noting that Leith, the Marconi operator, was also in the second-class dining-saloon at the time of the explosion. He speaks of but one explosion. In my opinion there was no explosion of any part of the cargo.

Orders given and work done after the torpedoing
The Captain was on the bridge at the time his ship was struck, and he remained there giving orders until the ship foundered. His first order was to lower all boats to the rail. This order as obeyed as far as it possibly could be. He then called out, 'Women and children first'. The order was then given to hard-a-starboard the helm with a view to heading towards the land, and orders were telegraphed to the engine-room. The orders given to the engine-room are difficult to follow and there is obvious confusion about them. It is not, however, important to consider them, for the engines were put out of commission almost at once by the inrush of water and ceased working, and the lights in the engine-room were blown out.

Leith, the Marconi operator, immediately sent out an S.O.S. signal, and, later on, another message, 'Come at once big list, 10 miles south Head Old Kinsale'. These messages were repeated continuously and were acknowledged. At first, the messages were sent out by the power supplied from the ship's dynamo; but in three or four minutes this power gave out and the messages were sent out by means of the emergency apparatus in the wireless cabin.

All the collapsible boats were loosened from their lashings and freed so that they could float when the ship sank.

The launching of the lifeboats
Complaints were made by some of the witnesses about the manner in which the boats were launched and about their leaky condition when in the water. I do not question the good faith of these witnesses, but I think their complaints were ill-founded.

Three difficulties presented themselves in connection with the launching of the boats. First, the time was very short: only twenty minutes elapsed between the first alarm and the sinking of the ship. Secondly, the ship was under way the whole time: the engines were put out of commission almost at once, so that the way could not be taken off. Thirdly, the ship instantly took a great list to starboard, which made it impossible to launch the port side boats properly and rendered it very difficult for the passengers to get into the starboard boats. The port side boats were thrown inboard and the starboard boats inconveniently far outboard.

In addition to these difficulties there were the well-meant but probably disastrous attempts of the frightened passengers to assist in launching operations. Attempts were made by the passengers to push some of the boats on the port side off the ship and to get them to the water. Some of these boats caught on the rail and capsized. One or two did, however, reach the water, but I am satisfied that they were seriously damaged in the operation. They were launched a distance of 60 feet or more with people in them, and must have been fouling the side of the ship the whole time. In one case the stern post was wrenched away. The result was that these boats leaked when they reached the water.

Captain Anderson was superintending the launching operations, and, in my opinion, did the best that could be done in the circumstances. Many boats were lowered on the starboard side, and there is no satisfactory evidence that any of them leaked.

There were doubtless some accidents in the handling of the ropes, but it is impossible to impute negligence or incompetence in connection with them.

The conclusion at which I arrive is that the boats were in good order at the moment of the explosion and that the launching was carried out as well as the short time, the moving ship and the serious list would allow.

Both the Captain and Mr Jones, the First Officer, in their evidence state that everything was done that was possible to get the boats out and to save lives, and this I believe to be true.

THE NAVIGATION OF THE SHIP

At the request of the Attorney-General part of the evidence in the Enquiry was taken in camera. This course was adopted in the public interest. The evidence in question dealt, firstly, with certain advice given by the Admiralty to navigators generally with reference to precautions to be taken for the purpose of avoiding submarine attacks; and secondly, with information furnished by the Admiralty to Captain Turner individually of submarine dangers likely to be encountered by him in the voyage of the 'Lusitania'.

It would defeat the object which the Attorney-General had in view if I were to discuss these matters in detail in my report; and I do not propose to do so. But it was made abundantly plain to me that the Admiralty had devoted the most anxious care and thought to the questions arising out of the submarine peril, and that they had diligently collected all available information likely to affect the voyage of the 'Lusitania' in this connection. I do not know who the officials were to whom these duties were entrusted, but they deserve the highest praise for the way in which they did their work.

Captain Turner was fully advised as to the means which in the view of the Admiralty were best calculated to avert the perils he was likely to encounter, and in considering the question whether he is to blame for the catastrophe in which his voyage ended I have to bear this circumstance in mind.

It is certain that in some respects Captain Turner did not follow the advice given to him. It may be (though I seriously doubt it) that had he done so his ship would have reached Liverpool in safety. But the question remains, was his conduct the conduct of a negligent or of an incompetent man. On this question I have sought the guidance of my assessors, who have rendered me invaluable assistance, and the conclusion at which I have arrived is that blame ought not to be imputed to the captain.

The advice given to him, although meant for his most serious and careful consideration, was not intended to deprive him of the right to exercise his skilled judgment in the difficult questions that might arise from time to time in the navigation of his ship. His omission to follow the advice in all respects cannot fairly be attributed either to negligence or incompetence.

He exercised his judgment for the best. It was the judgment of a skilled and experienced man, and although others might have acted differently and perhaps more successfully he ought not, in my opinion, to be blamed.

The whole blame for the cruel destruction of life in this catastrophe must rest solely with those who plotted and with those who committed the crime.

A French agent, Samuel Abramowitz, who was on a mission to New York for the French government, stands with First Officer Arthur Jones in Scott's Square, Queenstown, the morning after the sinking, both evidently very pleased to be alive.

Jones was at lunch when he heard a noise like an artillery gun. He dashed on deck and supervised the loading of the starboard boats. Having gotten 80 people into lifeboat 15 and seeing it lowered, he climbed down the boat falls to take command of the craft.

Abramowitz, who holds a French tricolour, was a furrier of Russian extraction. He had turned his place of business in Paris into a hospital for wounded soldiers. A father of eight, his eldest boy had volunteered for the French aeroplane corps. The Cork Examiner reported he had gone to America to 'buy medicaments or Red Cross necessities indirectly for the French Government'. His boxes, whatever they contained, went to the bottom.

'I went over to the saloon to have my dinner, and I heard a crack, and I see all those wooden chips go into the air, and the ship is gone to starboard,' he said. 'It was almost impossible for me to believe we had been torpedoed, because we had been talking about them, but in two minutes time those pirates, seeing that his work is not finished, he sent a second one.

'What followed is a picture nobody could believe. All those people, with their eyes to God and looking at death, were swallowed up by the sea.'

Appendix 3

Property Handed in to Police at Queenstown

Pocket-book, with cards and papers, bearing the name of Mr George F. Davies (missing), second-class passenger, leader of a Welsh choir [the Royal Gwent Male Voice Choir, only six of whom survived]. Forwarded to widow, Mrs S. E. Davies, Brynhyfryd, Beaufort Road, Cardiff, 19 August.

Bag, containing draft,. Bank notes and gold, belonging to Mrs Julia Sullivan (a survivor landed at Kinsale). Forwarded to Mrs Sullivan at Clounlea, Kilgarvan, Co. Kerry, 7 September.

Handbag, containing American Express Co. Cheques in favour of Miss Annie Robson (missing), second cabin passenger; also money and jewellery. Forwarded to father, Mr J. F. Robson, 1 North Row, Seaton Burn, Newcastle-on-Tyne, 5 June.

Handkerchief, keys, collar and links, property of Mr Percy Seccombe, saloon passenger. Mr Seccombe's body was recovered, cremated at Liverpool, and returned to New York on the *Lapland* on 19 May. The property was forwarded to his mother in Peterborough, New Hampshire, on 27 July.

Leather pocket-book, with name 'Thos. Brownlie', containing dollar bills, etc. [The wallet was found floating in the sea and was forwarded to his widow at Castle Street, Rutherglen, N.B., on 26 July. Mr Browlie's body was washed up in Mayo, and buried in Belmullet protestant cemetery on 10 July.]

Pocket-book containing dollar bills and notebook with name 'H. C. S. Morris' found floating in sea. Handed to Rev. H. C. Morris, survivor, 29 September.

Pocket-book with letters and papers bearing name of Mr T. McAfee, 42 Summer Street, Belfast. Mr McAfee was a third-class passenger (missing). Forwarded to sister, Miss S. McAfee, same address, 30 August.

Brooch (antique), with four moonstones, one ruby in centre, and four emeralds.

Lady's black cloth handkerchief bag, with expanding trellis work, nickel-capped top, containing lady's handkerchief with initials 'E. G.'; also gold brooch engraved 'Baby'; earrings, studs, links, etc. These articles were recovered from sea about the same time and in the vicinity of Body No. 224 [unidentified female, aged 23 or 24, buried in mass grave common B.]

Pocket-book, containing papers, etc, in the name of Mr W. Brown, survivor, third-class, found floating in sea. Forwarded to Mr Brown at 5 Bright Street, Middlesbrough, 1 December.

Gold pendant, handed to Chief Steward. Ownership proved by means of photograph enclosed and forwarded to Mrs Kate Cassie Duncan (survivor), second cabin passenger, c/o Cunard New York office, per *ss. Cameronia*, 24 October.

Draft in favour of Miss Nellie Fentiman (missing), second-class passenger. Cheque for amount forwarded to father, Mr F. A. Fentiman, Wealdstone House, Wealdstone, Middlesbrough, 7 June. [Nellie's body was recovered and buried in mass grave B in Queenstown on 13 May.]

Pocket-book belonging to Mr Samuel Max Kuebellick (missing), second-class, found floating. Forwarded to widow, Mrs E. E. Kuebellick, through Cunard New York office, 2 August.

Wallet found at sea, containing letter of credit in favour of Mr Leonard McMurray (survivor), second cabin passenger. Forwarded to Mr McMurray at 4 Queen Victoria Street, London, 12 June. Estimated value £500.

Papers, pipe, etc., belonging to Mr Frank J. Naumann (missing), saloon passenger. This material was found floating at sea on 21 August, more than three months after the sinking. Mr Naumann's body had been recovered early, embalmed and sent to London on 11 May. Mr Naumann was a principal of the firm of Messrs Naumann, Gepp & Co., at Fenchurch Street in the city. Effects found on the body were handed over to an accredited agent of the firm named Beadle who was sent to Queenstown in the wake of the tragedy.

Papers, etc, in the name of Mr Fred Isherwood (missing), third-class passenger.

Lady's satchel, containing cheque book in name of Mr Francis Fox (missing), second cabin passenger. Forwarded to Mrs A. Harris, 54 Exmouth Street, Swindon, sister of Mrs Fox, who also was a passenger and who was also lost. Neither body recovered.

Certificate, agreement and other papers in the name of Mr Robert B. Shirras (missing), third-class passenger. Forwarded to father, Mr Alexander Shirras, Whitehills, Belhelvie, 29 October.

Lady's handbag (leather).

Lady's satchel, containing gold watch, found floating at sea.

Lady's gold watch, case No. 1236, and inscribed 'Marc Chantre', Geneve. Initials on case 'M. D'. or 'W. D'. One small penknife and one cent piece.

Lady's half-hoop, five stone 18 carat diamond ring, with inscription 'J. T'. or 'J. S'. to 'M. M., 24-12-05'. [The inscription, for an apparent Christmas Eve engagement, was described as much worn.]

Also washed up, and handed to the coastguard on 9 May, was a wooden trunk, marked 'Francum family of *Lusitania*'. The Frankums were third-class passengers travelling from Detroit, consisting of parents Joseph and Annie Mariah and their three children – six year old Francis, four year old Frederick George, and Winifred Annie, ten months.

Mr Frankum saved his eldest son but the two youngest and their mother were drowned. The children were born in America and accounted for two of the US citizens lost.

Much of the *Lusitania*'s cargo was washed up along the Irish coast. Files in the Irish National Archives indicate that many of the non-personal, bulk shipment items found their way into people's homes.

Some salvaged goods were confiscated when the Royal Irish Constabulary became aware of such incidents, but prosecutions for alleged 'misdealing with wreck' were not considered politically expedient.

Crew survivors examine souvenirs. The roof of the Cunard passenger terminal is in the background

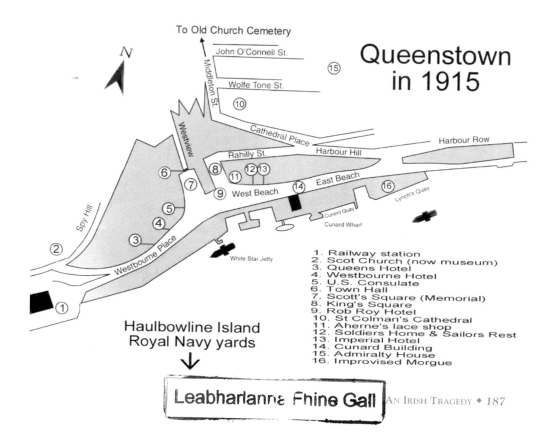

To Old Church Cemetery

John O'Connell St.

Wolfe Tone St.

Middleton St.

Cathedral Place

Westview

Rahilly St.   Harbour Hill

Harbour Row

West Beach   East Beach

Lynch's Quay

Cunard Quay

Cunard Wharf

White Star Jetty

Spy Hill

Westbourne Place

Queenstown in 1915

1. Railway station
2. Scot Church (now museum)
3. Queens Hotel
4. Westbourne Hotel
5. U.S. Consulate
6. Town Hall
7. Scott's Square (Memorial)
8. King's Square
9. Rob Roy Hotel
10. St Colman's Cathedral
11. Aherne's lace shop
12. Soldiers Home & Sailors Rest
13. Imperial Hotel
14. Cunard Building
15. Admiralty House
16. Improvised Morgue

Haulbowline Island
Royal Navy yards
↓

Leabharlanna Fhine Gall

Acknowledgments

I wish to acknowledge the kind assistance of the following: Anna Bale, Michael Barratt, Paddy Barker, Declan Cahill, Bella and Paudie Casey, Seamus Cashman, Luke Cassidy, Jim Crowley, Examiner Publications, Colleen Frew, Fr Tom Gaine, Jim Herlihy, Micheál Hurley, Marge McKindles, Paddy O'Sullivan, Mike Poirier, Noel Ray, David Snook, Jim Sullivan, Geoff Whitfield and the staff of the Cobh Museum, Kinsale Museum, National Archives, National Library and National Photographic Archive.

Thanks also to Mary Feehan, Aisling Lyons and the staff of Mercier Press.

Photographic Acknowledgments

Cover image of *Lusitania* courtesy of Examiner Publications; Captain Turner is courtesy of *New York Times*. Family photo Colleen Frew; Facing title page: *Illustrated London News*.

By page number, in order from top of page to bottom:
6 & 7: *Illustrated London News*; 10: *The Sphere*, Paddy O'Sullivan x 2; 12: *New York Times*; 14: *Irish Weekly Times*, *Life* magazine; 15: *Life* magazine; 16: National Library of Ireland; 18: Noel Ray, *The Graphic*; 19: *The Graphic*; 20: *Illustrated London News*; Poole collection; 21: *Ballymena Observer*, Author. 23: *Illustrated London News*. 25: Contemporary postcard. 28: *The Graphic*; 31: Library of Congress; 35: *The Sphere*; 36: *Larne Times*; 37: *Cork Constitution*; 39: *Cork Examiner*; 40: *Larne Times*, *Irish Post & Weekly Telegraph*, *Cork Examiner*; 41: *The Sphere*; 42: Mike Poirier; 43: Kilkenny descendants; 47: *The Sphere*; 49: *Lusitania* publicity brochure, *The Sphere*; 50: *The Graphic*, *Irish Post & Weekly Telegraph*; 52: *Daily Sketch*; 53: *Larne Times*, *Daily Sketch*; 55: *Cork Examiner*; 57: *Illustrated London News*; 59: *The Sphere*; 60: Contemporary postcard; 62: Colleen Frew; 65: *Cork Examiner*; 66: Marge McKindles; 67: *Illustrated London News*; 69: Examiner Publications; 72: *The Sphere*; 74: *The Sphere*; 76 & 77: *Irish Independent*; 78: Gaumont; 81: Louis Raemakers; 83: *Larne Times*; 84: *Shipping Wonders*; *Larne Times* x 2; 86: *Cork Examiner*; 87: *Irish Independent* x 2; 88: *Cork Examiner*; 90: *Cork Examiner*; 92 *New York Times Midweek Pictorial*; 96: *The Sphere*; 97: Noel Ray; 98: Private collection, E. Keeble Chatterton; 99: *Cork Examiner*; 100: Micheál Hurley; 101: *Cork Examiner*; 102: *The Sphere*; 105: Manx Postal Museum; 106: Manx Postal Museum x 2, Cunard Archives; 107: Poole collection, *Daily Sketch*, *Cork Examiner*; 110: Poole collection; 112: *Cork Examiner*; 113: *New York Times Midweek Pictorial*, Poole collection; 116: Oberlin College, Ohio; 117: *New York Times Midweek Pictorial*; 119: *The Graphic*, *Irish Independent*/Author reworking, *Daily Sketch*; 120: *Boston Globe*; 121: *The Graphic*, *The Sphere*, Poole collection; 122: *Cork Examiner*; 123: Poole collection; 124: *Cork Examiner*, Examiner Publications; 125: *New York Times Midweek Pictorial*, *The Graphic*; 126: Noel Ray; 133: Contemporary postcard; 134: Author x 2, Examiner Publications, *New York Times*, Lawrence Jolivet, Lockwood family; 135: *New York Times*, *The Graphic*, Poole collection x 2; 136: H. D. Northrop, private collection; 140: Horgan family; 141 *The Graphic*, Author, Jim Herlihy; 145: National Archives; 146: *New York Times Midweek Pictorial*; 147: Author/Kinsale Museum; 148: *The Graphic*, Mike Poirier; 149: *The Sphere*; 150: Author x 2, Cunard Archives; 151: *New York Times*, *The Graphic*; 152: National Archives, private collection; 153: *The Sphere*, Author, Cunard Archives; 155: National Archives; 156: Connor descendants, Little family, Author, *Sunday People*; 157: *Popular Mechanics*; 158: National Archives x 2, *Popular Mechanics*, Noel Ray; 159: *Popular Mechanics* x 2, *Shipping Wonders*; 160: *The Times*; 161: *Shipping Wonders*, Mike Poirier; 163: *Cork Examiner*; 164: *Engineering* x 2; 167: *The Sphere*; 168: *Illustrated London News*, private collection, Library of Congress, *Illustierte Zeitung* (reprinted in *The Sphere*); 169: Author; 170: Karl Spindler; 171: *Illustrated London News*; 172: Private collection; 173: Cunard Archives; 176: *The Sphere*, *Cork Examiner*, Marconi Archive; 179: Poole collection; 182: Author/Noel Ray; Poole collection.

Extract from *Fiche Bliain ag Fás/Twenty Years a Growing* by permission of Clólucht an Talboidigh/Talbot Press.

Index